THIRD SHIFT

ENTREPRENEUR

TODD CONNOR

THIRD SHIFT ENTREPRENEUR

KEEP YOUR DAY JOB, BUILD YOUR DREAM JOB

WILEY

Published by John Wiley & Sons, Inc., Hoboken, New Jersey.

Published simultaneously in Canada.

For general information on our other products and services or for technical support, please contact our Customer Care Department within the United States at (800) 762-2974, outside the United States at (317) 572-3993 or fax (317) 572-4002.

Wiley publishes in a variety of print and electronic formats and by print-on-demand. Some material included with standard print versions of this book may not be included in e-books or in print-on-demand. If this book refers to media such as a CD or DVD that is not included in the version you purchased, you may download this material at http://booksupport.wiley.com. For more information about Wiley products, visit www.wiley.com.

Library of Congress Cataloging-in-Publication is Available:
ISBN 9781119708360 (Hardcover)
ISBN 9781119708384 (ePDF)
ISBN 9781119708377 (ePub)

Cover image: Craft paper tear © voinSveta/Getty Images, Cardboard paper sheet © koosen/Shutterstock, Clouds © sharply_done/Getty Images Author Image: Courtesy of Todd Connor

Cover design: Wiley

Printed in the United States of America

SKY10026219_041321

Contents

Acknowledgements

The stories and content contained herein are inspired by the hundreds of entrepreneurs I have met, coached and learned from over the last 10 years. Their stories inspire me as to what a thoughtful and strategic approach to entrepreneurship, as well as to what a life well-lived, looks like. I'm deeply humbled to work alongside nearly 30 staff and 200 volunteer city leaders at Bunker Labs who selflessly bring their best each day to serve entrepreneurs in the military-connected community who are starting businesses like the ones you will read about in this book. They are by far the most talented, inspired, tenacious and humble group of people with whom I have ever had the privilege of working. Not a week goes by that we do not share deep belly-laughs as well as sincere tears serving our mission together.

I must also acknowledge the generous sponsors and partners of Bunker Labs who have endorsed our vision of what could be. They too share an urgency to see more dreams fulfilled and communities transformed through entrepreneurship.

Thank you to the team at Wiley, including Brian Neill, Deborah Schindlar, Tim Gallan and Gary Schwartz, who allowed for the broader vision of a book that was both a fictional story as well as a framework to be applied. You each brought rigor to strengthen the final manuscript for this neophyte author, and I am a far better, and more humbled, writer for it.

In addition, I must acknowledge Emily Drake, who runs The Collective Academy, the leadership consulting business I founded with which I remain a collaborator. She's brilliant, inspiring and hilarious. We all need *an* Emily Drake in our lives. I'm fortunate to have *the* Emily Drake in my life. She has taught me that it's not in spite of our flaws, but rather because of them, that people turn to each of us for leadership and support.

Thank you to my husband, Andrew, who has always been the touchstone to whom I return. There is no season of my life, and there have been many, in which I do not find him to be indispensable as well as the perfect companion. We all need a ride or die, and I'm grateful I have mine.

This book is dedicated to my son, Jasper. I hope he finds the deepest fulfillment in life, which is to be of service to others in pursuit of his peculiar interests, and to be fully and unabashedly himself in the process.

Finally, to you, the person reading this. I hope this book can unlock insights for you and illuminate small ways in which you can move forward toward the life you are meant to live. For what it is worth, I really believe that your dreams matter, and though you are undoubtedly inundated with reasons why you can't and shouldn't, I hope to be a persistent voice in your head that says you could and should.

—Todd Connor

Acknowledgements

Foreword

After serving as an officer in the Marine Corps, I launched my first venture, which was a free boxing gym for inner-city youth and young adults in Newark, New Jersey, called the IRONBOUND Boxing Academy. I was working full-time at a private school in downtown Newark, lived on campus, and oversaw a residence hall of 70+ teenage boys. I was also a graduate student pursuing my master's degree in American Studies from Rutgers-Newark. From October 2016 to the summer of 2018, my life consisted of work, school and boxing. I was the epitome of the Third Shift Entrepreneur, only I didn't know it at the time. I thought I was the exception, and worse than that, maybe I was doing it wrong. In June 2018, after I demonstrated it was working and with a nudge from my own Third Shift entrepreneurial community known as Bunker Labs (https://bunkerlabs.org/), I left my job to pursue the IRONBOUND Boxing Academy full time.

For the past two years, I've taught boxing to CEOs in the New York City metro area and, in the process, discovered other opportunities. I served as a part-time consultant supporting veteran entrepreneurship initiatives and moonlighted as a brand strategist with an e-commerce coffee company based in Atlanta. I even managed to launch my own podcast called *Confessions of a Native Son*, which is available on most podcast streaming services. When I shared what I had done for myself, other companies then asked me to help them build a podcast, and I built a small business doing just that. Some of these efforts have fizzled out, but others have taken off. I've built a professional life for myself that has impact, provides financial opportunity and allows me to continue to pursue what matters to me. I've built things without putting myself at risk, and I get better each time I do it.

Before you spend time, money and effort on starting a business, I encourage you to understand and embrace a Third Shift Entrepreneur mindset. The sad reality is that the majority of today's business literature does not reflect the vast landscape of our American identity, particularly for minorities. Socioeconomic and racial disparities exist across our society, which have excluded too many people from ever seeing a path toward business ownership. If we are going to overcome this reality, we will need a new way of talking about and teaching entrepreneurship.

Nothing is more freeing than generating income for yourself and your loved ones as an entrepreneur. You unleash untapped power and confidence in yourself when you can create a product or service and monetize it. The entrepreneurial journey is one of the most rewarding experiences, a true act of realizing your full potential. Everyone who has the aspiration should have the opportunity, and my hope is the strategies in the following pages will reveal an approach that will allow you to do so. If you have felt confused or left out of the entrepreneurship conversation, you are not alone. This book is an invitation, for you. You belong.

—"IRON" Mike Steadman

Introduction

This is a book about how to start something and, in turn, create an inflection point for your life toward living your fully expressed purpose. The mythology and assumption that starting a business requires outside capital, the blessing of a venture capitalist, a polished pitch deck and time in business accelerators is false. Those things represent the scaffolding for a specific kind of business and pursuit, which require outside permission. This is a book written for the vast majority of businesses, organizations and initiatives that exist beyond that narrow frame which you can start today, with the resources you have, as the person you are, and from where you are in life. This is a book about giving yourself permission, and learning to start small.

Over a 15-year period, management researchers Joseph Raffiee and Jie Feng tracked a group of would-be entrepreneurs to answer the question of whether quitting your job or keeping it, while pursuing starting your own business, was better.[1] They looked at more than 5,000 people in the United States who became entrepreneurs during this period

---

[1]https://hbr.org/2014/08/why-going-all-in-on-your-start-up-might-not-be-the-best-idea

of observation, and these entrepreneurs cut across age, gender, race demographics, industries and other controlled variables. The results were clear: Those who kept their day jobs were 33 percent less likely to fail in their new venture, which is significant. Adam Grant, the popular psychologist and professor at Wharton, says it this way, "Quitting your full-time job to start a company is like proposing marriage on the first date. . . . The most durable businesses are typically started by people who play it safe."[2]

Caution, then, is key. Yet the popular literature that heralds the courageous risk-it-all ethos of becoming an entrepreneur often diverges from the reality of that research and from what I have seen with so many entrepreneurs, which is the thoughtful, evidence-based advancements of starting a business from a cautious position that ensures financial security. Caution, to be clear, does not mean slow; it means aggressively focusing on the right things, which I'll explain. The false narratives that have been created about what is required to start a business are not benign. Rates of entrepreneurship have been on the decline for decades,[3] and it has become something of a national crisis today in spite of the explosion of support systems for aspiring entrepreneurs through universities, incubators, accelerators and entrepreneurship support organizations.[4,5] Not to mention, we've

---

[2]https://www.wired.co.uk/article/entrepreneurs-dont-quit-your-day-job
[3]https://www.bls.gov/bdm/entrepreneurship/entrepreneurship.htm
[4]http://www.unm.edu/~asalazar/Kauffman/Entrep_research/College_Scan.pdf
[5]https://www.bls.gov/bdm/entrepreneurship/entrepreneurship.htm

seen a surge in popularity of entrepreneurship-driven reality TV with shows like *Shark Tank*, *The Profit* and *The Apprentice*, all of which would suggest that more people, not fewer, would be starting businesses and yet here we are.

Fundamentally, it is hard to become an entrepreneur if you do not have people in your life to look to for inspiration and practical insights. As rates of entrepreneurship decline, this problem is exacerbated: the fewer people you know personally who are starting businesses, the more you are left relying instead on second-hand mythologies or television drama about what becoming an entrepreneur is supposed to look like. We celebrate these high-profile entrepreneurs but increasingly do not relate to them. We do not find the stories that successful founders tell of themselves to be either authentic or accessible. The chasm, as we see it, is too great.

Resigned, we tell ourselves a story that, perhaps, "People like me don't do things like that." That's tragic and false. I feel a particular urgency for systemically excluded populations to define their own futures and to pursue entrepreneurship on their own terms. Only about 20 percent of venture-backed companies have a female founder,[6] and only about 1 percent have a Black founder,[7] not to mention the under-representation of entrepreneurs in the military community, rural communities, or other communities feeling left behind. The pathway toward entrepreneurship, for too many, is not illuminated. We must do better.

---

[6]https://www.allraise.org/assets/pitchbook_all_raise_2019_all_in_women_in_the_vc_ecosystem.pdf
[7]https://hbr.org/2020/06/a-vcs-guide-to-investing-in-black-founders

My aim here is to make entrepreneurship relatable again and to invite real people like you, with real constraints in their lives, to start a business and, more important to me, pursue your own creativity and fulfillment. As I'll explain, being deeply concerned with a problem is the genesis of a good business. The problem I'm deeply connected to is in studying and coaching people toward those specific, uncelebrated and early moves you can take to express yourself and start things. Before a business, there is you. And it's you who I'm interested in. There is much you can and should build before you ever need to quit a job or make some public declaration about becoming an "entrepreneur." The question is not whether to quit or stay stuck but rather how to start.

I took a risk in choosing to write a fictional story, not being a fiction writer myself, because I believed in fiction as a powerful medium for teaching. Yet it is a vulnerability for me, having realized a number of deficiencies in the first version I soft-launched. Such is the choice we make, though, to discover the potential of our ideas. This process of creating original things will require a willingness to practice in public on occasion and get it wrong, which I regularly do. Know that I do this work alongside you.

This idea of becoming a *Third Shift Entrepreneur* is about choosing to step into this battlespace of being an original, a creator, an artist, an initiator. To cross this Rubicon is not a financial consideration or simply a question of your risk tolerance as much of the startup literature would tell you. Instead, it is an intellectual, deeply personal, often vulnerable and ultimately disciplined pursuit as you do battle not with competitors but with yourself. Becoming an entrepreneur is an act of cultivating this resilient cycle of putting things out there that matter to you and then assessing the response. The reward is not necessarily wealth or acclaim, although that can happen, but that you trade the latent stress of wondering if you are doing work that matters to you for the stress of wondering how your work will be received. It's a trade I'm willing to make, and I think you are, too.

How to Read This Book

As I've mentioned, some people learn through stories (I am one of those) and others want to see it broken into a set of applied strategies. In this updated version of *Third Shift Entrepreneur*, I do both. The first part of the book follows a fictional narrative, inspired by real people I've worked with and my own life, which hopefully gives expression to the human transformation that takes place through small and specific actions toward starting a business.

The second part of *Third Shift Entrepreneur* seeks to lay out the 12 Observations, which, if present, indicate you are on to something and the business has started. These are not sequential steps, per se, but a diagnostic tool to which you can return and ask yourself, "Is this true yet? Is there evidence of this?"

The third part of this book presents The Entrepreneurs, which gives life to how these 12 Observations appear for people starting different businesses. These, too, are inspired by people I have known, strategies they have deployed and, in some cases, the creative strategies I might have suggested they deploy. It is my hope you see yourself in one or more of these stories and this process of starting begins to feel tangible and accessible.

If you want to start with The Entrepreneurs, go to the 12 Observations and then read the story, that's fine by me. This book is meant to be used and referenced. Just as starting a business is not a linear and sequential pursuit, so too you should feel free to poke around this book for what feels interesting or helpful to start.

You can find more content and workshops at www. ThirdShiftEntrepreneur.com.

Let's begin!

Part I

The Story

Before there is a business, there is a person. Fifteen years ago, I was a management consultant who felt fine but not fulfilled. For me, this was the base condition that led to a controlled personal disruption, a few professional experiments and a messy but highly productive shift into the professional life I was meant to live. What I know looking back is it that was messy and un-strategic at the time, but the process toward stepping off of the assigned path and onto the chosen path yielded wonderful, surprising and impactful adventures. I have subsequently observed the patterns in dozens of other people who take the initiative and step into the work they are meant to do with their lives. This book is an attempt at explaining that alchemy and those earliest first steps.

Whereas most business entrepreneurship literature or business modeling tools start (understandably and perhaps obviously) with the business, I knew I needed to write a book that instead started with you, the entrepreneur. After all, you do not start a business in general or absent the realities of your life. You start a business in the context of your life: your financial realities, your insecurities and your deepest dreams. This is personal stuff, and to start with a market analysis ignores what I know is the background noise that can either propel you forward or hold you back.

What follows is a story, and a set of stories, about how people start things. I hope you see how you too can start things. Drama is in all of this, and the drama of your life unfolding is the most interesting of all.

Following this story, I'll offer you a more practical framework of 12 Observations, which indicate you are making forward progress. I'll then apply those 12 Observations toward another hypothetical set of aspiring entrepreneurs. Again, my aim is to make the big and intimidating idea of starting a business relatable, achievable and maybe even inevitable. You may find that starting a business is perhaps easier, but different, than you've envisioned.

Chapter 1

The Lingering Discontent

The alarm rang at 5:15 a.m., but Matt had been restless for two hours, constantly jolting himself awake in a panicked state, thinking he'd missed his flight. He could never sleep before an early flight. He'd never missed one, but that didn't stop the anxiety.

He laid in bed for a few minutes, feeling the heaviness on his eyes. He had done these one-day business trips dozens of times before, but for some reason this one felt different, harder. Maybe it was that he was about to turn 40. Maybe it was because this client had rescheduled this meeting twice. Maybe it was because of the fight that he and Sabina had last night, the fight about which he couldn't even remember any of the details this morning other than that Sabina reminded him he instigated these kinds of fights-about-nothing regularly before business trips.

Maybe it was the last thing he'd seen on Facebook before he'd gone to sleep: his old business school friend Amit celebrating the sale of the company that he had started eight years ago. At the time, he thought that Amit was foolish for leaving a safe job to launch the new venture. He looked at the photos and the 127 comments that followed of Amit celebrating alongside his wife and what looked like a dozen or so of the company leaders toasting and laughing. Matt recalled a specific conversation with Amit when they were in an entrepreneurship class together in which they each had to develop a business idea. Amit had a different version of a healthcare company that he was thinking of starting, and Matt had this idea for an adventure travel company that he put forward. Matt placed ahead of Amit in the competition, but he decided that starting an adventure travel company seemed like too much of a fantasy. Instead, he opted for a "real" job in consulting, and Amit ultimately persevered in starting that business in the healthcare space.

He felt a sort of familiar despair and self-defeating narrative rolling around in his mind. *"Others have achieved more,"* *"Sabina is right: 'You're miserable to be with and predictably so,'"* *"You should have started that adventure travel business,"* and the worst of the narratives: *"It's just too late"*. He felt lost. What would be his obituary if he were to disappear today?

Matt Carney. 39. It looked as if he was going to do exceptional things with his life, obtained some modicum of prestige, was sometimes more of an arrogant jerk than was necessary, paid off his mortgage, and ultimately played it safe. His friends mostly liked him. He took good vacations (and lots of pictures to prove it), and he had an average career as a consultant at Coopers & Tompkins. He served his country in the U.S. Army for 10 years. That mattered, and for that we are grateful.

The story he told himself, particularly as someone who once had bigger dreams of doing more, could paralyze him.

Enough, he told himself, rolling out of bed, careful not to wake Sabina.

He shuffled into the bathroom and looked in the mirror. His eyes were sullen, still piercing blue, but carrying a heaviness that seemed to only show up in the last couple years. He was 6'0" and was in trim shape in the military but his personal workouts had fallen off a bit these last few years with all of his business travel. The thick, black hair that he wore slightly long and combed back was now peppered with gray.

He turned on the shower and did the mental math on when he needed the Lyft to show up.

- 30 minutes to the airport
- Arrive 15 minutes before boarding starts
- 10 minutes for TSA pre-check
- Coffee inside the terminal
- Boarding
- Take off at 7:50 a.m.
- Land in Cincinnati at 10:07 a.m.
- Be at the client by 10:45 a.m.

He would lose an hour on the way out and gain that same hour on the way back. His life felt like a constant calculation of where he needed to be and by what time. Something about being in motion and en route to important client meetings offered him an emotional balm or temporary refuge from these larger, existential questions that would otherwise inevitably creep into his consciousness in the quiet intervening moments at the airport, in the Lyft, or in the shower. That foreboding question would be: *"To what end am I doing all this?"*

He finished his shower, dressed and gathered his things to leave, stopping for a moment to look at Sabina lying there in bed. She was blissfully unaware of the emotional journey her husband had taken in the 35 minutes since waking up and also unaware of how often he felt plagued by this void of not feeling that his life mattered, had some larger purpose, or that he would never know, or honor, his dreams.

That he had felt the opposite and full of purpose at one point in his life seemed to accentuate the pain. Sergeant Carney, the decorated Army Ranger with three deployments under his belt, could not have been a more different person than Matt Carney, the middle-aged management consultant living a typical middle-aged life. His life then was one of purpose: absolute loyalty to the men and women with whom he served and a pride that comes with working hard toward a shared mission. His performance in close combat, in which he brought every member of his team home while being under fire, had earned him accolades, an early promotion to E-6 and a rotation to the Pentagon where he would complete his schooling. He had watched as the men and women with whom he had served, and who he knew had extraordinary talent and tenacity, also return home to lives back in the United States that seemed "less than." Their fate mirrored his, and it was equally as disorienting to witness. He knew how great they could be and how great they were, a greatness otherwise unseen in the array of their present-day LinkedIn profiles.

The frequent inquiries that colleagues and friends had for things he had done while in uniform serving the country felt benevolent, but they presented Matt with this haunting question: *Are the best years behind me?* Maybe the Army had spoiled him, setting him up for a future life full of feeling underwhelmed. What made it all the more painful was the deluge of comments from people welcoming him home and expressing relief that he could finally put that chapter behind him. He didn't want that chapter behind him. Had he not met Sabina, he might have just stayed in.

At least in the Army, he thought, *you belonged, your life story made sense, and you operated in service toward something bigger*. Even for all of the dysfunction at times, at least it was a dysfunction where, Matt thought, you loved the people and they loved you back. He would reminisce about the deep camaraderie that was forged in making fun of the insanity of it all. More than anything, it was that feeling of belonging and that he was serving a noble mission that he missed the most. The welcome home hugs from civilians could not fully honor or fill the void he carried in his new civilian life.

Sabina always had a more coherent approach to her career and life. It was as if she knew instinctively what she was on this earth to do, and her career followed suit accordingly. On their first date in Washington, D.C., while Matt was working at the Pentagon, she sat patiently listening to Matt describe his decision to join the Army, his dream of starting his own business someday, and what he was learning about himself in the process. She seemed, simply, at ease with herself, her life and her identity. They would later joke that this first date was a therapy session for Matt, who did most of the talking and did not realize until later in the conversation that Sabina was training to be a clinical psychologist.

Their life together, first when dating and later when they were married and moved to Chicago, where they settled, would follow this pattern. Sabina, the preternaturally calm and steadfast one, seemed to advance on her career and life path without this inner conflict. Matt, privately and sometimes publicly, wrestled with an anxiety that his time was running out. He wanted to start a business, to become an entrepreneur, and that dream felt as if it was slipping away.

Blazer on, Matt paused to look at her in bed. Though he felt as if he had aged 10 years, she had not seemed to age a day with her short, curly black hair that she had kept the same way the whole time he had known her, her light brown complexion acknowledging her mother's Haitian heritage, and the way she slept on her right side, every night, with her wedding ring on. Her eyes didn't carry the anxiety, and she showed no signs of this existential crisis that Matt seemed to carry with him each morning. It all seemed so easy for her. She would wake up in 30 minutes, have a predictably healthy breakfast, one cup of coffee, and proceed to her office to see patients. She would be of service to her clients, write her notes, and return home. *She was enviably*, he thought, *normal. Why*, he wondered, *did his desire to do something, be something and build something occupy such a disproportionate place in his mind?*

He looked at her and smiled a pained smile, for how lucky he was to have her in his life and for how much he hated himself sometimes. He ordered a Lyft, poured a cup of coffee to go, and walked down the front steps of their vintage townhouse to wait for his ride and face his day.

Chapter 2

Small Talk

Standing in the early morning dawn, waiting on the corner for his Lyft ride, the spring air felt good to Matt, especially after coming out of a particularly harsh Chicago winter. He was excited about the client meeting in Cincinnati that had previously been put off. As a Senior Manager for one of the largest management consulting firms in the country, Coopers & Tompkins, Matt was on the cusp of making partner. He had built this relationship on his own with a large consumer packaged goods company and was going to pitch them a strategy project to optimize their pricing decisions around a set of household chemical products. He had done this kind of work before, and though nervous about leading the pitch for this new project, he felt comfortable with the subject matter. Winning this client would represent a significant achievement in the path toward the career milestone of making partner. The meetings would last all day, but he would still be on a same-day flight back home afterward to have dinner with Sabina.

In anticipation of this client meeting and the feeling of the accompanying hunt for this new potential win, Matt was energized. Why, he wondered in these moments of fulfillment in his professional life, couldn't he be happy with his job? Partner, after all, would represent a significant pay increase and arguably the culmination of his career transformation after leaving the Army, earning his MBA and working his way up through the ranks as a management consultant. Attainment of partner status was, after all, the prize, and he was close to securing it.

The Lyft, a black Prius, pulled up on cue. Matt looked at the app and saw that his driver matched the picture in the app with a goatee and red-rimmed glasses.

"Ken?" Matt said.

"Yes, Kenneth," the driver answered in a slightly high-pitched voice, gently reaffirming that he prefers to be called Kenneth more than Ken. "I assume you're Matt?" the driver turned a glance and answered.

"Yep. Good morning." And with that Matt slipped into the backseat and settled in for the 30-minute ride to the airport.

Matt's preference in these frequent Lyft rides to the airport was never to speak. The older he got, the more he hated the small talk, particularly with strangers. He would become anxious if he saw the driver had compliments for "great conversation." He could appear to shut down as a prevention strategy if it looked as if the stranger in the airplane seat next to him wanted to chat or find some commonality that, in Matt's mind, didn't matter. Discoveries like *What a small world! We both have relatives in Sacramento . . ."* Matt found pedestrian and irritable. He didn't particularly like this side of himself, but he was aware of it.

He grabbed his phone and opened up some of his favorite blogs. His preferred media consumption was a mix of management and strategy blogs, entrepreneur and startup business profiles, human interest stories and articles exploring natural wonders and adventure travel. He was a keen student of human behavior and deeply captivated by outdoor adventures. He had a natural curiosity about people with different life experiences than his own, something to which he had wider exposure in the Army and increasingly less so as he advanced in his professional career. Matt could be dismissed as a two-dimensional management consultant, but his heartfelt concern for others, his love of the outdoors and camping and his experiences in life represented more than what strangers might assume of him at face value.

Some of his male friends from the Army dove into sports, military history, or international current events. Not Matt. He had little interest in these topics despite his time in uniform. For Matt, he was more likely to be thinking about the intersections of innovation, the climate, entrepreneurship and human behavior.

Growing up in the Midwest, Matt cultivated a love of the outdoors, spending weekends camping in the Indiana Dunes, Starved Rock, or even the local forest preserves. He was more in his element outdoors, even in the unforgiving climate of the Middle East, than he would ever be inside of a corporate office building.

Matt was deep in an article about California wildfires and innovative community intervention strategies to prevent future catastrophes when the Lyft driver interrupted him.

"So, where are you flying to today?" he asked.

And here we go, Matt thought. *Here goes my peace and quiet by some Lyft driver who wants to chat.* "Cincinnati."

"Cool. For business?"

"Yes." Matt intentionally made his answer short.

His driver, Kenneth, seemed to get the message. He offered a furtive glance in the rearview mirror but otherwise sat looking straight ahead as he made his way down the street.

Matt felt a pang of self-loathing. *I'm such a jerk*, he thought. *What's wrong with people wanting to be nice in the world? Why do I always have these hostile reactions?* To redeem himself, he thought he would perk up and offer a friendly olive branch. "Nice car. How long have you been driving for Lyft?"

"A few months or so. The car is about a year old. I enjoy it. Plus, I get to meet new people like you."

Matt sensed the compliment was a throwaway line, but however disingenuous it might have been, it felt good to hear. He also noticed that Kenneth was wearing a blazer he liked, something he might want to have in his own closet and seemingly more formal than he expected from a Lyft driver.

"So," Kenneth picked back up, "I guess you must travel a lot for work?"

"Yeah," Matt offered, "almost every week."

"I know that gets tiring. So, what do you do for a living?"

"I'm a management consultant," Matt replied.

"Which firm? And what kind of consulting? Strategy? Operations? Human capital? Something else?"

Matt was a little surprised by the specificity of the question and the insider language that he seemed to know. "I work as a strategy consultant for Coopers & Tompkins, mostly looking at how companies implement better pricing strategies using technology platforms. But I've done strategy projects across a wide array of business challenges. A little bit of everything, I guess."

"Interesting. One of the big firms? Or a smaller firm? You a partner?"

Huh, Matt chuckled. *This Lyft driver apparently knows his lingo.* "One of the larger firms. Not quite a partner, but maybe this year. I've been a management consultant since getting out of the Army and going to business school. It's a grind, but it provides. Most days I like it." Matt paused and thought about the conversation with this driver, who seemed more knowledgeable than Matt expected. "You seem to know a lot about management consulting?"

"Not really. I just meet a lot of consultants on their way to the airport, driving for Lyft. I'm able to pick up a little of the language here and there. Nothing too crazy." Kenneth pivoted to continue the conversation, "My wife works in HR, and we were talking the other night about training and development. How do you get together with your colleagues for training and offsite retreats?"

"Well, we're on the road a lot so time at home is somewhat precious. Our clients, however, often do offsite retreats and occasionally they want the consultants there to facilitate the conversation or team building experience."

"Interesting."

Why is that interesting to you? Matt thought.

Kenneth continued and clarified, "So, let me get this straight. Some of your client's leadership teams want to do offsite retreats? Like on an annual basis?"

Matt thought about the question. "Well, it depends. Sometimes we are working with a client on a merger or acquisition,

13

Small Talk

and in that case, part of what we are doing is to get these two teams together to build trust, identify issues, and learn to operate as a newly consolidated team. As you can imagine, a situation like that can have tension or legacy resentment."

"I can only imagine, sure," Kenneth said, continuing. "I also imagine that finding the right environment to have that type of an offsite retreat would be important to create trust."

"It is. I mean we stay at lots of hotels all the time set up for corporate meetings and retreats."

"Does that work though? I mean, do you like the hotel environment for that kind of an offsite retreat?"

Matt thought about it. "Well, I haven't really thought about it but not particularly. It just tends to be what we do. I'm not sure I know other options. I did do an offsite retreat with the leadership team of a small subsidiary with whom we were working. The founder and CEO of the company offered to host everyone at her private ranch in the middle of New Mexico, and that was cool. She had something like 12 bedrooms, but of course, not everyone has that."

"Wow, that's cool," Kenneth affirmed. "So, just curious here. How much does it cost to bring a group offsite to a hotel for a few days?"

Matt felt it was an odd question, something of a non-sequitur, but weirdly enough he knew the answer because he had been tasked on one of last year's projects to assemble a plan to host a week-long summit and team-building retreat for a newly reorganized management team. He had the client manage the logistics, but he oversaw the effort from an experience standpoint. "Well, last year, I organized a leadership team retreat. We secured a block of about 20 rooms at a boutique luxury property in Tampa and went all in with catering and so on. We spent about $55,000 in all, not including flights. I think that was about the most the client wanted to spend for something like this offsite."

"That's not bad." Kenneth paused, as if to still be running the numbers in his head. "And is a full week typical, or do you sometimes do a long weekend?"

This guy has a lot of questions, Matt thought. "Well, usually two nights is about as much as we can get people to commit to being away. That full week was an exception, and weekends are hard. Our team usually prefers a Wednesday and Thursday night because they don't want to spend time away from their kids and spouses. And, logistically, it's hard if you want spouses to come as well because then you need to arrange for childcare."

"That makes sense. Most people don't want to give up their weekends for a work retreat," Kenneth offered in response, keeping his eyes on the road. For the moment, Kenneth receded from the conversation, sensing that Matt was into his phone or uninterested in continuing the dialog. He had seen those signals before and knew when to relent.

"Look. I know you're a busy guy, and you probably have a lot on your mind as it is. I didn't mean to bother you," Kenneth offered, glancing at Matt in the rearview mirror.

Matt, hearing the apology and even sensing that it might be rehearsed nevertheless acknowledged it. "No, not a problem at all. I appreciate your curiosity."

"Okay. One last thing," Kenneth grabbed the opening. "What other venues have you looked at locally for your corporate retreats?"

15

Small Talk

Matt, by now accustomed to the specificity of Kenneth's line of questioning, relented without even knowing what was driving this conversation. "Well, as I said, I'm not sure because I'm not the one who normally picks the venues, but I can tell you that I've led experiences at the airport hotels, downtown hotels, and a couple of more boutique luxury properties like one in Wisconsin and another one that is outside of Chicago, about 40 minutes west, called The Lodge. It used to be a hunting club. I'm not sure what the pricing was on those. I think I remember them being cheaper and more convenient than what we ended up paying for the Tampa retreat. But it depends on the client's preference. I've found that for the right venue, money isn't a problem. And the CEO usually gets involved in making some of these ultimate decisions, which means the budgets can grow."

"Got it. Thanks for the insight. I really appreciate it," Kenneth allowed, leaving Matt to finish his ride in peace and quiet.

After another 10 minutes, Matt looked up from his phone and saw they were approaching the O'Hare Airport. The sun was beginning to rise, and he could see the activity of planes on the tarmac getting ready to move thousands of business travelers.

The car drove into the airport and approached Terminal 1. "Well," Kenneth said, "Here we are. I appreciated the conversation and hope your meetings go well today in Cincinnati." And with that Kenneth turned back and smiled at Matt, making eye contact.

"Yes," Matt replied, "thank you as well." Talking with this Lyft driver, though not how Matt wanted to start his morning, nonetheless put him in a good mood. Matt jumped out of the car. Though Matt normally tipped the suggested 20 percent, he decided to tip him 30 percent and throw him a compliment for "great conversation." Matt waved and slipped through the sliding doors into Terminal 1, where he joined the sea of business travelers.

Chapter 3

Personal Readiness

Matt was able to catch the earlier 4:40 p.m. flight home from Cincinnati after a successful meeting, a small but gratifying victory. He decided that he would make dinner tonight as an act of apologizing for the fight that he had had with Sabina the night before. The fights were increasing in their frequency, and in his clearer moments, Matt knew he was the instigator. His apologies didn't follow often enough. He decided that tonight he would apologize and make it right.

As he was prepping the meal, he heard the door open and Sabina slip in. She was finishing her nightly call with her mom, and dropped her purse and keys and turned to grab a sparkling water from the refrigerator. Neither of them made eye contact.

"Okay, Mom. Yep, I know. Okay, well, I just got home. I'll call you tomorrow. Yep, love you, too." Sabina hung up, leaned against the fridge, and just gave Matt a slow, punishing look.

"Hi," Matt offered meekly.

"Hey. How was the trip?" Sabina replied, always ready to be the bigger person but not retreating from her position against the refrigerator.

"It was fine, good, actually. I think they're going to go with Coopers & Tompkins, which will be a big boost for my case for making partner. And I was happy to get the earlier flight back, so that was a bonus." Matt wanted to share more about how great the meeting was. But he could tell that Sabina was not engaged. "Listen. About last night. I was a jerk. I'm sorry."

Sabina gave him a long look. Her stares into Matt's soul could be piercing. It was part of the psychologist in her. If she chose to, she could wield this power with devastating effect. She uniquely could push past Matt's ego and confident male exterior toward a deeper level of insight and loving critique. He always knew that her intentions were pure. "It's fine, but you just have to know this is a pattern with you. You come home, you're unhappy, and then you spin it into some sort of conflict with me. It's not fair. If you're unhappy, then do something about it, but don't take it out on me."

"You're one hundred percent right," Matt said. "I know. And this morning in the shower, I just thought to myself how lucky I am to have you and that you don't deserve my BS."

Without directly responding to him, she picked up the pile of mail and began to thumb through it. *Had she moved on? Forgiven me? Was she bored by me?* Matt wondered. His insecurity in these moments of apology was pronounced.

He had planned ahead to do something special for her the coming weekend. Having just joined a climbing gym on the west side of the city, he was excited to see an email on the plane ride home announcing an open house social event they were hosting that Saturday for members as well as their guests to check out the gym for free. Rock climbing and hiking was something that they used to do regularly when they

20

first started dating, but as life intervened, it was one of the things that had fallen off. As part of his infamous string of New Year's resolutions, many of which inevitably involved physical fitness, Matt had recommitted himself to climbing at least a few times a week. He thought that bringing Sabina on Saturday would be a fun surprise and that he would probably get more credit than he deserved for doing something creative. Matt loved that Sabina was an adventurer at heart as well.

"I have a surprise for you," Matt continued. "Saturday we're going for a night of climbing at the new climbing gym I joined. We haven't done something original on a Saturday night in a while, and this will be fun." He waited to see if this would get the reaction he hoped for. It wasn't.

"Okay. I thought we were supposed to go to that co-workers' block party," Sabina responded without making eye contact.

"Forget the block party. I want to take my *amazing* wife climbing like we used to do." He grabbed her into an exaggerated, but loving, tight hug and kissed her head. She relented as he felt her muscles relax and hug him back. They were back to normal.

"Ugh. You're just insufferable sometimes," she said honestly, as she relented. "How did you know I would want to go climbing?"

"I didn't. But I knew I owed you an apology, and I miss climbing with you." Matt paused. "I don't know what the hell is going on with me. I think it's turning 40 and feeling like time is running out on the things I've wanted to do with my life. I always wanted to start a business, and you know that every six months or so I'm captivated by some idea. I think

21

about it and ultimately tell myself that it's not the right time or find some way to talk myself out of it. Then I get busy with work and let it slide off by the wayside. This is my pattern, and it's been my pattern for way too long. I want to start something."

Sabina stepped back, and now taking command of the conversation, held him by the shoulders and looked him in the eyes. "Matt, if it's starting a business that you want to do, then figure it out. No one is telling you not to do it. You just need to figure out how to start. Of course, if we finally get pregnant, that changes our financial picture."

They had talked about having a baby for years. Neither of them had before felt any rush, but at 34, Sabina was feeling a greater urgency and desire to start the process.

"A baby." Matt smiled. It wasn't that he didn't want children. It never felt like the right time. He held on to the idea that he wanted to do things before they started a family. *Maybe*, he thought, *it's time to let go of any delusions of grandeur and realize that this is your life. It doesn't get any better or different, so let that dream go. And maybe it's time you step up and finally have kids.*

"I promise. I want you to be happy. And I do want kids. I just don't know when. I know it will feel right at some point." Matt was suddenly flustered, sensing that their date night could end up in an argument about when to have kids. "Is this really the conversation we have to have tonight?" Matt asked, careful not to shut her down but also suggesting that they change the conversation.

"It's been 'someday' for many years," Sabina replied, almost under her breath. She was always careful in how she would approach the conversation about a baby with Matt, not wanting to pressure him, but also mindful of her own growing impatience.

Matt nodded at Sabina and continued, "You know, I'm seeing friends of mine from the military, from business school or even people I've known professionally, and so many of them are doing things I see as original, interesting and brave. I know my life isn't bad, but at the same time I feel as if I'm selling out or at least selling myself short. Even today, I was sitting with this potential client, talking about a big strategy project, something that could put me over the top for making partner. But I knew at the end of the day we would come up with a bunch of smart ideas, put them into a beautiful PowerPoint presentation, and hand them to the client. And then what? Who knows? Maybe they would do it or maybe they wouldn't, and frankly who cares either way? I think to myself, 'When will I make the decisions? When will I be in charge?' Doing something important or original based on my own talent, whether I succeed or fail, is what's important to me. In my current work life, I may never fail, but at the same time, it may never matter and that haunts me."

Matt began to walk away from the conversation, but Sabina pulled him back in. She had heard this enough to know this wasn't a fleeting thought: He was struggling.

"Matt," she offered, "I understand you're struggling. You know I've always told you I would support you, but I don't know how much I can do for you with this. You've got to get clear in your own mind on what's missing and how you get it. You keep talking about not wanting to be like your dad, and yet—." Matt pulled back. She had hit a nerve.

Personal Readiness

Sabina paused, and then Matt picked up the cue. "I know. My dad." His dad had worked at a factory job. He provided for the family, but he hated his job for all 28 of the years he spent working for the same parts manufacturer. He never found the path to being fulfilled. He talked regularly about the things he would do after retiring as if all the misery up until that point would finally yield the big return. Tragically, he died at age 60, three months before his planned retirement date, with Matt still in the Army. His death left Matt with a sense of deep sadness for a talented man he loved with a life professionally unfulfilled, but he also had a residual anger that his dad had not taken action sooner before it was too late.

"I'm not saying you are your dad, but I am saying that you need to take action. Though it's never easy, you are at a point in your life where you have the capability of doing something 'important or original.' And you haven't always seemed this depressed. What's changed? When was the last time you felt like your life mattered?" Sabina asked. She had a way of posing deep, existential questions that rolled off her tongue casually, as if totally normal and appropriate. She also sensed this was a bigger conversation, and she grabbed an open bottle of red wine, poured them each a glass, and lit a candle, which was her subtext for *I'm ready to talk.*

Matt didn't have to think, "In the Army. Every day."

"But you hated the Army," she countered.

"Well, kind of. Yes. It was a pain in my ass most days, but these soul-level questions never were there for me. You knew you mattered—."

"Okay." Sabina cut him off. The psychologist in her hated how his go-to emotion was shame. "Are you saying that you want to join the Army again? You know I would want to support—."

Matt almost choked on his wine as he let out a laugh. "Ha. Oh hell no. I mean, I'm glad I served and wouldn't change that for the world. But it's not about going backward into the Army; it's about learning how to move forward with a professional life that I'm proud of and in which I am making a real difference, like a new uniform I'm proud to put on each day. I want to control my future and not be subject to it, not just for me, but for us," Matt added, something that he had casually said in passing to Sabina but never with real intention. "I don't feel I'm even in the fight, and I want to be. I think I want to start a business. I know it sounds hard and financially challenging, but I keep coming back to it. I don't know. I just get excited by it, and there's not a lot else that gets me energized like that."

Sabina gave him a long look. "Well, if it's starting a business, then, I'm here for it. Whatever it is, this is real, and you need to do some work to figure it out. Or talk to a therapist or a career coach or someone. I'm here for you, but you've got to do the work for yourself. If it is starting a business, we will figure it out together, but you need to have a vision. Frankly, I hope you do take action because this lingering discontent is a bad look." Sabina smiled at him. *I've got you*, her eyes told him.

Chapter 4

Third Shift Entrepreneurs

The next day, Matt only had one meeting. Another senior manager in the Chicago office, Rebecca, asked if he could join in on a pitch presentation, along with some other consultants, for an upcoming merger for Delta Development Group that would have a variety of HR, pricing and enterprise technology implications. Matt had done enough projects for companies undergoing mergers and was known to be a great person to have in the room for meetings such as this one to offer his perspective on different issues that might crop up. Given that the client was in Chicago, Matt thought it could potentially be a good project to join if they won the business if for nothing but to avoid travel for a bit.

He grabbed a coffee to go, kissed Sabina, and left for the meeting. *If this goes well,* he thought, *I might just steal the afternoon back and perhaps go to the climbing gym or hide out at a coffee shop and read technology, entrepreneurship and current events blogs.* If he had time, he might also call and check in with other friends whom he knew were starting or thinking about starting their own businesses. Being connected to people starting businesses would give him the energy he found difficult to access otherwise.

The meeting was scheduled for 10:00 a.m., and it was located past O'Hare airport in a corporate office complex. Matt met Rebecca in front of the building under the large Delta Development Group sign, along with a small gaggle of about six consultants from Coopers & Tompkins who were also participating in the meeting. It might have been an unnecessarily large group, but given that the client had planned to have at least 12 colleagues on its side, Rebecca felt the strategic move was to show bench strength for this opportunity. Rebecca gave them the game plan as to who would speak and when, who would offer up insights if called upon, and how Rebecca would manage and land the meeting for a strong outcome. The group acknowledged the strategy for the meeting and headed inside.

They made their way to reception and were escorted into a conference room where a dozen or so executives from Delta Development Group were socializing, drinking coffee and reviewing documents before the meeting started. Lyla from the client team, who was presumably the leader of this merger integration team, invited everyone to get some coffee and grab a seat so they could get started.

Once seated, the meeting started and Rebecca went through and introduced each of her colleagues, including Matt, who simply nodded to everyone in the room. Rebecca turned it back over to the client, Lyla, who likewise introduced the dozen or so people gathered from her team. Lyla began, "Thank you all for coming to meet with us today. I know we won't remember everyone's names, but it is great to see the expertise gathered here. As we seek to ensure the success of this merger, we must have the right expertise assembled.

"What I'd like to do now is to ask my colleague, Kenneth, to walk you through what he sees as being the major work-streams for this merger."

With that, Lyla deferred to Kenneth, who began project-ing slides and giving context for the merger at hand.

Matt paused and looked at the presenter. *I know this guy. But how?* Red-rimmed glasses, a goatee, and speaking with a slightly high-pitched voice. And then it clicked: *my Lyft driver from yesterday. But is that right?* His mind swirled with the question of how this could be. He discreetly pulled out his phone, opened the Lyft app, and found the ride. *Yep. That's him. I'm thoroughly confused.*

With that discovery, he spent the rest of the meeting look-ing at Kenneth. Did he recognize him as well? What explained this? He held a senior role working in Delta Development Group's internal strategy group. Why would he be driving for Lyft? *I wonder if his colleagues know he drives for Lyft?* It was as if Matt had turned the volume on the conversation way down and moved it into the background, and he sat enveloped in that ambient noise just looking at Kenneth and wondering more about this man's story.

The meeting proceeded for another hour and a half with Matt making occasional contributions but otherwise strug-gling to focus. Eventually, Rebecca declared, "Well, I want to be respectful of your time, but I feel there are several threads here of how we can support this merger and assist each of you in your work. What I propose is a follow-up meeting, along with some of those documents I promised, which I will send to you by the end of next week. How does that sound?"

With that, they stood, shook hands, and concluded the meeting.

Rebecca leaned over to Matt as she packed her laptop. "Well, that could not have possibly gone any better. I've got a lunch back in the city I need to run to, but I appreciate you coming out here for this meeting. I'll keep you posted on next steps as it comes together. It would be great to have you on this project team if you're interested. I imagine this will be a substantial project."

"Yes, I agree. Great meeting. Thanks for everything. And yes, keep me posted. I'm going to shut down here, and I won't be long after you."

Rebecca and the other consultants made their way out of the conference room as did most of the other colleagues from Delta Development Group. Matt lingered a bit. Kenneth was shutting down his laptop and preparing to leave the conference room when Matt interrupted him. "Hey, Kenneth. Thanks again for a great meeting today."

"No problem, It's my pleasure. I think it's looking good," Kenneth responded.

"I agree." Matt lingered, awkwardly, for a moment. "Hey, so this is going to sound totally random, but I think you drove me to the airport yesterday."

Kenneth stopped and now looked up at him, slowly casing the environment around to see who else might have heard. "You know what? You're right," Kenneth answered. Matt could see that Kenneth was beginning to put the pieces together and felt slightly uncomfortable. "Let's, um, take a walk."

Matt followed him out of the conference room and out of the building. They walked through the parking lot and around the building toward a path that connected the different corporate office buildings.

Kenneth didn't say anything at first as they walked, and Matt decided to break the silence. "Look, it's obviously none of my business why you drive for Lyft. It's just that I wanted to place how I knew you. I enjoyed our conversation yesterday. It's just that—."

Kenneth interrupted, "You're surprised that I have a real job working in corporate strategy as well?" Kenneth smiled, relieving the pressure.

"Well, not that you have a job, but you have a big job. You leading the strategy team for Delta Development Group. I assume that you have an MBA. And based on just this one meeting, I would say that you're talented at what you do and, without getting into your personal life, I presume pretty well paid."

"What if I told you that my driving for Lyft has nothing to do with money?" Kenneth asked.

Matt paused, bewildered. "Then why do you drive?"

"Research," Kenneth offered.

Matt repeated slowly, as if trying to process, "Research."

They walked slowly outside, side-stepping about a half dozen geese crossing the path in between two manicured ponds.

31

Third Shift Entrepreneurs

"Look, I didn't want to talk about this inside the company offices, but my wife and I are starting our own business. I'm almost 40 now, and I realized what I want to do with my life. It has little to do with what I'm doing today, so I keep it quiet for the most part."

Pushing 40. Matt could relate.

"I haven't told anyone at work yet, but my wife and I are opening up a retreat center, about an hour from downtown Chicago."

"Wow," Matt offered, his interest genuinely piqued by this guy who, now having seen him twice in 24 hours in two totally different contexts, was proving to be as fascinating as he was mysterious. "That's cool. I think it's awesome that you are starting your own business. I'm also pushing 40 and, um, I'm sort of on my own journey of figuring out what I want to be when I grow up. Starting my own business is something I keep coming back to."

Kenneth didn't respond, unaware of the depths to which this conversation had the potential to tap something deep inside of Matt.

Matt continued, "But what does starting a business have to do with driving for Lyft?"

"Everything," Kenneth answered. "Yesterday, we had an entire conversation about retreat centers, the last time you used one, the kind of company you work for, how you use them, the decision-makers people involved, the price you are willing to pay and the ones in the marketplace that you have considered. You mentioned one I had never heard of, so when I got home, I looked it up online. I called them, pretended to be planning our next corporate retreat, and asked them for a pricing sheet. Thanks to you, I learned an additional price point for a corporate retreat. You gave me a lot of detail. In your mind, I'm just a talkative Lyft driver; but in *my* mind, I'm getting paid to pick your brain."

"But you didn't tell me any of this stuff yesterday," Matt said.

Kenneth laughed. "Why would I? I'm the one doing the research, customer research, that is. I only do morning routes from the North Side to O'Hare because that is when a lot of the management consultant types are taking rides to the airport. It's already on my way to work, so it's a matter of bringing someone else into the car with me to have the conversation. Occasionally, the person I am picking up knows nothing about corporate retreats or does not fit the business traveler profile, but more often than not, I learn specific and interesting things. Not just about corporate retreats but about labor laws, how to hire young employees, marketing and branding strategies, things about the hospitality industry. You name it."

Matt was taking it in. Kenneth continued, "As far as I'm concerned, I'm driving to work, and I need to be doing some form of customer research anyway, so picking people up and getting some insights is helpful. My research, which I also do at lunch and on coffee breaks beyond driving Lyft, into corporate retreats has yielded lots of other relevant details. So far, I've probably conducted around 20 customer interviews or so. I've cold-called or visited about 15 corporate retreat centers pretending to be planning a corporate retreat, and I've attended a few meeting planners conferences." Kenneth paused, and then as if sensing the absurdity that Matt might be sensing in this whole conversation, laughed and added, "And not that it matters, but I'm also a 4.8-star driver and have made about $450."

33

Third Shift Entrepreneurs

Matt was confused and amazed, all at the same time. "This is all so random that I just happened to get into your Lyft yesterday, that we happened to talk about retreat centers, that I happened to *know* something about retreats, and that I would run into you today."

"Actually, it's not random at all except the last part. I intentionally designed for those first few things. It's part of a strategy that I follow very closely, being what we call a *Third Shift Entrepreneur.*"

We, Matt thought, *who is we?* "Third Shift Entrepreneur," Matt repeated, curious. "How did you learn this stuff? What is your plan now?" Matt found himself thinking about the business that Kenneth wanted to start.

"It's a long story, but I am part of a network of people who are starting their own businesses. They are my people. People like me who are pursuing their dreams and doing the hard work to make them happen. We are willing to do things that others might not be willing to do, like driving Lyft and talking to strangers, because we are more invested in our dreams than our egos. It's not easy, but we are working together and following a playbook.

"To be honest, doing this out here is no joke, man. I didn't grow up with money or role models on how to start a business. I've had to work my ass off for everything I've done in my life: I'm proud of the life I've built and that my wife and I have built together. I feel as if I've done what I can on someone else's terms, and now I want to work on my own terms to build more of my dream for my family and me. It's personal for me."

Matt thought about what he had heard and, surprising himself, declared, "I want to learn more." Kenneth looked at

34

Third Shift Entrepreneur

him. Matt continued, "I know that we just met but I'm in this place of having my own, I guess you could call it an existential crisis, wondering what the next phase of my life is meant to be. I need some of what you're putting out in the world, and I don't know where to get started."

Kenneth pulled back a bit. "Well, here is the thing. I just met you. And for all I know you and I could be working together for the next six to 12 months banging out this merger and integration. This group I'm in is committed, and it's only for people who are serious about starting something: people who are serious about putting in the work. You seem, from our meeting today, good at what you do and committed to your career, so I'm not sure that there is any—."

"That's not true," Matt jumped in, cutting him off. He paused and continued. "I'm good at this job, yes, but something is missing, and I've known it for years. I'm a creator at heart, someone who takes on big challenges. I served for 10 years in the Army, and I just imagined that afterward, I would be running my own business someday. I'm not afraid of challenges. Honestly, I'm probably more afraid of not trying. I never even say these things out loud, let alone to a client, but I know I want to do more. I want to start a business. If something is working for you, I want to know more. It's a relief to think other people are crazy enough, no offense, to go out and take action in some form."

"Oh," Kenneth said, leaning in, "there most definitely are people taking action and starting things. For some people, life just happens. For *other* people, though, they *make* life happen. You've got to decide where you are on that continuum. I've had my moment, and it sounds like you are

35

Third Shift Entrepreneurs

about to have yours." Kenneth looked around, as both of them felt slightly suspicious for having this conversation after the meeting had ended 20 minutes earlier.

"If you are serious," Kenneth continued, "meet me tomorrow morning at 6:00 a.m. I'll text the address to the mobile number on your business card. We can pick up on our conversation then. I need you to decide, though. Only come if you are serious. This group doesn't mess around, but they do get results. New members are rare and only attend when someone vouches for them. I'm going out on a limb here, but I like you, and you seem sincere. If for some reason this doesn't work out, then let's pretend this conversation never happened, and we will get this transaction done as the professionals we are." Kenneth cracked a smile and extended a handshake.

"Deal," Matt returned. He watched Kenneth turn and dash back into the building as he stood there thinking about what had occurred. *Tomorrow morning at 6:00 a.m. What was this even all about?*

At home that night, Matt prepared dinner, played music to suit his mood and was in a dreamlike state thinking about his day, his conversation with Kenneth and the possibilities that lay ahead. Sabina walked in, threw her keys and purse down, thumbed through the mail, and looked over to catch Matt in a little dance with himself. He promptly went to her, kissed her, and told her he had made chicken marsala, her favorite, which Matt had learned to perfect. "Well, you're in quite the good mood," Sabina offered, with a tinge of suspicion.

"I am— it's weird. I had the strangest meeting today with a guy I met yesterday and who turns out was my Lyft driver."

Matt began to share his day, his pace quickening as his eyes opened wider with enthusiasm. "In any event, I'm there staring at him in this client meeting and then I put the pieces together. How crazy is that? And then we get to talking about how he is in the process of starting a business. He's doing some interesting things, and I feel I could learn a lot from him. In any case, he invited me to this meeting tomorrow morning at 6:00 a.m. and I'm going. I'm ready to make this move."

Sabina looked at him with loving confusion, still taking her jacket and shoes off. His story didn't make sense, but it didn't matter to her. She hadn't seen this buoyant version of her husband in a long time. It was as if he was suddenly, in a sense, unlocked. Nothing had changed, but in her mind, a rambling and excited Matt Carney was a better husband than the brooding, depressing one, who had roamed the house. It was a version of him she first fell in love with but she had not seen in some time: the optimistic, idea-of-the-week dreamer, and inspired man.

She looked at him. "Well, I have no idea what you just said, but if you feel like this and act like this, it's good by me."

"Right." Matt paused wanting to put his sentiments into words. "First of all, I feel meeting this guy Kenneth is a validation that I'm not crazy. Second, people are out there also feeling a deep desire to do more, be more, give more. Third, some sort of path might be available to me to help me achieve the goal of starting a business. It's a world I know nothing about. He's a person, frankly, about whom I know little, but knowing a group of people share the same sort of this aspiration or this struggle, whatever you want to call it, feels as if a world has opened up for me."

37

Third Shift Entrepreneurs

Sabina stepped around the kitchen island and moved closer. "Can I be a therapist for a second?"

"Are you ever not?" Matt asked with a coy smile.

"In your mind, the resolution for you is to determine a professional path forward for yourself, and once you have made those decisions and it's public, announced on LinkedIn, or whatever, it will be the moment you are fulfilled or resolved, as it were," she explained.

"As a therapist, however, what I would say is that the condition you are working to resolve is this discontent, anxiety and restlessness. All of these things and a few others. If resolving those conditions is the goal, then I would argue that whatever happened today has moved you forward even before you know what changes your professional future holds. And If I wanted to be a little condescending, I might say something like 'I told you so', that all you needed to do was to take action. It doesn't matter what happens next. That you are feeling you are making progress and on a path will in and of itself bring about resolution. So good job. Okay, I'm done preaching."

"I'm seeing why your clients love you," Matt said, smiling. "You can always preach to me. I know you always will."

Chapter 5

Real World Education

Matt was up early the next morning and ready to make the 16-minute bike ride to the address that Kenneth had texted him. He had not ridden his bicycle in what seemed like a year, which was odd given how regularly he biked everywhere when living in DC and Chicago, even through the punishing winters in previous years. Something about the temperate weather and the general motivation he was feeling had him grab the bike, inflate the tires, and head out at 5:30 a.m. as the sun was rising.

Upon arriving, he realized that the address provided was a residential real estate brokerage office. The lights were on, but he didn't see anyone. He cracked open the door and could hear loud talking in the back even though he was 15 minutes early.

"Hello?" Matt called out.

He saw Kenneth, his Lyft driver turned potential client and now turned personal coach of sorts, come charging out from the back hallway. "What's up, Matt? Glad to see you made it. To be honest, I wasn't sure if you'd show up." Though their interactions had been finite, Matt felt a deep kinship and trust for this new friend and guide.

"I thought I would be early, but it looks as if the other folks are here," Matt said.

"It's all good. We've been here since 5:30 a.m. Newcomers, like you, come at 6:00 a.m. But you're fine. This is good timing. Come on in and I'll introduce you to everyone."

Matt walked into the intimate conference room with whiteboards on two of the four walls, folding chairs scattered around, the smell of fresh coffee, bright lighting, sticky notes, notepads, open laptops, and a general mess around the room of tear sheets, journals, backpacks, and other office supplies.

Matt looked around and observed a collection of people who, on the one hand, did not appear to have much in common. On the other hand, they seemed to be deeply engaged with each other. They took turns listening enthusiastically to updates, interrupting each other, fondly ribbing each other, and intently congratulating and encouraging each other. Something about this group gave him a strong sense of a shared community, belonging, and an elevated sense of purpose. He felt like an outsider initially, but he was quickly welcomed into the fold.

A woman who Matt estimated to be in her late 20s made her way over to Matt first. She was fashionably dressed and had a powerful warmth and illuminating smile. Her hair was pulled into a tight bun, and her vibrant yellow earrings and matching oversized necklace matched her yellow-toned sundress. "Good morning, Matt. I'm Yisel. Welcome. You ready to do this or what?" She laughed a loud, fun laugh and extended both hands toward him for two high fives.

Do what? Matt thought. "Ha. Yeah, I think so," he said with a big smile while returning her high fives with enthusiasm and a bit of awkwardness.

A man in his mid-50s came over next. He appeared reserved and focused with a dead stare but also welcoming. He introduced himself with an aura of formality. "Good morning. I'm Chad. It's a pleasure to meet you. Welcome." They shook hands.

"Good morning, Chad. Nice to meet you," Matt replied.

Next, a vivacious and confident woman, who appeared to be in her late 40s, made her way over with a big, warm smile. Matt extended his hand, and she pulled him in for a hug. "Sorry, but I'm a hugger," she offered with a laugh. "Welcome. I'm Kim. I'm excited to support you."

Support me? Matt thought. *I wonder what Kenneth must have told these people?* "Well, thank you. I appreciate that," Matt said over her shoulder as she still held him in an embrace.

Next up was a man who appeared to be in his early 30s, tall with a heavy frame, shaved head, and dressed in a white-collared shirt with a brand logo sewn into it. He walked around the chairs to greet Matt properly. He appeared to be a bit shy and soft spoken, *a gentle giant of sorts*, Matt thought. "Good morning, Matt. My name is Alberto. I look forward to getting to know you."

"Well, thanks, Alberto, and likewise," Matt replied.

And last but not least was a man who seemed to hang back and observe the scene while the others were coming over and offering their greetings. The man let his folded arms fall to his sides and casually approached Matt with purposeful intent. "Welcome, Matt. Kenneth says good things about you. You're new to the process, but I understand your wanting to make a move. My name is Regis. Are you ready to do the work?"

Regis. Matt looked at him and immediately sensed this was the leader, a man in command of himself and the environment around him. He appeared to be in his mid-60s, slight in stature, well-groomed, sporting a salt-and-pepper goatee and a white flock of hair. He was also more formally dressed, wearing small half-moon glasses and a sweater underneath a blazer. He had a confidence and command of himself and the environment Matt found inviting and slightly intimidating.

Matt caught himself still taking in Regis and the scene, forgetting for a second he had been asked a direct question that was awaiting an answer. "I appreciate that," Matt replied. "I'm not sure if I know what this is all about, but I'm definitely interested."

"Interested," Regis picked up, "is what allows you to come today. But committed is what will be required if you want to come back. I don't mean that to sound intimidating, but this group has been let down by leaning on other people who are not as committed to building their businesses as we are. We set a standard for ourselves, and then we stick to it and it gets results."

"These five people, or six if we include you," Regis continued, "are putting in the work to realize their dreams and start businesses. The only expectation is that you work as hard as they do and you follow the rules. That's the price of admission." Regis paused. "We are what we call *Third Shift Entrepreneurs*. The first shift is your day job, the second shift is your life: family, friends, life obligations, commitments to causes you care about, the community in which you live, and so forth."

Regis continued, "And the Third Shift. This is what you do in the nooks and crannies of your day, in the waning hours, at 5:00 in the morning or 11:00 at night, when most people are sleeping, on social media, or reacting to the world around them versus building something for their future. The Third Shift is the staging ground where you start a business, build your future, and pursue your dreams. It's the time you invest in yourself while you are executing on the now and you are building what is next." Regis took a breath, paused, and smiled.

"To be clear," Regis continued, "many people are content with their careers and their status quo. That can be a wonderful thing. We joke among ourselves that we envy those people, but the people in this room want to build something. They have an idea they cannot stop thinking about. They have something they need to see in the world. They feel a different calling. They want to take action but do not know where to start. Sometimes they think their choice is between a safe and unfulfilled life or a daring life full of risk.

"I have realized," Regis continued, "that is a false choice, and that you can start right from your current place in life, with your current job, or perhaps at another job that's closer to your dream, by taking the right steps. In fact, that is the strategic play. This group is not necessarily more talented, but maybe we are a little more courageous and more disciplined in how we reclaim any white space in our days and weeks. It is not about being willing to take risks. It's about doing the work." Regis looked at Matt to assess what he might be thinking. Matt returned the look as if to imply that he was hearing it yet not understanding it all. Regis continued, "I'm blabbering. Are you ready to dive in?" Regis broke his intense, locked gazes, flashed a wide smile with that last invitation, and placed a firm grip on Matt's shoulder. "Let's get started."

"Okay," Matt said, taking in the words and the boldly expressed point of view. Regis broke away from Matt to call the session to attention.

"Welcome Third Shifters," Regis declared, as everyone sat around a large conference table and pulled out notebooks in preparation for the session. Matt glanced at his watch: 6:00 a.m.

Regis continued, "I want to start by welcoming our newest *prospective* member, Matt Carney who is currently a consultant for Coopers & Tompkins. Team, for Matt's benefit, would you tell him what you do today and what you are building for tomorrow?"

Kenneth took the cue from Regis and began his introduction. "Well, I think Matt knows what I do. I work in strategy for Delta Development Group, which is about to go through a merger and has been the focus lately. The job is great, certainly on paper, but my third shift passion project is that my wife and I are planning to launch a retreat center. I have a passion for leadership and bringing teams together to build trust and she has a passion for hospitality. This has been a dream of ours for some time, and we're committed to make it happen this year. Also, as Matt knows, I occasionally do customer research while driving for Lyft to determine things like pricing, flesh out my go-to market strategy, and learn about potential channel partners and other customer needs for retreat experiences."

Matt nodded in acknowledgment, unsure of his place in this meeting but nonetheless taking it in. Kenneth turned to his right where Yisel was seated.

"I'm Yisel. I work as an account manager for an ad agency downtown. That's my day job. I like it and have a good career there, but my passion is coffee." Matt heard the emphasis as Yisel's posture shifted and she underscored the words: *my passion.* "I'm working on building a coffee business based on my grandmother's special roasting recipe. She passed away, which still weighs on my heart, but she came from a family of coffee roasters in Guatemala. Many of my relatives had been tasters, which is a big deal there. My grandmother had a palate that she cultivated from a lifetime of tasting coffee brewed from various beans and making coffee blends. She was a special person in my life, and I want to bring her essence to life through coffee. In my spare time, I'm working at a local coffee roaster and also holding coffee tasting events for catering managers."

Yisel smiled at the group and motioned Chad to go next.

"Good morning, folks," Chad started rather formally, looking over the rims of his glasses. "I'm an intellectual property attorney at a boutique firm, and I have been practicing law for many years." The career matched what Matt presumed based on Chad's demeanor. "In the meantime, however, I am building my business as an antique map dealer. I've always had a passion for cartography and rare and fine maps, and I'm working to make a business doing the thing I love." This interest in maps struck Matt as fascinating and unexpected. Chad deferred next to Kim, who was seated to his right.

"Well, good morning again, Matt. My name is Kim, and I retired from the Army after 20 years on active duty." Matt smiled, knowing they had this in common.

"Hooah," Matt bellowed, giving the verbal nod offered from one soldier to another.

"HOOAH," Kim replied, louder, bursting into an even bigger smile and laugh. "That's right. Go Army!"

Even though the Army is a large institution, Matt always felt a special kinship when he came across anyone else who had served. He sensed an immediate rapport with Kim and was curious about what she did in the Army and where she served, and to learn more about her career since separating.

"After my 20 years, I knew I wanted to do something to be of service to others, which is what fueled my career in the military and which I knew would be something that I would miss upon getting out. I secured a day job working at a hospital, managing a team of people who do the check-in process, working with patients. I like my job, but my real aspiration is to help young women coming out of the foster care system."

Matt noticed in Kim's story, like Yisel's and Chad's, how she lit up and came to life as she began talking about her passion project.

"I grew up in the system, so I know the good and bad people who were in my life growing up. When I was 17, I joined the Army because I knew that could provide me with a stable path forward. With that and my faith in God, I built a productive and fulfilled life for myself. But I know that is not always the case for young people coming out of foster care. One adult who decides to advocate for a child can make all the difference in the world. So, I want to build an organization that works with women between the ages 15 and 18 who are preparing for life on their own after they age out of the foster care system at 18."

Matt was inspired by Kim's passion, as well as the others, but he was confused, assuming, coming in, this group of entrepreneurs would be talking about technology or raising venture capital dollars. What he was seeing instead was something deeply human. Still, he wondered: *What do these stories have in common? Antique maps, foster care, Guatemalan coffee?*

Alberto went next. "Morning, Matt. My name is Alberto as I mentioned to you. By day, I manage a wireless phone store. I started in retail and have always been interested in consumer technology and wireless phones. Eventually, I was promoted to run a store. My passion, though, is technology-enabled reality experiences, things like escape rooms where you put people into a simulated environment, and they must solve the challenge. As a kid, I loved haunted houses. While other people were waiting for the next thing to jump out at them, I was constantly thinking about how they had put this whole thing together like the graphic effects, smoke, costumes, and the rest of it." Alberto opened up as the passion started to pour out of him.

"I went to an escape room a few years ago with my wife and some friends," Alberto continued, "and I absolutely loved it. I mean, I really loved it. I also thought of how to change and improve it, and I kept returning to it as an idea. Then, I had an idea for an Apocalypse experience with zombies and all kinds of crazy stuff. My wife, though thinking it was crazy, also saw the potential in it, so she joined me in the effort. We converted our garage into an experience we call the Apocalypse Escape and are selling tickets to the neighborhood. We'll see where it goes, but at least we have started." The group offered some affirmation for the progress as Alberto added, "Oh, and I still manage the wireless store, probably for a few more months at least."

Regis grinned as he took stock of his protégés around the table. "So, Matt, there you have it. We have a coffee roaster, a Zombie Apocalypse escape room, a cartographer and antique map dealer, a foster care transition program, a retreat center, and then whatever you are deciding to do, which we will get to."

"Regis," Yisel jumped in, "you have to tell Matt your background as well."

"Sure." Regis didn't seem eager to share his own personal story but opened up. "Well, one of the first jobs I had out of graduate school was running a safety program for a large manufacturing company. This was back in the late 1980s. I realized the time-consuming process was manual, and had lots of holes in it. I would spend most of my time tracking down employees to ensure they had completed their required safety refresher training for us to be compliant. It felt ineffective.

"So, instead, I built a better way of managing a safety program using the technology version of Scotch tape and bubble gum. With the company's permission, I built a database management platform to manage employee safety training records. It worked well, and I made the move, again with the company's support and a little bit of its capital, to spin out this solution into a business that grew from there. Over the course of 18 years, we developed the technology platform, expanded into consulting for safety programs, and became the industry standard for safety program software. I decided I wanted to move forward and spend my time

48

doing what I love most, which is coaching and mentoring people like you: the Third Shift Entrepreneurs," Regis said, his arms spread wide to encompass the entire gathering. "I had a lot of people help me along the way, and I knew I owed something to the next in line. Besides, if I'm honest, this is my perverse idea of fun."

"And when he says, 'it was time to move forward,'" Kim interrupted, "that's code language for he sold his company, SafeTech, for several million dollars. I'm just saying."

The group laughed, and Regis conceded a smile.

"Well, thank you, Kim, for always clarifying." Regis returned the discussion to the topic at hand. "So, Matt, this is what we are here to do: to learn and grow our businesses together. Each week, you will learn some of the observations of the Third Shift Entrepreneurs. Sometimes, people talk about rules of starting a business or the steps to starting a business. However I talk about the *observations* of starting a business. We need to clarify certain things. Once they are, then you are good and you move on. If they are not clear, then that is where you will spend your time. The first observation is you must begin with what you are interested in: some connection, passion, or obsession even. As you listen to each of these entrepreneurs, you can feel their passion, curiosity, or personal connections to the things they are building," Regis explained.

"This is about having a specific idea of some problem you want to solve. It's not about a great solution or at least not yet. It's about caring for youth in foster care, continuing your grandmother's legacy through coffee, offering a thrilling one-hour experience, selling a beautiful antique map, or

Real World Education

creating a better corporate retreat. And you'll know you're *obsessed* with it when you stay up late thinking about it, you wake up early thinking about it, and you get excited talking about it. For me, that's what building a safety program software management solution did. I saw I could do it better, differently and felt passionate about pursuing that. I kept thinking about it.

"And you must be obsessed," Regis emphasized for dramatic effect. "The word is intentional in this context. Someone who *likes* an idea will do it for a little bit, meet some inevitable resistance, get frustrated or bored, and then decide to spend their time somewhere else. Someone who is *obsessed* with an idea will persevere beyond the inevitable obstacles. Someone who has that passion for an idea will pursue it with an almost irrational fervor even though other people can't understand why someone would care so much or spend so much time.

"It's the thing that you can't get out of your mind. You think about it even when you wish you wouldn't. It's often something that touches you personally." Regis panned across the conference table, pointing at the Third Shift Entrepreneurs as he went. "Kim's story, Yisel's passion for coffee, even Chad's deep commitment to antique maps. Each of their stories compels them to proceed. Though some people would say, 'why bother?' Our people say, 'I can't *not* do this.' Work, for them, is its own form of play or even a mission: They do it for the sake of doing it. I wouldn't invest in any business or support any person who was not on some level *obsessed* with the thing they were doing or building." Regis paused to gauge the receptivity of the group to what he was sharing.

"Sometimes, I talk to a group of business school students, and they think it works the other way: 'Shouldn't you look at the market, do the gap analysis, and then decide what the right business is to start according to the gaps?' I respond, 'Absolutely not.' The question is not whether the market needs a given business. The market might need a business, but that's the wrong approach. The right question is, what is the right business for *you* to start? The answer has everything to do with what you know, what you care about, the markets or patterns you uniquely understand and your weird, unique and compelling vision for the thing you want to go and build. Building this thing, Matt, should be what you would still choose to do even if money was not involved because you feel so strongly about the value, experience and service you are bringing into the world."

The room was quiet. Clearly Regis had shifted into teacher mode, and the students were capturing his lesson.

Regis paused and leaned in, looking straight at Matt across the table. "But let me make an important point, which might seem paradoxical. You must be obsessed with the problem you are solving but at the same time be *unattached* to its solution. For example, Yisel can be committed to bringing the traditional Guatemalan coffee roasting process to the United States to share her grandmother's gift to the world, but if she gets stuck on *how* it will happen, she will inhibit her ability to solve the problem.

"If, for example, she decides she must have a coffee shop, sell the coffee through retail channels, or offer coffee roasting classes, she could miss the right opportunity. You only know the right opportunity by talking to customers and running some experiments to see what sticks. Yisel has to be committed to bringing her grandmother's coffee and its 'essence' to the U.S. market, but *how* that happens will be revealed through her controlled experiments. She will make those decisions eventually. A lot of entrepreneurs get this wrong and miss the opportunity to make small modifications that would have made their businesses successful. Loving your business idea does not mean being fixed and inflexible on the details of how that business comes into the market. Just the opposite."

By this point, Matt realized the others had begun scribbling notes in their notebooks to capture some of the lessons that applied to them. Matt was, on the other hand, transfixed listening to Regis's perspective. This was a man with wisdom, someone who shared a strong point of view, not because he had any ego invested in the answer or from any desire to be right, but because he was an experienced professional pleading with his students not to repeat the mistakes he had seen made dozens of times over the course of a colorful career.

"So, my question for you, Matt, is simple: What have you been thinking about these past 10 years or even this past week? What can't you stop thinking about, or what do you keep returning to?" Matt felt the weight of the question hang as the group looked at him. He wasn't sure if this was meant to be a rhetorical question or if it was one he was supposed to answer right here at 6:28 a.m. in this storefront real estate office.

"I want to start a business. That feels clear to me," Matt led, with clarity about his aspiration, whereas he might otherwise have hedged in talking with friends and his colleagues. "I don't have the specific idea yet, and I generally like being a consultant, but for me it's not really a mission. At work, I offer some insights, deliver a PowerPoint, but I don't really see the work through. I'm a team player. I want to be in the trenches with people, helping them figure out the bigger challenges and feeling more ownership over my work." Matt paused. This was as much as he had ever articulated to anybody, perhaps let alone himself, as to what he wanted to do and build. He continued, "Again, I don't know how to turn that into a business, so I'm getting started."

Regis jumped in. "You don't have to answer this right now, but you will soon. More importantly, not liking your job is not the right reason to become an entrepreneur. What does *entrepreneur* even mean, anyway? People who chase that title and that status will fail. It's a title, and it says 'I don't want to work for other people.' It's like wanting to be a famous actor but not wanting to act. The real starting point *must* be the problem you are here to solve, the beautiful thing you are here to build, or the people you are here to serve. If you start there, then the business, as well as the title, will follow. But don't get the sequence twisted. Figure out what you care deeply about and what you might have thought about more than anybody else. I'm not interested in brilliant ideas in the abstract. I'm interested in brilliant and specific problems that are close to you, especially the kinds unique to who you are, what you've lived through, and what you know how to do."

In some ways, Matt felt like he was being scolded. Regis's voice had become elevated as he emphatically clarified his points, yet Matt felt a deep sense of gratitude for the stern and focused insights as if he were listening to a coach pleading with his players because he knew what they needed to know and the only question would be whether they were open to hearing it. Matt felt this was all in his best interest, and this was the coaching he had been needing even if he barely knew this man or knew where he was headed.

"Ah, but enough time on the soapbox for one day," Regis chuckled at his own professorial tendencies. "Let's get into the homework. Each of you has your accountability partner for the week, correct?" Regis looked around the table as the cadre began to make eye contact with each other. "Okay, let's see. Alberto, you and Chad are together this week. Kenneth, you can join them as well. Kim, you and I are spending time this week. Matt, why don't you and Yisel meet this week to start? Go ahead and get with your partners to figure out your plan."

Yisel to turned to Matt. "Any chance you can meet me at the coffee shop and roasting facility I'm working out of? Can we say tonight at 8:00 p.m.?" She gave him her card with her number.

Matt thought to himself, *tonight feels soon*, but he was eager to dive in and start. Matt had assumed this would be some weekly meeting or even less than that, but Yisel was operating with a greater sense of urgency, and Matt felt this as well, and he was grateful for that. "Okay. Sounds good. I'll text you my number, so you can send me the address."

The group began to gather their things to prepare to leave. Regis pulled Matt and Yisel aside. "Matt, listen. I want you to spend some time on what you've been thinking about or with what you are obsessed. It does not need to be creating world peace. Better if it is small, specific and interesting to you. It might be something that's right in front of you, or maybe even something people keep asking you about. This is important. Come with a list. Yisel has been through this exercise before."

"Okay. Got it. What I keep thinking about or what I am obsessed with. I will give that some thought for sure."

"And be specific," Regis pushed. "Don't just say something like 'accounting.' What is it about accounting? Is it spending four hours on a budget document, or is it talking to a new client? Is it developing a strategy to reduce the tax obligations of a company, or is it leading a team of accountants? Oh, and don't stay anchored in what you are good at. That's the easy mistake to make. People confuse what they are good at with what they like to do, but those are different. I expect to see some things on that list you might even consider hobbies or distractions, like refinishing your basement, helping to organize a family reunion, or taking on some cross-fit challenge. There's important information in those observations about yourself." Regis packed up his things.

"Okay, got it. Will do," Matt obliged as Regis gave his shoulder a gentle slap and turned to walk out.

"Oh," Regis added, turning around. "A couple more things. I've given you your first strategy, but I'm also going to share behavioral changes with you required if you are going to shift your life into starting your own business. The first two are these: What got you here won't get you there. You need to break a couple patterns. So, if you are used to being home at 6:00 p.m., drinking two beers, and watching TV all night, don't expect a different outcome for your life. Break patterns. Try different routes to work. Get up early. Stay up late. Go visit different neighborhoods. Do things that put you into a state of discovery."

Matt listened to this seemingly personal advice. Regis had the presence of someone who had been there and done that.

"And the second one is this: Every minute matters. I see that you rode your bike here. I wonder what you were listening to. Were you mindlessly entertaining yourself, or were you learning something relevant? Did the learning value of what you heard supersede what you might have been reading had you taken public transportation or drove here? You might think that's obsessive, but when you get going and start your own business, every minute will matter, and excuses like 'I don't have time' won't cut it. Most people don't know how much time they have, and they have far more of it than they think, but they aren't exacting in how they use it."

Matt took this in and was grateful for the lessons. Regis turned to walk out but had another insight. "Oh," Regis said, looking Matt in the eyes again, "and I presume by the ring that you are married? Ask your spouse what you love to do and what others see in you. She'll know you better than you know yourself." Matt nodded.

"Okay." Regis laughed. "Now I am done with my soapbox."

As the Third Shift Entrepreneurs made their way out the back of the small, residential brokerage office, Matt realized it was only 7:10 a.m. He had the whole day ahead of him. Walking out of this small office and into the spring air, watching the city wake up, Matt was filled with an optimistic energy things were about to shift. He didn't know how or what was to come, but he knew his journey had begun with this most unlikely group of individuals. *Why were they so willing to help him? Who were these people? What was to come next?*

Chapter 6

Breaking Patterns

M att returned home by 5:00 p.m., having begun the day at the Third Shift Entrepreneur meeting and going into the office to catch up on work. He grabbed the mail and changed from his work clothes and into something casual before his meeting with Yisel that night.

He stopped himself, hearing Regis's voice: *Break the pattern*. What did that mean? Regis gave the example of coming home, watching TV, and drinking two beers. Matt thought he wasn't that guy, though making dinner and drinking a bottle of wine was not out of the norm for Sabina and him. He loved those nights. Was that bad? Was it wasting time to spend a night cooking with your spouse? *I get the point if I were some lazy bum who mindlessly watched TV*, Matt thought, *but I'm not, so do I need to break this pattern?*

Resolved not to fall off Regis's wagon before he had even started, Matt was intent on breaking a pattern. He looked at his comfortable sweats calling him and at the bedside clock: 5:15 p.m. Looking out the window showed a beautiful spring day, temperatures in the mid-60s. *Scrap the normal routine.* He had not been for a jog after work in as long as he could remember. Running was something he enjoyed, but running after work was something he almost never did because he was usually too exhausted by then, at least that's what he told himself.

So, with a strong resolve, he rustled through the bottom drawer, pulled out running shorts and a shirt, threw on his running shoes, and grabbed his earbuds. The decision to break his normal pattern felt small but exhilarating.

He went to his playlists and clicked on the first one. There it was again, like the voice of God: Regis. *Scrap the normal routine and intentionally make choices.* He stopped the music and went to his podcast app. He loved podcasts, but he didn't always take the time to listen to them. He wasn't always intentional in what he listened to either, usually choosing the podcast recommended by the app based on his prior listening trends. In fact, Sabina had suggested a podcast to Matt called "More Than Business" by Kara Jones. Sabina had said her podcast blended psychology as well as advice for aspiring entrepreneurs, mostly targeted at women, but she'd suggested it because she knew some of the self-doubt he faced and the wisdom he needed. "Just trust me. There is something in this for you," Sabina had told him at the time. Kara Jones had started and sold a few different businesses while raising kids, and she was something of a guru for aspiring entrepreneurs. Though Matt might not have identified himself as someone who listens to self-help podcasts, the reviews of this one were nonetheless strong, and he trusted Sabina would know what he needed. Given that Matt now identified himself as an "aspiring entrepreneur," he needed the infusion of insights and inspiration, so he hit play.

As he stood on the front stoop stretching, he breathed in the air and took in the scene around him. Young people in the neighborhood were coming home from work in business casual with their headphones in. Two kids across the street were drawing a picture with chalk on the sidewalk. Some neighbors down the street were sitting on their stoops listening to music. Live music came from somewhere. The neighborhood was alive. For some reason, it felt new to Matt. That was, perhaps, the most interesting part. He had been living in this neighborhood for several years, but for some reason, standing on his front step, listening to a podcast about aspiring entrepreneurs and preparing to go for a run, something had changed, like a fresh chapter had begun.

He took off and headed toward the lakefront path. He was not used to running without music. For the first several minutes, he tuned the podcast out, enjoying the beautiful sites and scenes of Chicago: people walking dogs, outdoor cafés, sports fans dipping in and out of local bars, and the ebb and flow of professionals getting off trains and buses, coming home from work.

When he hit the lakefront path, he finally tuned into the podcast. "So, fear. That will hold you back," Kara Jones said as she punctuated her comments with a dramatic pause. Her tone was that of a sympathetic coach, compassionate and welcoming, yet authoritative.

Matt continued at a steady clip down the lakefront path toward downtown, letting his mind wander off and into the words of the "More Than Business" podcast.

"It's the fear of being embarrassed. The fear of failing. The fear of 'What will my friends think?' It's the fear that holds us back. For many entrepreneurs, the greatest fear is not that they will lose their money or even that the business

Breaking Patterns

won't work. They are stuck in the paralysis of not wanting to update their LinkedIn page to say, 'I'm starting a company,' because at that moment, they are accountable. They are accountable to the thing they have said. It's the emotional risk they are signing up for at that point."

Kara Jones continued . . .

"Here is the deal: You need other people to create your business and people *want to help you* create your business, but if it's just in your head, they can't. Starting begins at the point at which you do something outside of your head, which you *can't take back* because you are accountable to what you have said to other people and to your own reputation. Too many entrepreneurs give themselves the excuse that it never really worked even though they never really started. Worse than that, we can self-sabotage. We would rather kill the idea ourselves than suffer the pain of someone else telling us, 'I don't like it' or 'I don't need it.' This is what makes starting something, actually starting something, so scary, because you might fail. You've told the world that you are doing it, and as a result, the world might ask, 'Hey, did you stop doing that thing?' And you might have to look that person in the eyes and say 'You know what? I did in fact start that thing. And I tried. And I put everything into it. But it didn't work.' And it's that *very sentence right there*, which is why most people don't ever start something. But if you want to get into the arena and *actually* be an entrepreneur, then that is how it must be. The only other option is not starting. There is no such thing as *kind of* starting. No such thing. You cannot do this without a willingness to put yourself out there and put your reputation on the line."

Matt continued at a steady clip, listening to Kara on the podcast, taking in the waning spring day in Chicago. He was lost in his own thoughts, oscillating from the sheer excitement that he might be starting a new journey to some psychological cocktail of fear, anticipation, anxiety, and the guilt and shame that he hadn't done anything yet.

The fervor of the podcast continued in his ears while Kara continued her appeal:

"Fear. That's what we are talking about. It's fear. But here's the good news: It's easier to manage because it's all in your head. Just think about this: It's you versus yourself. Because other people, when you do start something, will find it courageous, bold and exciting. They will admire you for it, yet we struggle to admire ourselves. And listen: all of those people who you think will criticize your '*failure*,' they are not the people for whom you do this work. Who cares what they think! They are in the cheap seats; you are in the arena. You are doing the important work. But you—*you* need to decide that your own fulfillment matters more than what society tells you is success. Their version of success might be your own personal prison. So, I get it: you're scared. The only remedy to dealing with the fear is to practice the thing that makes you afraid. Practice it in small ways and then bigger ways. What you *learn* by putting yourself out there is that, hey, guess what, if it doesn't work, you're still alive and something else good may come of it. At least, you get to go to bed telling yourself that you didn't live your life on the sidelines.

Breaking Patterns

So, do your planning and be smart, but at some point, you need to start. Don't confuse busy activity or even quitting some job you don't like with making progress. You might say '*I made a plan*,' '*I built a website*,' '*I filed some paperwork*,' '*I finally quit my job*' to which I say fine, okay, do all that stuff. But that isn't the same as starting. *Starting* is when the world knows you've staked a claim. You're tethered. You can't just delete it. But that's when the good stuff starts. Most people don't even get to that point. They let the thing fail before they even start."

Something triggered in Matt. He knew he had to take action, and that this reservoir of self-pity in which he dwelled had been a pathetic excuse to take no action. He felt his heartbeat increase. He had once been a motivated soldier. He knew how to take action for himself and get it done, yet these last few years had been a comfortable slide sideways.

"Get going," he said to himself, surprised at the directness and that he had said it out loud. He kept talking to himself: *You know what you need to do. Now go be the adult. Take action.*

When he finished the run and came upstairs, he noticed the time: 5:50 p.m. He thought, *I feel great, different, in control, and it only took me 40 minutes*. He had broken a pattern, and he saw the wisdom of doing so. *Why would this simple and even obvious idea have seemed so non-negotiable just last week?*

Sabina came home a few minutes later as Matt finished showering and was prepping dinner.

"Hey, babe," said Matt welcoming her home, more chipper than Sabina had seen him in some time. "I just went for a run and followed your recommendation and listened to that Kara Jones podcast. There's a lot of wisdom there." Matt was moving quickly. "Dinner will be ready shortly, and then I have to run to meet my new friend for coffee at 8:00 p.m."

Sabina didn't know what had gotten into him, but she liked the change.

"You're in a good mood," she noted.

"You know what, I am. It's hard to describe," Matt reflected. "The meeting this morning was unlike anything I've ever experienced. I feel as if I am coming alive and I'm not sure why other than I met these people who are interesting and who are starting their own businesses at night. There are six of them, and the leader, Regis, is this successful guy who built and then sold a technology business several years back. They call themselves the Third Shift Entrepreneurs, and they're a little tribe who support each other in this process. Each one of them is pursuing something interesting and specific to who they are and what they want to do in life: everything from coffee roasting to a retreat center, to a lawyer who is becoming an antique map dealer."

Sabina listened with curiosity and some skepticism. She had seen Matt fall in love with ideas-of-the-week only to lose interest shortly thereafter. She had learned not to become emotionally invested in these flights of fancy. *When it's real and sticking, I'll know it and support him then*, was generally her disposition.

"Cool," was the one-word response, neither hostile nor enthusiastic. Sabina offered it as a bland acknowledgment.

Matt continued in an animated fashion as he pulled together a quick dinner. "My challenge is that I don't know what I want

Breaking Patterns

to do. I know it's something more than what I am doing now. They didn't ask me what business I want to start. It didn't seem to matter to them, but I know I need to figure that out and I desperately want to do so. Having this conversation with a group of people has changed how I feel. I feel different today than I did last week, like I'm not stuck, or at least some sort of path or option exists even if it isn't clear yet."

"I'm happy for you, honey," Sabina replied.

Matt could hear the cautious support in her voice, and he didn't blame her. Hell, he didn't believe himself half the time. Why should she? "Okay, so I have homework tonight. I need help. Regis told me to catalog what I love to do or have been continually thinking about. It's sort of a simple exercise, but he underscored how important it was and that I needed to be specific. I need your help. He told me to ask you because an outside perspective would be helpful."

Sabina looked at him. "Okay. Sure. I'm here for it."

Sabina's apparent nonchalance for Matt's newfound enthusiasm didn't bother him. He smiled to himself. *She'll see the difference in time.*

An Obsession

Having made a quick dinner, Matt and Sabina sat down for a conversation, mindful that he had an 8:00 p.m. appointment to meet Yisel. Matt brought out a notepad, specifically for this process, following the lead of the other Third Shift Entrepreneurs.

"Okay, I'll start. I'm obsessed with—." Matt tapped his pen and thought out loud. "Obsessed is a strong word. I'm not sure I'm obsessed with anything, though Regis did say it's the thing you keep thinking about. I love parts of my job. I love winning new clients. I love talking with people, understanding where they feel stuck and helping them design a strategy to help them achieve great outcomes. I like being creative and finding unconventional ways of solving what look like typical challenges, like a merger or an acquisition."

Sabina interrupted him. "You hate mergers. Two years ago, I barely saw you when you were working through that complex transaction with that gourmet snack company. You were grinding it out at all hours, and when you did come home, you complained about it."

Matt paused to reflect back. "Okay, that's fair, but I want to think about that. I hated the hours, true. Though, if I'm honest, I probably came home and led with complaints to justify that I was never around. The last thing I would want you thinking is that I'm having a blast while never being home."

Sabina looked at him with that skeptical squint he was used to. "So, you complained for my sake? Hmm."

Matt continued, "No I'm not saying that. I'm saying that if I'm honest with myself, I loved parts of that deal. I loved the work and got lost in it. It was challenging, lots of personalities involved. The details of the transaction made it complicated, but at the end of the day, it was the most satisfying thing I did. Did I love working crazy hours? No. But I know I poured myself into it because I liked it. It was interesting to me. Some of the personalities I could have done without, but the CFO was awesome and is one of my closer friends today." Matt paused and thought again about the experience.

"Actually, I loved everything about it except that I couldn't be around to see it through. I felt we worked so hard, and, poof, I was out of that project and into another one within a week. The part I hated was not being able to stick around to see the outcome. Also, if I'm honest, I feel I killed myself for that project, which I was happy to do, but my pay didn't reflect the effort. Several executives received enormous payouts; meanwhile, the managers and consultants at both companies nearly worked themselves to death and hardly received a bonus for the effort. It was unfair. I'd like a more direct correlation of the reward for my effort."

"Okay," Sabina conceded. "So, keep going then. What else?"

"I like understanding the people involved and what makes them tick to design a solution that makes everybody happy.

Well, maybe not everybody, but most of those involved. I liked the wide array of considerations for everything from enterprise technology to human resource issues to strategic product positioning. I guess I liked touching many dimensions of the business and being something of a generalist."

Matt paused, made some notes, and kept thinking out loud. "I love spending time on a budget. Not all of the time. I can geek out diving into a spreadsheet, running numbers and doing correlations and analysis, which might be buried in the numbers. I also love feeling I'm in a pursuit, going for something, whether a new client or a new solution." Matt stopped himself. "I do love pursuing new clients, but I hate the feeling of walking away from the projects I've just completed. I want to know how it all turns out. I guess that's the nature of management consulting though—."

Sabina was listening. Matt's self-assessment seemed more accurate than she would have thought him capable.

"What else?" he asked himself out loud.

Sabina perked up. "Remember when you first made senior manager and you took it upon yourself to organize the social outing for the new associates? You loved that. I don't know everything that went into that, but I know you talked about it for months."

"You're right. I love helping people think about their careers and mentoring them along the way. I loved planning the social outing, and we did many thoughtful things to make those new consultants feel connected to the firm and to each other, which was fun and different from what we normally do."

They sat in quiet for a second, both thinking.

"This doesn't sound terribly original at this point or any-thing that would give me some future direction. What else? I mean, I've dreamed of being my own boss and building my own team. I've wanted, in my core, to start my own business and be able to move as fast as I can possibly move or as fast as the clients want, not slowed down by mediocre perfor-mance around me," Matt added, "I think I like smaller clients. I'm not excited by projects that don't have the CEO involved in some way. It feels like the work can get lost."

"I love other things, but they don't have anything to do with work, such as camping, being outdoors, human psy-chology, and leadership in general. It's hard to stay active with those things, and part of me thinks those are lost dreams from college or my youth. Of course, I dream of going camp-ing more than we do and exploring national parks."

He looked at Sabina. She knew how much passion he held for hiking, exploring parks, and camping, anything hav-ing to do with being outdoors, which was much more a part of their lives when they first started dating. That part of Matt had not shown up in a while, and she sensed that it was part of his low-grade, mid-life crisis. Being in an office or on the road and constantly in and out of airports was not part of who Matt was or what made him tick. It had taken a toll. He was smart and liked strategy consulting, but he was a soldier at heart and wanted to be outside and working with his hands.

"I'm sure that all former college athletes love a sport but know they will never play it again," Matt continued, as if to dismiss the idea preemptively, "so I'm not sure things like playing in the dirt or being out in nature belong on the list of what is possible, but I'll capture it for now. I don't want to sound like one of those people you ask what they love, and they answer, 'being on a cruise or on a beach on vacation.' As if that's some insight into a future career. I do love being outside, and you know as well as anybody how I lose my mind a little if I can't get into nature in some form, but I don't know how that translates."

"There is something there," Sabina jumped in. "You're not a guy who sits in an office. Your health, being outside, being physically active has always mattered to you. Don't ignore it."

Matt listened and took in what Sabina was saying before responding confidently. "I think you're right. This does matter. If I think about my best days, it mostly involved doing something physical or outdoors. I have no idea how that relates to management consulting, but there's something there."

Matt and Sabina continued this conversation as they each pulled from increasingly specific anecdotes. At one point, Sabina thought about how she appreciated the novelty of sitting and talking with her husband instead of whatever else they might have been doing like watching TV. She could see something coming alive in him.

She also thought it surprising he was going to an evening meeting at a coffee shop to meet a woman whom he had met that morning. Matt thought it strange as well but trusted this newfound process. He invited Sabina, but she declined, sensing this was his thing, his journey. Even stranger was that he realized the address Yisel had given him was close to where they lived, though he had never ventured there. He was excited to try it, even if he could not yet understand how going to see coffee being roasted had anything to do with his professional future.

By the end of the conversation, Matt had pages full of notes, and he and Sabina had shared a few good laughs about some of his previous adventures and misadventures. They recalled with nostalgia some sweet memories that informed who he was and what he loved, many of which he had forgotten or had lain dormant and neglected in the back of his mind. Some of the things he got right, some of the things he got wrong, between his Army years and his movement into management consulting after business school. He thought about his adventures outdoors and his false starts with business ideas over the years, which he would passionately pursue for a week and then lose interest. This will be different, he committed to himself. Somehow, this *will* be different.

Chapter 8

The Internship

M att locked his bike and looked at the bustling coffee shop with a neon sign in front that identified *Viva*, the coffee shop and roastery where Yisel had told Matt to meet her. It was set inside an old warehouse building with industrial glass garage doors opened to let in the warm spring air. Young professionals and students were scattered about, some working on laptops, others engrossed in conversation or reading.

"Matt," Yisel called from behind the long coffee bar. She wiped her hands and came around to greet him. He was probably at least 10 years older and had just met her that morning. This and coming to her for entrepreneurship coaching and life lessons didn't seem strange in this moment.

"Come on back." Yisel led Matt through the busy coffee shop, through a set of swinging double doors, and into the warehouse where an extensive coffee roasting operation was set up.

"Do you own this place?" Matt asked, never having been given a full explanation as to what Yisel was doing here.

"Oh no," Yisel said, laughing. "I wish, but no. I still work in marketing during the day, but I work here at night where I also make my own coffee blends. Come here. I'll show you."

Matt was captivated by the fresh, rich smells of roasted coffee beans. Yisel led him over to a staging area with what looked like 20 to 30 burlap sacks in barrels filled with coffee beans and covered with airtight lids. Yisel began to open the lids, scooping up beans and lifting them for Matt to smell.

"This is from Kenya. You smell that? It's a large bean, has some sweet fruity notes, and makes for one of the cleanest coffees in the world."

Matt inhaled through his nose, absorbing the rich scent.

"Or this one," Yisel continued. "These are Geisha coffee beans from Panama. These carry a natural tea-like body with lots of clear, bright flavors like citrus, peach and jasmine." Yisel was in her element, excited to present the diversity and specific contributions of the different beans. Matt leaned in to smell the roasted coffee beans as she presented them.

"Here you have these delicious smelling and tasting Kona beans from Hawaii. Hawaii has the micro-climate for growing coffee beans with its rain and sun, fertile land and volcanic soil."

Yisel opened another container off to the side with a little dramatic flair. "Smell this one. This one is mine," she offered with pride. "Guatemalan beans: full-bodied, hints of chocolate, nutty, and sweet. In my biased opinion, they're the best coffee beans in the world. I love this blend. I tinker with small batches to get this blend just right. My grandmother spent her life tasting coffee, and she was locally renowned among growers and sourcers. I want to bring her standards and spirit to consumers in the United States."

72

Though Matt regularly grabbed brewed coffee all throughout the day, he had never been particularly discerning. Seeing these beans, facilities, and Yisel's passion for the craft, he realized how little attention he had been paying to the coffee that was part of his daily life.

"But," Yisel interrupted herself, "you didn't come here to talk coffee. You came here to talk business." Yisel, with her naturally commanding flair, led them to two stools near a coffee-tasting bar opposite where the beans were staged.

"Let me tell you how this started for me. I was unhappy in my job. I still am, but that's a longer story. I wanted to start a business, and since I know and love coffee, I knew this was a connection to my grandmother and something I cared about. I also knew my grandmother could discern a well-roasted bean and that coffee can represent a bigger story about a place, something much more than just a caffeine hit.

"So, I did the things I assumed an entrepreneur was supposed to do. I looked for places to lease space, examined hiring a director of sales, and searched for coffee equipment to buy. I even paid a marketing person to create a website and a brand. I applied for and got approved for a small business loan, which I was excited about at first because everybody needs money to start a business." Yisel paused and looked at Matt to see if he was picking up the storyline. "Sounds great, right?"

"Well, yeah. I mean it sounds you were on your way to starting a business," Matt responded.

"Ah. And you see, that is the fatal flaw of most entrepreneurs," Yisel perked up in refute. "I did these things that look like starting a business: getting a loan, signing a lease, buying equipment, incorporating the business legally and hiring people, all of which, if you notice, involve *spending money*. None of this is important nor had anything to do *making money*. And *none* of it had to do with customers. My thought was that I'll build it, which is the spend money part, and then I'll sell to customers, which is the make money part. And that, Matt, if you don't learn anything else from me, was backward."

Matt was listening intently but was confused. "Okay. But how do you start a business or sell something to customers if you haven't built the business? It doesn't entirely seem irrational what you did."

"Ha!" Yisel, lighting up with some exaggeration, slapped Matt's arm and smiled. "Definitely rational but definitely not right. There is a different way to do this. What I will tell you, having spent time with the Third Shift Entrepreneurs, is that there are strategies that exist to sell to customers or get them excited and committed before you go and spend money. This stuff isn't necessarily obvious, and people get it wrong all of the time. Fortunately for me, I got lucky."

"Lucky?" Matt asked. "As in the business worked somehow? Or that you met Regis and the crew?"

"Exactly," Yisel replied. "The second part, not the first part. My business didn't work. Well, to be fair, it never fully started, but I didn't get in so deep that I couldn't pull back and start over. I did, however, as you said, meet Regis and the Third Shift Entrepreneurs. What I learned, almost immediately, was that I had it all wrong. Regis gave me some diatribe about needing to do this differently, which I resented at first.

I just thought he was being overly controlling. Later, I realized he was protecting my own interests. He has been my biggest advocate. It was a loving concern for my own success as opposed to some sort of, I don't know, scolding," she said, closing the lid on her proprietary blend.

"He brought me back to reality in a big way. The first thing he told me is that the only time you celebrate is when you get money from a customer. Everything else is a false signal. Second, he told me not to buy all this stuff until I understood the business and had customers. I should figure out the key questions of this business, like how to roast coffee, what kinds of customers are buying it, where to source it, what the industry trends are, what the industry supply chain looks like and, importantly, whether or not I like doing this. I needed to figure that out before I spent any money. That, he told me, is my education or my self-imposed 'internship.' And I can get that education free. He told me, in fact, that I can get paid to get that education. He advised me to go learn on someone else's payroll and with someone else's equipment and investment. And, as part of that, find strategic partners who can do other parts of the business I don't want to do or don't know how to do."

Yisel paused as one of her co-workers delivered two espressos in front of her. "Ah, you're the sweetest. Thank you, Alana. Here." She put one of the espressos in front of Matt. "Enjoy this. I know it's caffeine and it's late, but trust me, you're going to love it. If you can't sleep tonight, then consider it an opportunity to do some work on your business. Savor it first. Really smell it, taste a little, and start a little relationship with this coffee in front of you. Show some gratitude for the hands that made it and from the faraway places these beans come from."

Matt and Yisel each took a slow sip. Yisel was in a state of pure delight, and Matt found himself having an entirely different experience with the coffee as well.

"Hmmm, that's good." Yisel put her cup down. "Okay, so the third thing I learned quickly from Regis was this: understand that different channels exist for selling coffee. I couldn't be good at more than one of them to start, so I would have to pick. Selling to individual consumers is different from selling to hotels, which differs from selling coffee online, which differs from selling it to local grocery stores agreeing to put it on the shelves, which is also different from running a coffee shop. If I tried to do all of those things at once, I would be unsuccessful at all of them. If I knew what I was doing, I would say no to opportunities that don't fit my strategy.

"Finally, Regis said, make sure you know how to make damn good coffee. If you can't do that, then all of this is a waste of time and money."

"Wow. Sounds as if he was pretty hard on you," Matt acknowledged.

"Yeah, it felt brutal at the time to hear that, but I have come to appreciate his advice because he was the one person who helped me save money and lower the risk of starting the business. I needed his advice even if it felt as if he was taking away my dream."

Yisel, politely, gestured to Matt to start taking notes. Matt pulled out his notebook and his pen.

"Okay, so let's recap." Yisel shifted to teacher mode as Matt prepared to take notes.

"Lesson 1: Don't spend money on stuff until you have a customer base that requires you to make those investments. Spending money on a business is not necessarily progress. Ditto for borrowing money or even getting an investor. That isn't necessarily progress. The only real progress is in learning about and getting customers, which you can do in most cases without spending money for a while. If you can, borrow someone else's infrastructure and get paid to learn the business, which is what I'm doing by working here at *Viva*.

"Lesson 2: Turn your life into an internship. This doesn't have to be an actual internship, but the point is to be thinking about how you get closer to understanding the market you want to enter: the people involved, the supply chains, maybe the technologies, the sales cycle, all of that. You can't go from your day job to something totally different without context. You need to get the context."

Yisel paused, took a sip, and gave Matt a second to catch up on his notes.

"Lesson 3: Understand who specifically is buying what you are offering. You can't sell to everyone, and selling to businesses is different from selling to individuals, so you have to decide. Entrepreneurs don't want to limit their options, so they say, 'I can sell to anyone!' because it seems like more business or more opportunity. That's wrong. The more specific you are, which involves saying no to opportunities in order to get focused, the more successful you will be."

Matt was scribbling notes. "Okay, I think I got it. You have to understand where you will sell the coffee or product and be willing to say no to grow or say yes to opportunity."

Yisel perked up. "Ooh, I like that. Say no so you can say yes. That could be our new tagline. You should tell Regis. Okay, there was one more thing, an obvious thing that a lot of entrepreneurs get wrong as well."

Matt thought, *It wasn't a rule*. But it was the last thing she said, "Make sure that your coffee is damn good."

"Exactly," Yisel said. "Some people get the business part all figured out, develop sophisticated plans, line up investors, create marketing materials, and the rest of it. But if the product is no good, who cares? I have a friend who started his own boutique marketing agency and sold marketing projects without success. He was frustrated because he was actively selling and working hard but couldn't get any business. Because he's a friend of mine, I said to him, 'Do you want to know what I think is your problem?' He sort of paused and said, 'Sure.'" Yisel took another sip.

"I pulled up his website and said, 'Randy, look at your website. I say this with love, but it sucks. There are broken links. The stretched photo looks janky. And you're a marketing company who is offering to sell this service to other organizations. End of story.' It was harsh, and it hurt saying it, but he kind of laughed at how obvious it was to see. He told me that I was right, and he hadn't focused on his own marketing because he was in sales mode. If he were a coffee company, sure you can have a crappy website to start. But a marketing company? It won't work that way." Matt kept taking notes.

"By the way, I'll never offer advice to someone who doesn't ask for it. What's the point? That's why I asked Randy first if he wanted the advice. You'll beat your head against the wall otherwise. The good entrepreneurs want the advice; the bad ones keep selling you on why what they are doing is the right and smart thing even though it's not working." Matt nodded.

"The point is," Yisel continued, "and this is Lesson 4: you have to be good at the thing you want to bring to the world and to your customers. If you're not good at it and if the thing doesn't work, or no one wants it, then you'll be wasting your time and everyone else's. So, make sure the coffee is damn good." Yisel looked serious for a second, took a sip, and then she let out a laugh at seeing Matt looking intimidated.

Matt laughed in return, but he continued taking notes to capture the lesson. "This is good. Really good stuff. Thank you."

Yisel finished her espresso with one final sip. "You're welcome. Okay, so you don't get to sit and listen. Tell me what resonates for you. What does all of this mean for you?"

Matt looked up at the ceiling, wanting to crystallize his thinking. "Well, I'm still not sure what business I want to start, but I do know I want to do more to bring something unique into the world. Getting paid to learn is a great lesson. It's sort of obvious, but I would have missed it. I've assumed this would require a big capital investment or quitting my job, but the way you said it makes it seem more attainable. I met Kenneth because he was my Lyft driver, and that is part of what he was doing as well."

Yisel jumped in to build on the point Matt was making. "Get paid to learn. Yes. It was so obvious, but it wasn't anything that I had thought about. I knew my grandmother had this expertise, her coffee was amazing, and people would

79

The Internship

want it, but there were a million details in between I didn't know. It wasn't just deciding to work here at *Viva* at night. I had to reorient my time with my regular job. With my day job in marketing, every day there, I'm learning new things and gaining expertise, but I never thought of that as training toward starting my own business. Though, it is. Once I decided I wanted to start my own business, this coffee business, I started to gravitate toward projects at work involving startup businesses and anything related to food or beverages, so I could gain that expertise. It has helped to think of my day job as the place where I am getting the training I will need to start my business. Regis told me to get a Third Shift job where I could learn about the coffee and roasting industry. Six boutique coffee roasters are in Chicago, and a couple from South America own this one. I went to all six and spent a night just hanging out, tasting their coffee. The coffee here was the best, and they had a real commitment to culture. I talked to the owners and shared stories of my grandmother and how I wanted to learn about the industry. I even told them I would work free if they would let me learn how to roast coffee."

"What happened?" Matt asked.

"What happened was amazing. They offered me a job on the spot. And here is what you learn along the way. Opportunities will show up, and you will be given what you need but you have to know what you want and be specific. I have learned to be more specific and transparent with what I am hoping to learn and have found that people show up and honor you in the process. For the owners, they were always struggling to find people who loved coffee as much as they did or understood how important culture was to roasting coffee. So, when I showed up saying I wanted to learn, it was an incredible gift for them. We each thought we were doing the other one a favor."

"So, what happened next?" Matt asked, finding himself interested in this unfolding drama.

"Well, I started the next week, about three months ago. I work three nights a week, and I have learned every part of the business. I know how to source roasting equipment, roast coffee, source beans and people's flavor preferences. I have learned the importance of the name you give a coffee for how customers decide to buy it as well as how to get packaging and branding for coffee. I've also come to understand pricing and profit margins *and* understand I don't ever want to run a coffee shop. It's too much work. It drains me, and it isn't what inspires me."

Matt paused as if this revelation was somehow a defeated ending to an otherwise uplifting story. "So, what do you want to do then?"

"I'll tell you what I want to do. I want to package and sell the best Guatemalan coffee at a premium price point to boutique hotels and upscale neighborhood grocers right here in Chicago, at least to start. I can't be competitive on price selling to large grocery stores, so that's not my goal. I don't want to do that kind of volume, and I don't want to compete on price. I want the difference between my coffee and others to come down to quality. I want to be in fine restaurants, hotels and boutique stores that care about the story and quality of my coffee.

"And," Yisel continued, "here is what else I have learned. I don't need to build any of this stuff. The owners right here at *Viva* are happy for me to roast my coffee here during off-hours in exchange for brand recognition on my labels, '*Roasting by Viva,*' with their logo attached. They see it as a win-win to get their brand out there in the marketplace more widely."

"So, you seem to have more than an idea. You have a business?" Matt asked.

"Well, it's getting there. I have one hotel that will source my coffee. I will generate about $700 a month in revenue from them, and I have another boutique upscale market here in Chicago where I expect to do about $1,000 a month. My margins are about 30 percent right now, so it's a small business but a real business, and I have my day job working in marketing."

"How do you juggle all of this?" Matt asked.

"Well, I told you I didn't like my job, but that was before when I felt stuck. I appreciate my job a lot more than I ever did now that I know it is enabling me to build something for my future. Knowing that it's part of my education, or 'internship' as we call it, makes me more motivated to learn about this industry. Coming to work with my own learning agenda, beyond what the company expects me to do, has fundamentally changed the experience for me."

"Huh." Matt was curious about this last point, and he admired Yisel. What she had accomplished in a short period, her tenacity of taking on this goal and being focused on how to achieve was terribly impressive. "That's incredible."

"Matt, it's not incredible. It's doable and it is teachable. It's about being focused and pursuing the 12 Observations of the Third Shift Entrepreneurs. The best part of this is I have not taken on any debt. *Viva* has been selling my blends from the start. I've been making money while learning how to start this business. The only thing I am giving up is time and some brand exclusivity by including *Viva* on the label, but if that's the sacrifice I have to make to bring my dreams to reality, then I am more than willing to make it."

"I think that's awesome. Seriously," Matt said.

"Thanks," Yisel said, "and I had to sacrifice one other thing besides time."

"What's that?" Matt asked.

"My ego," Yisel answered in a deadpan voice. "I used to work service jobs in high school and college to support myself and to cover my cost-of-living expenses. I thought working in an office and in a marketing position was progress and that I would never have to work in a service job again, which I thought of as 'lower level.' I had to get over that to realize that if this is what it takes to learn, then I would need to check my ego at the door. A lot of people want to run a successful business, but not a lot of people are willing to put in the ego-threatening work required to get there."

After a contemplative pause, Yisel continued. "I remember the first time I was working here. Someone I knew from grade school came in, looked at me, and didn't know what to say. The look on her face suggested she was looking at me and thinking, *'I'm surprised she works at a coffee shop and not in a professional career of some sort.'* It bothered me and I felt insecure, but I turned, took her order, smiled, chatted with her a bit, and privately reminded myself I was playing the long game of being a successful business owner. It wasn't about her, and someday she would understand why I made the decisions I made or she wouldn't, and that would be fine, too. I realized any insecurity I had was about my own ego or a story I told myself. The story you tell yourself, if you aren't careful, will keep you hostage to a reality in which you aren't even happy."

Matt listened to her words and the truth in them. He knew how much making partner had been a public milestone that everyone would celebrate with him: in person, at the firm, in LinkedIn accolades and with old friends from business school. He would take a public bow for his accomplishments. What would it look like to go back to the world and say, "Change of plans. I'm not that happy, and I want this new, scary and, maybe to you all, inexplicable thing"? Would it look like a mid-life crisis? Probably. Was he willing to risk that? That would be the question that would linger for the next several days.

Yisel stood up and poured two small cups of coffee from a small pot that had been dropped by another server nearby with a nod to Yisel. "I know it's almost 9:15 p.m., but you need to try this, too. Just a little bit. This is also my blend."

Matt held a delicate cup and took an intentional sip. The coffee was delicious. "Wow. You have a gift for this."

Yisel sat back. "So, before I let you go, let's talk about you for a second. You had homework, right? Regis asked you to think about what you love, so let's hear it."

"Right." Matt flipped back through his notebook for the notes he had taken with Sabina earlier in the night. He began to share the list of things that he loved, starting with situational things at work, elements of management consulting, being physically active, being in nature, exploring and other situations specific to his personality.

"So," Yisel said, taking a long sip, "you work as a management consultant for Coopers & Tompkins which is a big firm, and you have these other things you love, including camping and the outdoors. I explained the strategy of getting paid to learn. Have you ever considered offering to do a consulting project for an outdoor gear company or a travel company that focuses on outdoor excursions, or maybe get a job running strategy for a resort in the mountains? I don't know if such a thing exists. In other words, could you take what you do now, which is management consulting, but do it for clients who share your passion for the outdoors?"

Matt stared at her. *What an obvious suggestion*, one that he had never thought of. He sat in contemplation.

Yisel could see that he was processing the advice before breaking the silence. "We talk about these things as micro-movements."

"Micro-movements," Matt repeated.

"Yes, micro-movements are a little strategy that smart entrepreneurs have and use to win out there. We have this misconception that starting a business is about some big dramatic change. We quit our jobs, cash in our bank accounts, and go for broke. That's not smart and not how we think about it as Third Shift Entrepreneurs. We prefer micro-movements instead: the small, specific, and incremental things you can do to shift your thinking, shift your time allocations throughout the day and shift your opportunities. Small changes lead to big results."

"Hmm," Matt said, thinking more.

"What I heard you say, and tell me if I am wrong, is you like certain parts of your job but miss a connection to nature and want more autonomy to be in control and be the decision maker. You also said something important, which is a belief statement. You said you believe, as humans, we need to be in nature to be healthy and whole. That will resonate with people. You need to get to the other people who *believe* the same things you do. So, a micro-movement would be to focus on getting a client in the outdoors or camping space. Maybe the next time you have a client meeting, let them know you're interested in camping and see what conversation ensues. That way, you are applying what you have expertise in without quitting your day job; instead, you are focused on an area in which you have real passion. When you begin to speak about your interest, the world can respond. You'll be surprised at what comes back. The universe, or other people, can't help you if they don't know where you want to go or what you believe."

Matt wrote *micro-movements*. "I like that idea, but I don't necessarily get to pick my clients, so I'm not sure—."

Yisel could hear him stuttering and looking for excuses. "Well, Matt, I don't roast coffee at a coffee shop until I decide I do. Who is your boss again?"

"Well, I am a senior manager. The projects I am assigned to mostly determine who will be my boss, per se. In my position, I am trying to bring in new business to make partner."

"Oh," Yisel jumped in. "So, you definitely could talk to a company or an organization with some connection to nature, the outdoors, or camping. In fact, you don't know this, but part of your visit here is that I get to give you homework." Yisel laughed at the surprise on Matt's face. "It's true. Regis lets each of us give the new guy homework. So, my homework for you is to go have a meeting with someone who could become a client of yours at a company with some connection to the outdoors. It doesn't matter which company. Get beyond your normal routine. Find a company or organization you're interested in and go have lunch with the CEO, the CFO, or some other person who would normally hire management consultants and see how you can add some value. It's a brave and focused conversation. It can't hurt, right?"

"Okay," Matt obliged. "I'll do it. I joined this climbing gym on the west side and it's a hobby for me, but I have never talked to whoever owns the place. It might be interesting to talk to them."

"Well, there you have it. That's a great start," Yisel responded. "Go climbing at the gym and talk to the owners about their business. You're a smart guy who helps companies think through their strategic questions. Maybe they'll have questions you can answer. Plus, remember my story about working here. They thought I was doing *them* a favor. If you're paying to go to this climbing gym, you're doing the owners a favor in that you're already a customer of theirs. Of *course* they will talk to you. Entrepreneurs are used to connecting with people they've never met before. It's only those corporate types, of which you might be one, that think it's weird." Yisel smiled, even as she gave this not-so-subtle dig at Matt. He smiled back and appreciated the ribbing. He could see the inherent wisdom she carried, so much of which she had shared with him in this brief hour together.

After a few parting thoughts and Yisel making him promise to do his homework, Matt left the busy coffee shop.

When he got home, he was tired and mentally exhausted, yet his heart was full and the caffeine kept him thinking. He didn't have this lingering anxiety about what he was meant to do with his life, which would normally be his parting thought before falling asleep. Though he didn't have answers, he knew he had started a journey, a journey that began before 6:00 a.m. and ended this same day after 10:00 p.m. with new friends he didn't know a day ago.

Sabina was asleep, and Matt changed clothes and crawled into bed next to her. Though he was exhausted, his mind was still racing. He pulled out his journal to capture some of the key lessons from the day. He thought about the things Yisel shared and admired the progress she had made by jumping into a job to get paid to learn. Though he admired what she was doing, he was a bit unsure about how any of this could be related to him. "Get paid to learn," he wrote. "Don't start a business before you prove that you can solve the problem." *Trust the process*, he encouraged himself, as he drifted into a deep sleep.

"Meet me and Regis tonight at 1824 N. Willow Street at 7:00 p.m. Business casual attire. See you then. Kenneth."

This was the text Matt saw after he woke up at 6:30 a.m. Kenneth sent the text at 4:30 a.m. *Who are these people*, Matt thought. *Do any of them sleep?* He rolled over. Sabina was in the shower getting ready for the day. He got up and shuffled into the bathroom. "*Huh*," he said under his breath.

"What? And, by the way, good morning . . ." Sabina offered.

"I have to go to another event tonight. These people are intense."

"What event? A client event? But you were gone last night, too," Sabina prodded.

"No. It's from Kenneth with an invitation to join this new group of friends tonight. Presumably some Third Shift Entrepreneur event. I don't know the details. He just texted me at 4:30 this morning with the address and told me what time to be there. Part of me wants to say I can't, but that's not how this group rolls. They were clear they can unlock a future for me, but I have to play by their rules."

"Interesting group. If I didn't know better, I would have said you just joined a cult." Sabina chuckled, happy at least to know that Matt was taking action for his future.

"No, it's not like that," Matt offered as he reached for his toothbrush. "They are intense though. They are committed to doing what they have commited to doing. And they seem to have fun doing it, which I can see."

Matt shared his visit last night with Yisel and some of what he had seen and learned. In particular, this idea of starting a business using someone else's infrastructure, in Yisel's case someone else's coffeeshop, fascinated him.

"Interesting," Sabina offered, "but how do you do that if you're a management consultant? I mean, I don't think seeing clients at night is realistic, and you know I love you, but I don't have to tell you we can't afford not to have your salary for any extended period of time."

Matt heard her, and it didn't need saying that they needed his income. Though she might have, in theory, supported the idea of quitting and starting a business, it was not something they were financially in a position to do.

"Yeah, I know. The idea of quitting and starting something scares me, and I don't want to lose the income, though part of what I'm learning is I don't have to do that. It's not about quitting and starting something new. It's about continuing to do what you're doing while exploring what you are building for yourself. It's about starting something before you quit something."

"Interesting," Sabina responded, "but how do you do that if you're a management consultant?"

"I don't have an exact idea, but it requires some creativity." Matt was pulling on some of the lessons he had learned and was beginning to develop his own point of view. "It could be taking on more clients aligned with what I am interested in, talking to people about my interest, or perhaps something more public like starting a blog or giving a presentation at a conference."

Sabina was dressed and finishing her makeup, moving faster than Matt. "Well, you'll figure it out. Are we still on for Saturday night? It sounds like it might be the next time I talk to you for more than five minutes at the rate you're going."

"Yeah, we are still on for Saturday. Hey, I want you to know I appreciate you tolerating me as I figure this out. I don't know what it all means, and this morning I was a little exhausted and maybe confused, but I want to trust the process. Even if it is a cult." Matt smiled and gave Sabina a kiss.

He looked at himself in the mirror as he finished brushing his teeth. *You're breaking patterns. Trust the process. Keep making micro-movements.*

Chapter 9

The Space to Discover

Matt spent a full day at the office. It was as if the workload had caught up with him after a couple of days of being mentally checked out of work and checked into the Third Shift Entrepreneur group. He had lost track of time and had spent the better part of the afternoon in his office with the door closed, cranking through PowerPoint presentations and client deliverables. When he looked up, he realized it was 6:20 p.m. He put his things together, including some work to take home, and dashed out of the office to make the 7:00 p.m. event that Kenneth invited him to. Though he didn't know a lot, or anything for that matter, about what to expect at the event, he knew he had to be on time.

Matt jumped in a cab and gave the address. He recognized the neighborhood, a swanky part of the Near North Side of the city where people lived in four-story row homes on tree-lined streets even though they were only blocks away from piercing skyscrapers. "Here we are," offered the cab driver. Upon arrival, Matt took in the broad and dramatic poured-concrete staircase that led up to an oversized oak door with a brass knocker the size of his fist. Gas-fired lamps flickered on either side of the door, and Matt could hear people bustling about as classical music emanated from within.

As Matt stood there, the door swung open as a woman propped it open with one hand while holding a tray of champagne with the other. "Welcome. Please come in."

Matt stepped into the house, picked up a glass of champagne and made his way into a large main living room with high ceilings, candles burning throughout, a staged fireplace and oversized, comfortable furniture. About 20 to 30 people were socializing. Antique maps were staged throughout the space on tripods. Servers moved trays of hors d'oeuvres throughout the cocktail reception. Matt cased the place for any sign of Regis and finally spotted him in the corner of the kitchen chatting with two people that he recognized as Chad and Kenneth.

"Gentlemen, pretty stunning home here. Thank you for inviting me." Matt extended a handshake to each of them.

"I'm glad you made it. It was Kenneth's idea," Chad smiled, as he gave credit for the idea to his friend.

"Well, thanks, Chad. I appreciate it. I'm honored to be here even though I don't quite know what this is."

"Oh, you'll find out shortly," Regis answered. "Chad, why don't you go and do what you need to do, which is talk to your customers." As Chad made his way to greet guests and answer questions they had about the various maps on display, Matt saw him step into his passion for talking about the intricate details of the artifacts he so passionately adored.

"This is an antique map show, salon style." Regis began, turning to scan the reception as the guests gathered. "These individuals fashion themselves as cultured people who want to be in the company of other cultured people. Chad has organized this as a way to showcase antique maps, teach people about the art of cartography and, hopefully, sell some pieces."

"Is this Chad's home?" Matt asked, looking around while absorbing the splendor and the architectural details.

"No. This home belongs to the senior partner of Chad's law firm. He's that gentleman over there in his mid-70s." Regis pointed to a man in a cable-knit sweater sipping champagne and entertaining two other guests his age.

Kenneth jumped into the conversation. "Before we get into tonight's event, how did it go with Yisel? What did you learn?" he asked.

"A lot. Definitely one of the big lessons while watching her was you can get paid to learn, which is what she has been doing by working part time at *Viva*. I also learned about creative ways to start a business without spending a lot of money. She told me about borrowing what other people have built and paid for, in her case the coffee roasting equipment. I mean she's essentially started her business, but it doesn't seem she had to take any real risks. She's given me at least one example of how it's possible to reduce the risk of starting a business."

"Boom. That's it," Kenneth responded resolutely while Regis was nodding in satisfaction at the progress of the newest member of the group.

Regis added, "You're about to see another example of how that is possible. But what about Yisel? What did you learn from observing *her?*"

Matt thought for a moment about the question, "Well, she's passionate about coffee, and her coffee is excellent. She brings an intangible energy, which is contagious. She's also willing to put her ego aside and do the work. And it is, from watching her, a lot of work."

"Correct," Regis offered. "It is a lot of work to work two jobs effectively and give up your mornings and nights. Right, Kenneth?" Regis smiled as Kenneth smiled in agreement.

"At its core, however," Regis continued, "that is the choice you have to make if you want to pursue something that gives you fulfillment and lowers the risk of getting started. To be clear, she could have done it differently, and most people do. She could have taken out a loan or borrowed money from friends and opened up a coffee roasting facility of her own, diving in that way. In my view, that's expensive, risky and unnecessary, but most people assume it needs to be done that way, which is why we don't have more people starting businesses in this country. Starting seems overly intimidating or risky because, when done that way, it certainly is."

"I can see that," Matt replied. More guests had arrived as Matt, Kenneth and Regis were talking, sipping champagne and walking around to observe and study the old maps on display.

Kenneth took the lead in the conversation. "So, what we have here, Matt, follows those rules as well. Chad has had this real passion for antique artifacts, specifically maps. He spent years thinking about quitting his job to open a map shop." Kenneth paused. "I want you to think about that statement for a second: quitting his job to start a business. Isn't that how everyone dreams about it happening? One day, like a fantasy, we will quit our jobs and be free to pursue what matters to us. With the Third Shift philosophy, we reject the idea that starting a business is some linear pursuit where you stop one thing and start another. If you have a passion for doing something or creating something, then start doing it today. Don't blame your current job. Smart entrepreneurs pursue multiple projects at once." Matt watched Chad talking with a client.

"They keep the current thing going while curating the next thing. They get comfortable 'practicing in public,' as I call it. What they find out in running these little tests about their passion project is which ones have legs. You need to discover the business, in a sense, and you can only discover it by getting out there and starting in small ways. If you don't do it that way, then you concoct some idea in your head about the business you want to start and how great it will be, and you know exactly how you think it should work, but all of those assumptions limit you, and most of them are wrong. There might be a business that could work, but it's not exactly the one you've envisioned in your head. Your customers need to help tell you how the business should work, according to their needs and not according to your grand vision. Think about Yisel. She couldn't have known that someone would let her roast her beans for free had she not stepped out in smaller ways."

Kenneth stopped as Regis looked at him impressed, smiling. "Well, I couldn't have said that better myself, Kenneth."

"So, back to Chad," Regis picked up. "He was stuck in this paradigm of unhappiness, wanting to be an entrepreneur selling antique maps and the like, but he couldn't figure how to get off the starting block. So, we talked about what would it look like to start immediately. At first, he was confused by this. He pushed back, saying that he couldn't afford to quit his job and open up a cartography shop." Regis shook his head and smiled as he prepared to deliver the punch line. "I told him *opening* a map shop has nothing to do with his passion for talking about and *selling* antique maps to people. 'If that's what you are passionate about,' I told him, 'then go this week and sit down with people who might be interested in buying a map and sell it to them. After you sell one map, sell a second one. And a third one. Then, you might need a store, but you can do a lot before you take on all of that overhead and personal financial risk.'"

"So, he took the advice?" Matt asked.

"Sure did. He's still a lawyer, but here we are at the home of the senior partner of his firm, Karl, who is hosting a sort of salon gathering for him to sell maps."

"How did that happen?" Matt asked, genuinely curious about how this all came about. "Why would his current boss want to help him start a business?"

"Well, I was having a lot of conversations with Chad. He was scared to say something. He thought work was work and personal was personal, and he should keep the two separate. I challenged him to mention his passion for maps to Karl and see his reaction. Well, Karl thought it was interesting. He didn't know much about it, but he had one friend, a neighbor down this street, whom he knew to be himself a collector of antique maps. They got to talking more about this interest of Chad's, and in the course of the conversation, Chad mentioned he likes to sell maps as well on the side. Karl, far from thinking that was threatening, thought it was fascinating and something the firm could leverage. Chad then floated this idea to host a wine and cheese reception with key clients or prospects who are interested in maps so he could talk to them, build relationships, and in turn sell to them if appropriate."

Matt looked surprised, given his assumption that starting a business would have to be something that he kept quiet and hidden from his co-workers. He looked at Kenneth, knowing that he did not seem public yet with his desire to open a retreat center. "That sounds easy, but in reality, it's hard to do in our line of work as management consultants. I think if I say I want to start something separately, Coopers & Tompkins would probably want me to leave." Matt pushed back a bit, including Kenneth in his defense, because he presumed they had a shared understanding of how things work for guys like them working in strategy roles, either in-house or as consultants.

"You don't know that," Regis explained. "There's a smart way to do it, and a strategic way to time it. You'd be surprised at who would become excited by hearing about what you want to start. It shows passion and creativity. It might help differentiate you from your colleagues because you have a dream you're pursuing."

The reception continued to unfold. On the other side of the room, Chad explained to a small group of people, hovering over a map, some specific details that seemed to enthrall them.

Kenneth added, "Chad's biggest challenge when he started was in being too linear in his thinking. He kept daydreaming about some perfect scenario or some doomsday scenario. Regis had to pull him back to reality several times."

Regis affirmed Kenneth's point and continued, "There is a psychological blind spot that most of us carry, and Chad did, in which we essentially view most decisions as having two outcomes: good or bad, win or lose, success or failure. For people thinking about starting a business, the danger is that we think the business will be wildly successful or a terrible failure. That's binary thinking, that we will win or lose, and that only two possible outcomes exist. But it's flawed thinking, and it's not the way the world works. The reality is 10 if not 100 outcomes are possible when you start a business, most of which are good, and many of which you would not have expected. The more you practice starting things, the more accustomed you become to seeing how things unfold in interesting and unexpected ways. Like this event. It's somewhere on the road to starting, not a total success yet, but not a failure. It's *incremental progress*. Learning to expect this outcome gives you the courage to make more, smaller steps forward. People will see you as brave, courageous, or just interesting for stepping out with something to offer. Or they might not pay attention, which is fine, too. For the Third Shift Entrepreneurs, this is the path to discover that unknown opportunity on the other side."

Matt nodded, hearing these themes and reflecting how he had seen some of the principles at work with Yisel the night before. The serving staff began inviting people to congregate in the living room for a presentation.

"Looks like we are starting," Regis said. "But I want to call out one thing before we do, and this is related to sales, which is something every entrepreneur has to do. You have to create the space where you are engaged with those who will be your customers. You need to open the relationship before you sell to them, and in Chad's case, he's doing that through education and these social events. It's hard to sell maps, or anything for that matter. Nobody likes being sold to. People do, however, appreciate learning about something they're interested in while socializing. People want to be in a community with other people who care about, or think about, the same things." Regis watched Karl move to the front of the main room.

"So, I always say, if you want to sell something, become a convener and an educator of the community who cares about what you do. Ultimately, with that trust and connection, they will naturally buy from you. What Chad has done here is to convene people, invitation — only, who are interested in maps or in theory could become interested. They are here because they enjoy learning, maybe talking about antique maps, but most importantly, this is where they can be among those whom they view as their peers. I want you to observe how people interact with each other; they like being a part of this little community gathering here. It fulfills some part of their self-identity, which is important to them. Don't underestimate the extent to which all of your customers, including when you are selling to a business, are making buying decisions in part based on how they feel and the emotional and reputational need that you might fulfill for them personally."

"That's good advice," Kenneth affirmed, looking at Matt, "and something I'm working to figure out for myself."

From the corner of the room, Matt heard a spoon clanking on a glass of champagne. "Excuse me. If I can have your

The Space to Discover

attention." People gathered in the main room and sat on couches and chairs assembled around the fireplace.

Karl, the host, took center stage, "Welcome everybody. We are delighted to welcome you to our home. I can't think of a better evening than to spend time learning about the richness and history of our world, connecting with new and old friends alike and maybe an excuse to enjoy an evening out together on a weeknight," Karl smiled.

"I'm particularly excited that Chad, a colleague of mine, can share his passion for the ancient art form of mapmaking. A few months ago, he shared with me his interest in cartography, and since then, I have become interested in maps myself. Frankly, I had not given antique maps or antique anything much consideration before, but talking with Chad has sparked my curiosity, and I hope it sparks yours as well."

Karl spoke for a few more minutes and then turned it over to Chad, who began to walk around the room, positioning himself at different maps, explaining some of the intricacies and elements of the maps that make them special, their historical relevance and their provenance. His presentation was followed by questions from the crowd and more mingling.

Matt observed people coming up to Chad, continuing to pepper him with questions. *"How much is that one piece? I love it."*

"Would you ever consider doing a similar event at our home? I think our friends would find this interesting."

"Have you heard of this art dealer downtown? She hosts monthly auctions. I don't believe she has added old maps to her repertoire, but I have to imagine that she would be interested in a conversation at least. I can connect you if you'd like."

Regis, who had also been chatting with some of the guests, made his way back to Matt. "Pretty cool, huh? Chad is like a celebrity here."

"Yeah. He knows his stuff, and these people seem pretty hooked," Matt observed.

"And to think that a few months ago, he was thinking he had to quit his job and open a store. Today, instead of accruing debt and hoping that someone comes into his store, he's getting out in front of those people who can be his customers, building better relationships with them and sparing himself the overhead. At this point, he is making a little money, refining this salon pop-up concept and building a prestigious reputation, and he has several more events booked over the coming months. Will he open a retail shop at some point? Maybe, but that's not the goal. The goal is a thriving business and doing what he loves, which is talking about and showcasing antique maps. And by building the community first and curating the demand, the business will follow in some form. Teach, then add value to the people you engage by making them look good or be better, and then sell. Every person here is getting value, including the host, those who buy, and those who don't buy. Everyone. Including you." Regis smiled and raised his glass to Matt.

Matt observed the room and saw the level of engagement and enthusiasm. He wondered if Chad's boss, Karl, would change his attitude if at some point Chad left the firm, but for some reason he didn't think so as long as Chad continued to host these types of events, which created value that pointed back to the firm.

As the reception slowly dwindled, Matt went over to thank Chad for allowing him to be a part of this evening's experience.

"Chad, I want to say thanks for allowing me to drop in on tonight's event. An impressive evening all around. You've got me intrigued by maps actually. More than that, I learned a lot in the whole approach tonight. There are lessons in all of this for me."

"Thank you, Matt, for coming," Chad replied, and then still holding his hand in a handshake, he added, "And you're right. There are lessons in this for you. You are much closer to starting your own business than you think. Follow the strategies of the Third Shift Entrepreneurs. This stuff works, it really does. I've been holding on to this passion of mine for years and only saw paths forward that terrified me. I was paralyzed, but I met Regis, hooked up with the group, and he said some obvious things that got me started in small ways. Don't get me wrong; I still have moments of fear, like coming in tonight and wondering whether people will show up, whether I'll know what I am talking about, or whether I'll embarrass myself somehow. But those are reputational questions in my head I can resolve. I'm clear about my passion and clear about my path, which doesn't feel outlandish or risky."

"It's evident," Matt replied.

Matt began to thank Chad again, but Chad interrupted him, "Oh, Matt, one more thing before you leave. You have homework." Chad smiled and pulled out some notes from his pocket. "I need to give you your homework."

"Okay," Matt agreed, "I'm ready for it."

"Become an expert at something and go public with it. I'm not sure what that will be. Maybe it's something in your day job or maybe it's some private passion of yours. Whatever you think you might want to start a business around, go public with some form of expertise. If you wanted to open a bakery, I would say make some live video on Facebook about how to bake cookies. If you want to start your own management consulting firm, then publish an OpEd piece about a challenge that companies are facing these days. Get out of your head and go public with your ideas in some way. I spent hours studying maps and thinking about them, but it was all in my head. Regis pushed me to go public with it, which, in my case, was talking to my boss, which led to events like this."

Chad paused while Matt was listening and taking in his advice. Chad, with a warm smile, motioned to start writing.

"Ah, right. The notebook." Matt pulled out his notebook and wrote down the instructions from Chad. *Become an expert at something and go public.*

Chad continued, "There is a misconception about what constitutes expertise and authority. At one point, I was thinking I needed to get an advanced degree to be considered an expert at antique maps because there are people who are far more expert at it than me. But it's not true. Expertise is awarded to the person who holds the conversation. If I'm the one who is out here talking about maps, showing maps and selling maps, then I'm looked upon as the expert. No one stops to say, 'But wait, is he qualified?' The key is that you have to be out there sharing it with other people. That's the part people miss. Otherwise, you're just in your basement or in your head accruing all of this knowledge people won't know how to access from you." Matt kept writing.

The Space to Discover

"It's not just that most people fail when they start a business. It's that most people never get out of being stuck in neutral, and part of what can keep you in neutral is thinking you need to get another degree, another certificate, more studying, more expertise, or whatever. If you can solve the problem today, whether it's making great coffee, helping a small business with its accounting software, or selling antique maps, then you are qualified. Nothing short of solving the problem for someone can give you the expertise or the authority otherwise. So go public with your expertise, whatever that is, so the people who need you can find you."

Matt finished scribbling some notes, and along with having captured his homework from Chad, turned again to thank him. "This has been great. I appreciate your taking this time to talk with me, especially knowing you could be talking to a lot of other people right now."

Matt thanked him again and made his way out of the home and toward the street, which, now being 9:00 p.m., was quiet. He looked around to hail a cab, but not seeing one, thought about taking public transportation. *Break a pattern*, he told himself, and knew that he could take the bus and be home in about 30 minutes.

On the bus, Matt was tempted just to scroll news feeds, but he heard the advice of the Third Shift Entrepreneurs group again: *Take advantage of every minute of your day.* Matt laughed to himself: *These people are getting to me.* He went to his podcast lists and found Kara Jones looking at him again. He clicked on a random episode of hers, entitled "Victim," and he started listening about halfway through.

". . . and you're sitting there wondering to yourself, how the hell did she get that job? Why does he have so many followers on his podcast? How did she become this successful entrepreneur? How did that person get elected?"

Kara was animated with her energetic voice and tough-love coaching ethos.

"And you might be sitting and thinking to yourself, *but I'm smarter and more talented than half these people.* And you know what? You're right. You probably are. But they did something you probably have not done, which is that *they put themselves out there.* They started the podcast, ran for office, offered some service, made some product, started a company, or self-published a book. Whatever it is, they did the thing. It's not a talent competition broadly speaking. It's only a talent competition between the people who have put their hat in the ring, and that turns out to be very few people. Most people are working hard but hoping someone notices and picks them. It doesn't work that way. *You* have to pick yourself."

Matt sat on the bus watching the city scenes pass by, absorbing this advice.

"And that's the good news; You *can* pick yourself. You don't like the way it's done? Great, do it differently. You don't like my podcast? Great, start a new one that's better. I can't listen until you start making one. Most people are content to complain about the options. Others will create better ones and earn credibility and expertise in the process."

Kara became uncharacteristically quiet for a moment, slowing her pace for dramatic effect, "Stop waiting for permission. Give yourself permission. People cannot come alongside you and join your cause until you show them what you believe in and what you're building. But they are there. Trust me, they are there."

Chapter 10

The Team

Matt was up by 6:00 a.m. and so was Sabina. She was going to be seeing clients all day, and like most days, he admired how she woke up in a generally good mood, ready to do the work at which she excelled, the work she enjoyed and the work that was of service to her clients. He envied the ease with which she approached her days and the evident alignment of her professional life to her natural gifts.

He thought about Yisel's coffee roasting, Chad's private reception to showcase antique maps and his conversations with Regis and Kenneth. In his mind, he could hear Kara Jones's tough-love wisdom. He had a lot to process in a few short days. Was he making progress? It was hard to know.

He had homework to do, talking to someone who works in a strategy role for a company having some connection with the outdoors or camping and going public with some form of his own expertise.

"What time will you be home tonight?" Matt asked Sabina as he poured her a cup of coffee to go.

"I think 6:00 p.m. My last client is at 4:00 p.m., but I have to wrap some things up after that."

"Okay, sounds good. I'll probably be home about the same time. Don't forget we have climbing and date night tomorrow." Matt reached for a spoon to hand to Sabina who, unlike Matt, took her coffee with cream and sugar.

"Right. Got it. That was sweet of you. If you're tired, we don't have to do it," Sabina offered.

"No, I want to," he said, and he meant it. He was energized by doing something new and by the opportunity to spend some quality time with Sabina.

Matt got to work by 8:00 a.m., threw his bag down on the chair in the corner of his office and pulled out his journal. His head was a bit all over the place, and not much at work. He read some of his notes from the week to refresh his mind on what he was learning. He thought about how he would find someone to talk to who works in finance at an outdoor-related company to do his homework. Maybe a former management consultant from Coopers & Tompkins?

As he was thinking through these things and making a list of what he needed to do for his Third Shift Entrepreneur homework assignment, he heard a knock on his door frame. He looked up from his desk and saw Saul, the managing partner of the Chicago office, standing in the doorway. He was holding a cup of coffee and held a stack of papers and magazines underneath his arm.

"Good morning, Matt," Saul offered with a smile. Saul was one of the people in the world for whom Matt had infinite respect. A son of immigrants, he had grown up poor and had started his own management consulting business with no real assets except for a sincere desire to build a life for himself and his family and to help other business owners along the way.

He started as a CPA doing accounting work for businesses but, over time, expanded his portfolio to do more advisory work, and to help business owners sell their businesses. In particular, Saul grew his business in the logistics area where he developed a wide network of business leaders who implicitly trusted him because of his personal character and because of the high-quality work he and his team did.

His firm was something of a home-grown anomaly in the Chicago market, and it had been acquired by Coopers & Tompkins, their now current employer, some 10 years ago. Though some thought Saul, like most founders whose companies have recently been acquired, would fade to the background or worse yet, become a distraction, he maintained an active role helping mentor new consultants coming up the ranks and helping win additional business.

Widely beloved and now in his 60s, he seemed to be slowing a bit and appreciated spending time with people at the firm like Matt in whose careers he had been so personally invested over the past several years.

In spite of the privately held aspiration of starting his own business, Matt never doubted that Saul was a wonderful and supportive leader and that the firm had treated him well. Saul had been something in between a professional mentor and a father figure for Matt. These facts alone made pursuing a career change and starting a business, whatever that could be, sometimes feel irresponsible, foolish, or even selfish. "Good morning, Saul," Matt replied, sitting up at his desk.

"How's Sabina?" Saul asked, always mindful that relationships superseded work. Saul never started a meeting without first asking about family, a loved one, a sports team you cared about, or something else personal.

"Oh, she's great. You know, busy, seeing lots of clients, but good," Matt offered. "Hey, Saul can I ask you a question?" Matt ventured, thinking about the homework he had been given. "Have we ever had any clients that do things in the outdoor segment, like sell gear or anything related to camping, adventure travel or the outdoor segment?"

Saul paused to think. "You know, I don't think so. Or at least not that I can recall. I'm trying to remember. There was one guy whom I helped sell his RV camping ground about eight years ago. It had been a family asset, kind of a run-down, old place, but I was amazed at how profitable it was. They had loyal customers who came back year after year. I'm not sure if you'd consider that related to the outdoors."

Saul thought a bit longer. "Well, you know. Sharon is on the board of the Parks Foundation here in Illinois and has been active with them for years as a volunteer. We did a pro bono project a few years back to help them structure their finances as part of a consolidation they went through."

Matt had forgotten that Saul's wife was an active environmentalist who spent time serving on the boards of various organizations. Matt was also intrigued about the pro bono work at Coopers & Tompkins, something he knew other consultants had participated in but something that Matt never seemed to have enough downtime from client projects to explore. Saul had regularly done charitable things quietly for causes about which he and Sharon were passionate, including environmental causes. Saul had built this incredibly loyal network of clients and friends, partly because of his big heart and desire to step forward and support causes that mattered to him and his clients.

"Why do you ask? About clients in the outdoors sector?" Saul asked.

The question startled Matt. "Oh. No real reason. I mean, I guess I was just interested."

Saul didn't react to the answer, waiting for Matt to say more.

"Well, you know I'm interested in the outdoors, whether it's climbing, hiking, camping, whatever. In the Army, I was constantly physically active, and that's just not something that happens for me anymore. I mean I work out and I joined this climbing gym, but something about turning 40 has me assessing things differently and asking myself what I'm passionate about. A friend of mine reminded me of how passionate I used to be about exploring parks and being outside and how I've kind of lost that piece of myself. She challenged me to find ways to bring it into focus again, including through my consulting projects if possible. Sabina and I used to do a lot more of that stuff earlier in our relationship. So, I'm not sure what that looks like, but I was curious."

"Actually," Saul replied, now homing in on Matt, "I didn't know you were interested in camping, climbing, and all that. That's great. Let me think on it. If that's something you have a passion for, you've got to listen to that." Saul paused, and then continued.

"You know, when I started my firm, it was built through the network of other immigrant business owners. I was so passionate about them and their businesses. That community was there for me and helped me to get off the ground. Sharon and I knew what it meant to come to this country and struggle, and we were committed to helping others fulfill their dreams as well, so we took on all kinds of clients: immigrants who owned restaurants, manufacturing plants, cab companies, a little technology company. You name it. Mostly from Southeast Asian countries. We helped each other. We broke bread together. We felt we were all in this together. Nobody ever seemed to have any money, but we kept doing the work for each other." Matt listened and made mental notes.

"They couldn't have even told you what I did but that they trusted me with all of their finances and more strategic business challenges. There was, I'm not sure how to describe this, a sort of loyalty born from people in the bad times as well as the good times. And I'll tell you, back then, many of those fledgling little businesses did unbelievably well. The firm I built was successful only because of the bets we placed in those business owners, because we cared about those people. I still do."

"I didn't realize all of that backstory," Matt replied.

Saul lit up. "Trust me there's a lot more back story than that. I'm still close friends with so many of those old business relationships. That, to me, is the good stuff. Well, anyway, you don't need to listen to me go down memory lane, but whatever it is you're passionate about doing, let me know. In fact, carving out your lane in something around the outdoor category could be helpful and strategic as you look at making partner."

Saul checked the time on his watch. He was one of the few people Matt knew who didn't walk around with a mobile phone glued to his hand. "Well, if you'll excuse me,

I've got a call in a couple minutes. And please do tell Sabina hello." With a wink and a wave, Saul turned and left Matt to his thoughts.

Matt smiled, grateful for Saul's perspective. "*Let me know how I can help.*" Was it really that simple? Matt couldn't decide how small or big of a deal it was that he shared with his boss he was interested in getting outside and being connected with the industry that supports that. *Why did I keep this to myself?*

He thought about Kara, whom he'd listened to the other night talking about the fear of starting, and admitting you're starting, and how people can't help you unless you tell them where you're headed. Maybe he had made one "micro-movement" in the right direction by telling Saul he was interested in the outdoors. In return, Saul offered to co-author or at least support the journey. It was a small step, but it felt like a big one.

Matt's desk phone rang. "Good morning, Matt Carney."

"What's going on, man? It's Kenneth." Matt could hear that he was on speaker phone, and that Kenneth was clearly in his car.

"Kenneth. Hey!" Matt was surprised but delighted by the phone call. No one ever called his desk phone, but Kenneth had the number off his business card. *Who are these people?* he laughed. *This is my prospective client and previous Lyft driver turned executive coach, and now he is calling me at my desk at 8:15 a.m.* He was grateful for the novelty of this experience, even if he didn't understand it.

"I'll keep this brief. I only have a few minutes. I got to work after dropping off the head of the Training and

Development for a major hospital system who told me all about how frustrated they are not to have a better facility for leadership retreats, small support groups, and addiction recovery experiences. She laid out their blueprint for me, where they currently go, what they pay, how they need privacy, which weekdays they usually need. Everything. It was gold." Kenneth continued, "And I told her what my wife and I were looking to do. She was all in, and she spends time in the area where we are looking to acquire our property. She told me if we can put something together, she would commit to at least bringing a group or two out to experience it. Not to mention, she gave me five stars and a 25 percent tip." Kenneth laughed at the last part, knowing he was not driving Lyft for the money but found it quaint to have made a few extra dollars while cultivating a business opportunity.

Matt was genuinely excited for his new friend. "Kenneth, that's wild. Congrats."

"Appreciate it. Anyway, that's not why I called." Kenneth turned serious. "I wanted to check in with you and see how you are doing on your homework."

"My homework. Right. Well, I'm working on them. I've got a couple homework assignments . . ."

"What do you mean you're working on it?" Kenneth interrupted.

"Well, you know, Yisel wants me to talk to someone who works in strategy or management at a company related to the outdoors, and Chad told me to become an expert at something and go public with it. He also told me to add value to the people I meet by helping them look good or be better for the people who matter to them. I'm going to reach out to the owners of the climbing gym I joined. And I'm putting together a plan for people to reach out to. I'm pretty busy, so I'll have to juggle how I do this with my current job."

"Matt, listen," Kenneth interrupted. "I'm only going to say things people have said to me, and only in a spirit of friendship, so don't take this the wrong way. You have the time if you make the time. It sounds like you're moving forward, but I think you can do more."

Matt didn't respond and felt a little irritated at the push, given how jammed he felt his days were with work and Third Shift Entrepreneur events and meetings. What was he supposed to do?

"Listen. When did you meet with Yisel? A few nights ago?" Kenneth continued. "When she tells you to go talk to someone, you have a choice. You can say, 'That's something I'll do in the next month, next week, this weekend, tomorrow, or right now.' Third Shift Entrepreneurs do it with urgency."

Matt listened to the answer. He knew this in other parts of his life. With clients, he was always right on it. He could be maniacal about pursuing things that needed to be handled with them. That was the culture of the Army, and also the culture at Coopers & Tompkins. His strong performance as a management consultant had been driven by his willingness to meet the client's needs no matter what the circumstances.

"You see," Kenneth continued, "for us Third Shift Entrepreneurs, no one gives us deadlines. Because of who you are and the big firm you work for, you know how to put in the long hours to please a client. I'm only asking you to give your future that same priority. You can slide sideways for years, thinking you're making progress. Other people will create urgency in your life for their problems, but you have to create that urgency for yourself. The question for you is this: How will you create urgency in your own life for your own goals? How will you learn to prioritize your future?"

Matt overheard the Google Maps voice giving Kenneth directions. Matt got the point, but he didn't feel he had been wasting time or blowing off the work. He actually felt he was moving quickly.

"So, Yisel says go talk to someone who works in strategy at an outdoor company," Kenneth continued. "Do you know anyone who fits that profile? What is your exposure to companies or organizations working in nature or outdoor-related endeavors? Who do you know?"

"Well," Matt thought about it, "I don't know people myself. I'm not sure. My networks there aren't that good, or at least I haven't had a chance to dig into it."

"Matt," Kenneth cut him off, "this is an easily solvable thing. It's customer research, which is my specialty. Right now, I need you to do this. Go to the *Chicago Journal* and look at its lists of large public and private companies and find a few that could be a fit."

"Okay," Matt responded, "I'll log in now."

"Okay, cool. Look at all of the business lists in Chicago: privately held, publicly traded, mid-sized. Go through, read about the companies and note the ones that sound interesting to you because they do something related to the outdoors. Then look at the foundations and nonprofits that sound interesting to you, ones with a mission or something that excites you. If you stop what you are doing and do this, it's maybe an hour of your time and you will have a better idea as to what the landscape in Chicago looks like for your future business."

"Okay, got it." Matt had pulled out his notebook and was taking notes as Kenneth kept moving.

"But even after you do that, that's not good enough because you're just doing some research at your desk. You need to go and talk to people. It's not about having 100 conversations, necessarily, although that can be helpful in gaining context in certain instances for your customers. In your case, it's about one or two strategic conversations that unlock insights for you. Stay focused on getting to those one or two right conversations and you'll capture some magic. You said you're going to a climbing gym?"

"Yeah, Saturday night with my wife," Matt replied

"Okay, talk to the owner. Make that your goal," Kenneth ordered.

"That's what Yisel told me, too," Matt replied.

Matt could hear Kenneth laughing at what he presumed was either Matt's innocence or his stupidity. He wasn't sure. "Yeah, good. Yisel is right. You should talk to a few other people who own gyms as well. I'm not sure how many are in Chicago but probably a bunch of them. I don't know. My guess is you can find their names on their websites or on LinkedIn. This is simple. You find them and you send them a note. I also want you to find a CEO or head of strategy at an outdoor-related company. After you build your list of companies, just drill down to get some names of people."

Matt was feeling eager and energized. He wanted to pursue his dream of becoming an entrepreneur, and some themes were emerging. He was all in to reach out and do what was necessary even if he didn't know what to do. "What do you say to these people when you do find the right ones?"

"Matt, think about what Chad told you. Add value. Make them look good, be helpful, or help them to be better at what they do. That's all. If you add value, they will want to connect with you. The value can be to buy them lunch, help them in their career, help their organization, float an idea or offer access to your skill set to pique their interest. Maybe suggest that you think they're a smart, interesting person and that you would like to learn from them. That's flattering, and people will appreciate it. You're not trying to get lunch with the Pope. People are available more than you think. Just add value."

"Okay. Thanks, Kenneth. This is helpful. I appreciate it." Matt was grateful for the push and the clarity as he prepared to end the call and think about his next steps.

After hanging up with Kenneth, he spent some time searching online for the right contacts and organizations, including the Forest Preserve District, which he wrote down, as well as a list of privately held companies, including Adventures Unplugged, an outdoor gear company.

After a quick search, he found the CFO for the County Forest Preserve District, Cory Schneider. He appeared to be in his late 30s. He pulled him up on LinkedIn. They had three mutual friends, including one guy with whom Matt went to college, a former co-worker, and a woman who was a friend of Sabina's. He didn't feel he knew any of the three of them well enough to ask for the introduction.

Matt started a note along with a LinkedIn request "Hi Cory. I don't think we've met, but I'm a big fan of the

Forest Preserve District and the mission it serves to get people outside. I work as a management consultant at Coopers & Tompkins and would be interested in connecting." Matt read the note before hitting send. He thought about Kenneth's advice to give him something of value, and added a line, "We've done pro bono projects for public agencies in the past, and this could be something we could explore over lunch."

Not sure what to expect, Matt took a breath and hit send and leaned back in his chair.

Matt began to get himself organized for the day. He had important client meetings and other matters to attend to he had let slip this week. He organized the paperwork on his desk and thought about his course of action for the day when he heard a LinkedIn alert on his phone. He looked at it: a LinkedIn message from Cory Schneider with a short note, "Matt, thanks for the note. I would be happy to connect. Please shoot me an email and let's get something scheduled."

Matt was delighted and surprised. It shouldn't have been a big deal, perhaps, but it seemed like a minor triumph that Cory would have emailed him back right away. He had played this interaction up in his mind as something aspirational and challenging to make happen, and here in fewer than seven minutes he had achieved it.

Channeling Kenneth's advice, he immediately emailed, something he previously might have put on a to-do list and taken care of in a few hours, days, or weeks. Not now. Though it might have seemed a little bold, Matt let Cory know that tomorrow he and his wife were going to this new climbing gym he had joined on the west side and asked if Cory would potentially be interested in meeting there as Matt's guest. Otherwise, he offered to schedule lunch.

Cory replied, noting that he and his partner lived near the gym but hadn't had a chance to check it out. He took Matt up on his offer immediately. It struck Matt as unconventional that he and his wife would be spending Saturday night with another couple they had never met, but he thought about breaking habits and chalked this up to the part of the journey where he stepped outside himself and into what was possible. He confirmed to meet Cory at 5:00 p.m.

Matt then thought about Chad's advice: *add value*. How would he do that? Matt spent a few minutes thinking about Cory. *Who was this guy? What were his challenges? What could he be wrestling with? How could I add value for him? What do I not know about the Forest Preserve District that I need to learn? Whom do they work with to support their financial needs?*

This was the kind of project Matt loved: researching a new client of sorts. He spent the next several hours scouring through everything he could find out about the Forest Preserve District and, thinking as a management consultant, what pressures and opportunities it faced. He had done a little bit of public finance work even though it was by no means a specialty of his. He dug into everything he could find about this quasi-public entity.

He researched the history and impact of the Forest Preserves with over 70,000 acres of natural land and an estimated 62 million visits every year. He learned about the size and scope of their trails, nature centers and campgrounds. He dug into the finances, annual plans and strategy documents related to the future of the Forest Preserves. He learned about the revenue streams from taxes but also that they earned some revenue through operating the camps and through other partnerships. He also dug into Cory's background as well as the backgrounds of the other executive staff at the Forest Preserve. From what Matt could gather, Cory appeared to be someone who had been quickly promoted through the ranks at various public sector agencies. Though Matt had done this kind of research for dozens of clients in the past, such as consumer packaged goods companies, something about him being passionate about the mission of this organization elevated this experience.

Matt was in a state of flow, finding himself immersed in this research and losing track of time; no detail felt benign to him. He found everything he was learning to be interesting, leading to new threads of inquiry. When he finally looked up and pulled himself back into reality, he saw that he had been at it for several hours. He had never thought so completely about the financial challenges and opportunities an organization like the Forest Preserves might be facing. He felt ready, fascinated and excited about the conversation with Cory. *I wonder if this is what being obsessed as a Third Shift Entrepreneur looks like.*

Chapter 11

Monopoly Advantages

Later that day, Matt went for another run after getting home from work. Matt searched for another podcast from Kara Jones. This one was titled, "The Monopoly of You." Matt bounced down the front steps of his townhouse, dropped in his earbuds, hit play and was off running.

"Listen, I want to talk about monopolies. *'But Kara*, you say to me, *aren't monopolies for big utilities, and aren't monopolies a bad thing?'* Well, maybe before, they were. But today, in a talent economy, if you create something that is so distinctly *you*, something no one can copy and paste, then you can create a monopoly. And it's in the monopoly that we create value for ourselves. Every great artist has done this, creating his or her own style. Something so helpful, needed, precious, or desired that it doesn't have competition, *per se*. It may not be big, but people will come to you and your company because they don't know where else to find what you are offering and in the way you are offering it. Average artists focus on following existing forms, and they improve on them with greater technical skill. *Great* artists create their own new forms and, in turn, create new markets. Average businesspeople do business the way school taught them to. Great businesspeople break those rules to do it on their own terms and they create breakthrough value as a result."

Matt picked up his pace, feeling an energy spurt.

"My guess is that if you are listening to this podcast, you're a little insane like me, and you have some burning desire to do something with your life. My other guess is you have some weird idea that has been tumbling around in that brain of yours. And this idea, this thing, is your monopoly. I'm not saying you should go out there and do what you love because I want you to feel good or because it sounds nice. No. I'm saying you should pursue that idea because you are sufficiently obsessed with it to keep going even after the stuff hits the fan, which it inevitably will, and even after it gets harder than you could have ever imagined.

"Loving this idea and being obsessed with it are the fuel to keep you going another day. When you pursue it, you'll become the expert and create a nice little monopoly for yourself. You won't succeed because you are smarter or better, but you will succeed because no one did it the way you did it and no one had thought about it as much as you had. Certain things only you have: your personality, your networks, your life experience, your weird ideas and your specific passions. If you put those things together in a way that makes sense, people can't compete with you. Only you will have done this pattern recognition that assembles this specific business in the way in which you would put it together. And that's your little monopoly of one. The *monopoly of you* in the world."

Matt hadn't noticed his increasing pace. The podcast continued and Kara told story after story of people pursuing specific ideas tailored to their personalities: a woman who built a YouTube channel with cats doing puppet shows, a guy who operated an unsuccessful taco truck until he moved it to the roof of a building and an older couple who opened a nursing home with an onsite waterpark to entice family and grandkids to hang out. Matt was winding back toward home, absorbing the ideas.

A "monopoly of one." That was an interesting idea. *What was that for him?* He hardly felt unique; being a middle-aged management consultant wasn't original. Being interested in the outdoors, treks, or camping wasn't original either. So, where was *his* monopoly in all of this? That question would carry him through the night.

As he was ending his run, he got a text message. "Hey Matt. Alberto here. Hey, I'd like for you to come see the Apocalypse this weekend. Sunday at 7:00 p.m. I have two tickets for you and your wife. It's near 43rd and Halsted. Text me when you get there."

Matt laughed at the tone. The people in this group always surprised him. They didn't ask; they commanded, but he found himself eager to comply. "See you there," he texted back.

Apocalypse: The Experience. He began trying to imagine what to expect, but he couldn't.

Matt now had two appointments on the books for the weekend ahead: one with Sabina to go climbing with another couple he'd met on LinkedIn and another to go to an escape room on Sunday in a neighborhood he had never visited at the invitation of a guy he'd met less than a week ago. Strange as this all seemed, however, this was the first weekend in a while where he felt excited about what lay ahead.

Chapter 12

The Hypothesis

Saturday night, Sabina and Matt showed up at the climbing gym ready to go. They were decked out in their respective gear, and something about the night felt like their early days of dating when they used to go exploring and do new things all the time. As they got older, it seemed they did new things together less often. He was excited to be breaking that pattern with Sabina.

The gym was filling up with climbers coming for the Saturday night open house. Matt looked around the room for Cory Schneider, whom he had only seen on his LinkedIn profile. Sabina warmed up on the low practice wall. Matt was looking around and spotted two guys who made their way into the gym, one of whom he guessed could be Cory.

"Cory?" he asked.

"Yes. Hey, you must be Matt. Good to meet you. This is my partner, Jesse." Matt shook their hands and called Sabina over to meet them as well.

For a moment Matt thought, *What am I doing here? I asked for this night and this meeting, but I'm not sure why all of a sudden—*.

Sabina, used to getting people to open up in her therapy practice, broke the ice. "Is it me, or does this feel like an awkward first double date or something?" The awkward, but funny, comment broke the ice.

Soon, they were chatting, getting suited up to climb and finding numerous points of connection about the gym, the neighborhood and other outdoor activities throughout the city that interested them. Sabina and Jesse, in particular, hit it off and were laughing together. They paired off to go climb and spot each other on a challenging wall.

Matt and Cory similarly made their way over to another busy wall, with couples climbing and spotting each other.

"Hey, again, I appreciate you guys joining us," Matt said.

"We've been wanting to come here since it opened but hadn't found the time and so your note prompted us to try it out. We thought, what the heck. Let's go."

"Well, I appreciate it." They stood lingering among a group of folks waiting for their turn to climb. People were offering to spot and support each other, so couples could climb together if they wanted.

"You know, to be honest," Matt started in, "I'm on a little bit of a journey. I'm working on starting a business, exactly what I'm not sure. I have this good career as a management consultant at Coopers & Tompkins, and I have this dormant passion for the outdoors and nature. I'm figuring out if a business intersection exists between those two. So, as strange as that sounds, I saw your profile and thought you would be a good person to talk to."

"Ha. Well, I'm not sure I have any insights. My career has been pulled from one thing to another, almost all in the public sector. To be honest, I'm inspired some days, but other days come when I want to pull my hair out. I've been thinking a lot about what is next for me as well."

"I think that's the story of most people's careers. Sabina, on the other hand, has it all figured out. She's a therapist, does a great job with clients and doesn't seem to have these existential crises that I do."

"I can relate," Cory said. "Jesse has been an interior architect since graduating college, and he loves it. He designs interior office spaces, is passionate about design, does a great job, and doesn't ever want to do anything else. Any time that I complain, he gives me this deadpan look of 'Really? We're going to have that conversation again?'"

Matt laughed, knowing that feeling all too well from his own experiences with Sabina. The gym activity was picking up, and Matt and Cory continued to share more about their professional journeys and what they were hoping for in the future. At one point, Cory revealed his own desire to be an entrepreneur. Not that he had much experience with randomly meeting up with people through LinkedIn, but Matt assumed the conversation would be about supporting Cory in his current professional role. He never considered the possibility that Cory, too, might have had his own thoughts about leaving and starting a business. He found himself suddenly collaborating with a kindred spirit who had enjoyed some professional success but was wondering "what's next?"

"To be honest," Cory continued, "I think I could be a good entrepreneur, but it scares the hell out of me. I love selling, I love problem solving, and I have many networks I could tap into. The Forest Preserves is an amazing institution.

The Hypothesis

I'm passionate about the mission, as well as the nature preserves themselves, but I feel it's increasingly difficult to get outside and stay connected with that mission."

"Well, I'm not sure how this could evolve, but I'm committed to starting small and continuing this train of thought with you if that interests you," Matt offered, as they continued talking.

The gym was bustling with climbing and socializing. Matt remembered his homework to connect with the owner of the gym. *Was he or she even here? What would he or she offer or ask?* Over by the folding table that hosted the impromptu bar and hors d'oeuvres that people had brought, Matt spotted a woman who appeared to be the manager talking to a few employees.

Matt went over and introduced himself. "Hey, I know this is random," Matt began, feeling himself getting nervous, "but I was wondering if I could talk to the owner of this gym? I'm a new member, and I'm interested in how it got started."

The woman was tall, decked out in climbing gear, wearing a hat over her red hair and had a bit of a Southern accent. "That's me. I'm Jodie. Thanks for joining. How's it going so far?"

And with that Matt was into a conversation with the owner of the gym. What seemed so intimidating as a homework assignment on paper unfolded with ease, both the conversation with Cory as well as the one with Jodie.

"So, I'm interested in this gym and how you brought the whole vision to life. I work as a management consultant, and I was excited to join this place. I admire that you went ahead and built it." Matt offered some flattery, which

130

Third Shift Entrepreneur

had been encouraged by the Third Shift Entrepreneurs, but he meant it.

"Well, thanks, I appreciate that. Honestly, it's a dream come true to open and run this business, but it has its challenges," Jodie responded, and with that, she opened up with full transparency about how the gym came to be. He discovered this was her second climbing gym and how she was looking to grow it through a franchising strategy. She viewed working with corporate teams for team building experiences as a key and underdeveloped market. Her passion, in addition to climbing, was leadership development, and she saw the intersection of climbing experiences as a way to unlock new conversations, vulnerability and trust within teams. Matt immediately thought about Kenneth and wondered if there could be an intersection for his startup idea.

Cory and Matt listened with interest. "Question for you," Matt started. "Could we organize a group of professionals, such as people who are management consultants or work in strategy for different companies, to come climb here every couple of weeks? It could be a chance to network with like-minded finance professionals who care about climbing and physical fitness, and maybe they could explore new ways to work together."

Matt didn't come into this night thinking this is what could come together, but in this moment, something emerged, a hypothesis of sorts as to what could be possible. Seeing Jodie's desire to bring more professionals to the gym and his desire to expand a more intentional network of professionals working in strategy consulting who have a personal interest in climbing, it seemed reasonable. Jodie jumped on the idea and offered, "I'll give free time at the gym if you bring in professionals who are decision makers at their companies. All I ask is that you let me share our corporate offering with them and let me build my own relationships with them as well."

With that conversation, even before the night had ended, Matt and Cory were partners in some kind of a climbing networking group. They figured that, regardless of what their respective futures held, building a strong network of management consultants beyond their current sector could help.

Sabina and Jesse, who had been out of sight for an hour or more, came laughing hysterically from across the room.

"What's so funny?" Matt asked.

"Oh, don't worry about it. It's too much to explain, but Jesse's my new best friend," Sabina said. Matt hadn't seen her this free or laughing this hard in some time, and though he had no idea what she and Jesse were up to, he was happy to see her relaxed and having fun.

She smiled and said, "You guys seem pretty serious."

"I think we just launched a networking group that will be meeting up here in the climbing gym starting in a couple weeks. So yeah, while you've been off doing your thing, we've been busy." Matt put his arm around Sabina.

Cory added, "You reaching out to me seemed random, but I really feel as though we could be at the start of something good. If nothing else, I know that Jesse and Sabina will insist on getting together again, so it looks like we're stuck together."

Chapter 13

Running Experiments

M att poured a cup of morning coffee, and thanks to
Yisel, he wondered where the beans were grown, what
roasting process was used, what flavors he could detect and
whether the store-bought coffee he had sitting around was
good. *Not likely*, he mused, and he made a mental note to
buy some of Yisel's coffee that week.

The phone rang, an unknown number, but given the local
area code and that it was Sunday at 7:30 a.m., he figured the
call must be relevant and picked it up.

"Matt, it's Regis. How are you?" Regis asked, calling from
what sounded like his car.

"Regis. I'm doing great, thanks," Matt answered, no longer
surprised by these unexpected intrusions by the Third Shift
Entrepreneurs. "Thanks for the call. How are you?"

"I'm fine," Regis said.

Matt listened into the silence, waiting for Regis to explain
the reason for his call.

"Well?" Regis asked, as if the reason was self-explanatory.
"How was the week? What's happening? What have you
learned? How's the homework going?"

Matt began to recount his last several days, talking faster as he detailed each surprising turn. Regis listened quietly for a few minutes as Matt ran through the unfolding events. "And you'll never believe this. It was the most incredible and random thing. As he and I got to talking, he shared that he was also exploring his next steps professionally and would love to start his own business. But he didn't know how or where to start. So, we have partnered on building this networking group, and I feel it's a beginning to see what could be possible, getting people in the room who work in strategy and who have some interest in climbing." Matt paused, wanting to gauge a reaction from Regis.

"I'm happy for you," Regis offered. "It sounds like a great week, and I agree with everything you said except for one thing."

"What's that?" Matt asked.

"That I'd 'never believe.' I totally believe, and I'm not surprised one bit. You see, when you've been doing this for a while, you come to appreciate the method to this madness of starting things. You're using the strategies of the Third Shift Entrepreneurs, and they work. Breaking patterns, opening channels of conversation with people, adding value to their lives, overcoming your fear to initiate something and just trying. Some people talk about ROI as return on investment; I talk about it as return on initiative. By starting things, whether conversations, thoughts, businesses, relationships, or new habits, you create an incredible set of opportunities for yourself. Of course, you don't know where it will end up. By sharing it with the world, however, you allow other people to co-create the outcome. Like the way you invited this guy from last night into the journey."

Matt took a sip of his coffee and let Regis's words sink in. Regis knew all along that this week would yield something productive, even if he didn't know what.

"Thanks, Regis. Yeah, I guess none of this surprises you, but let me tell you, it feels new and exciting to me. I'm a believer."

"Good, not for my sake but for your own. You can take or leave my advice. I have no ego in this. It gives me joy to know that you are learning what allows you to make progress in your life."

Sabina wandered into the kitchen, confused about why Matt was on the phone, to which he whispered, "Regis." Nothing at this point in the week seemed to surprise Sabina, who proceeded to pour herself a cup of coffee.

"I have homework for you," Regis continued. "Are you ready?"

Matt grabbed his notebook. "Ready."

"Okay, here is an important Third Shift Entrepreneur strategy: Put it on paper. It sounds as if you had a great conversation last night with your new colleague. That's wonderful. The question becomes, 'So, now what?' The way you answer this is by putting whatever you think you plan to do next on paper in terms of this networking group. You have to define what 'it' is. Give it a name, give it a price, give it a scope, describe it, attach pictures to it. Do it in a notebook or as a Word or PowerPoint document or make a video. I don't care. But do something to add detail and make it real. Put up a website quickly if you want. Your willingness and ability to put it into writing, or not, is the difference between being someone who thinks they are innovative, sharing his or her good ideas verbally, and the person who does something about it." Matt kept writing.

"I can't tell you how many times people say things like 'I was going to do that' when the reality is they were going to *talk* about doing it. I call this *productizing your idea*: giving it definition, shape, boundaries, and a name. Often, I hear people who have a good idea, but until they put it on paper, it's insufficiently defined, and the work therefore cannot begin. People can't react honestly and critically to something if it doesn't have the requisite level of detail. Presenting it in detail, with people's ability to say yes or no, like or dislike, is how you run the experiment to know whether you will have traction. So, the homework is to go and put it on paper."

Matt hadn't thought about putting anything on paper but wasn't opposed to doing so, and had assumed he'd have to at some point. It just felt fast. Then again, this was the Third Shift Entrepreneurs. "I'm meeting with Cory again this week. Shouldn't I wait for that?"

"Uh-uh," cautioned Regis. "Remember the rules. Do it now. That's a rule. Writing it down is a forcing mechanism to make you define 'what' you are doing, 'who' benefits, 'how' it works, and 'what' it costs. Give it a name. You can and will change this, but you have to make this real, whatever 'this' is. Having something on paper allows other people to react to it and agree, disagree, or ask questions and make suggestions, all of which are productive outcomes. And you need to practice talking about it. You need the 10-second story, the 30-second story, the 2-minute story and the 10-minute story. Your job is to perfect each version of the pitch. How you talk about it will be based on the audience and the amount of time they are willing to give you."

"Okay. Got it. I'll put it on paper. Then I'll bring it to the meeting or send it in advance so that Cory can react to it," Matt said.

"Good." Regis was ready to end the call as abruptly as he had started it. "Well, I'm off for a bike ride. Beautiful day out. I'll see you Wednesday morning with the group, yes?"

"Yes, I'll see you there." Matt started to end the call but felt compelled to add, "Oh, and Regis? I can't thank you enough. I mean, I don't know how I even ended up meeting you, the group, and all the—."

"Ah, Matt, it's nothing," Regis cut him off. "You'll return the favor soon. Have a wonderful day." And Regis hung up.

Sabina looked at Matt quizzically as he finished writing a few notes and broke out his laptop. "Sending an email?"

"Nope," he said, "writing the plan for this new networking group."

"Huh," Sabina said in return.

"I don't know what we are doing with this thing, but I suppose that's the point of getting it out of my head and onto paper. I'll find that out as I go, apparently." Matt laughed without taking his eyes off the computer screen.

Chapter 14

Proof It Works

Matt showed up a few minutes early at the address Alberto had texted him earlier. The mostly quiet residential street was tucked in an industrial business corridor with a number of cars parked on both sides of the street. As he approached, he could hear the ruckus of sound effects and squealing laughter coming from the back of the house. Walking up to the front of the house from where the noise emanated, he saw a prominent backlit sign that said *Apocalypse: The Experience* in blood-soaked letters along with an arrow pointing down the side alley toward the garage in the back. A small crowd had gathered, consisting of high school kids, young adults and some couples in their 30s. All told, maybe 15 or 20 people were there.

A woman with white ash covering her face, pierced only by red contact lenses that gave her eyes the eerie appearance of something from the dead, was busy warning the assembled crowd, "It's coming! It's almost here!" She wore a white jumpsuit that looked part paramilitary uniform and part prison outfit. People seemed skittish, frantically laughing, grabbing hold of each other and delighting in the nervous excitement.

"And you must be Matt," she said, never breaking character and seeming to look right through him. *How did she know?*

"Yeah, I'm Matt. Alberto invited me," Matt answered, a little taken aback by being confronted by this apocalyptic space figure.

"Alberto, yes. From Zoron, the planet nearing extinction? He wants to take over our planet. We must expel him," the woman shrieked, still in character.

Matt didn't know whether to laugh, jump into character, or get in the car and drive away. The other guests were squealing, watching this woman interrogate Matt.

"Hurry! Hurry!" the woman screamed. "The time is coming! Get inside! Go! *You must go now."* With a scream and a frantic waving of her hands, she directed everybody into the garage. Once inside, she closed the garage door, which triggered a dramatic light show with accompanying sound effects, as if to imply everyone had boarded a spaceship preparing for takeoff. The garage was made to look like a kind of modern holding cell, the inner chamber of some spaceship.

What ensued was a 30-minute mental journey unlike anything Matt had ever experienced. A 3D holographic projector flashed images, accompanied by sound effects, while a storyline unfolded of a dark overlord figure coming to prepare for the escape to another planet as extinction loomed. Another wall projected the time limitations with a series of challenges the group had to resolve against a countdown clock: repairing a ceiling rupture, a clue that required silence, and building an energy tower. Objects flew overhead, surprising noises came from different corners of the garage, smoke effects and even scented effects filled the room.

It was kitschy in so many ways, but within 2 minutes, Matt was enthralled. At one point, a challenge appeared for who would remain behind, a mental trust game, for which Matt volunteered. Toward the end, the walls appeared to collapse inward as people freely screamed and lost their minds in the moment. It was 30 minutes of pure exhilaration that culminated in some sort of gangly alien creature with an oversized boar's head emerging from the opposite corner of where the group focused, screaming a booming "NOW!" that nearly floored everyone.

Slowly, the room lit up, and a set of beautiful and calming space scene images were digitally displayed on the wall.

"Congratulations," a robotic, deep throated and calm voice announced. "You have survived the Apocalypse Experience. Many others have not been as lucky. You have earned your citizenship on the Planet Zalta. But remember, new citizens, though your taxes are voluntary on this planet, limited room exists on future space escapes, so we recommend you tip your guides generously."

The lights came on and the boar's head mask came off, revealing Alberto, who grabbed the hand of his wife. They took a bow to thunderous applause and handed everyone a home-printed citizenship certificate for the Planet Zalta. People filed out of the open garage door, picked up a postcard encouraging them to share their experience on social media, grabbed a 10 percent off coupon for their next visit and passed a jar suggesting a $20 tip.

"What'd you think?" Alberto asked excitedly.

Matt was still coming off of the high of the experience. "Man, are you kidding me? That was so well done. I mean, I had no idea what to expect, especially when you came into the garage, but it was probably the most intense 30 minutes I've had in a long time."

"This is Maribel, by the way. She's responsible for much of the vision behind the whole show. She's also the mother of our children." Alberto smiled as Matt shook her hand.

"I used to do community theater," Maribel explained, "and Alberto is into science fiction and fantasy. We were with our kids at Disney and were talking about its different shows and effects, and we were curious about how they made it so entertaining. I don't know how it started, but we thought we should create something experiential. We could entertain ourselves in the spring and summer and get our kids involved as well. We spent about six months researching, going to other escape room concepts, reading, thinking and designing, and we ultimately designed this whole experience."

"It's amazing. Really well done," Matt said.

"I'm going to get the kids' dinner." Maribel waved and made her way into the second-story apartment behind the garage.

"It's been a journey to get here, let me tell you," Alberto said as he shook his head.

"There was a time when I thought the strategy would be to rent out a storefront next to one of those Halloween superstores. I was looking at signing a 12-month lease for a show that might have lasted a couple months. I thought about hiring a production company and had a fixed image of what it was supposed to be. I wanted the floor to vibrate, which would have been cool, but that would have created a lot of complexity and increased the cost, not to mention the liability. I spent two months alone trying to figure out that floor. I was stuck working on the wrong things, but I didn't know it."

"Then you met the Third Shift Entrepreneurs?" Matt asked.

Alberto nodded. "About five months ago. It's funny, but Regis simplified it for me. He said, 'What do you want to do?' I went into this elaborate story about the retail storefront, vibrating floor, production values and everything else. He interrupted me. 'You told me *how* you are doing it, but back up and tell me *what* you want to do,' he said, 'and answer that in terms of the people you are trying to impact.'" Matt waited.

"I struggled with that. I had to reframe it in my head and think of it differently. What I landed upon was I wanted to create a surprising, exhilarating and futuristic experience that left people excited enough to tell their friends about it," Alberto explained.

"'That's it,' Regis told me, 'That's your answer. The rest are small details. Your challenge is to go create that experience for as little money as possible. In business,' he explained to me, 'we have the *Minimum Viable Product*, and this would be the *Minimum Viable Experience*. Create it with duct tape and Band-Aids, see if you can deliver it, and then spend more money scaling it up from there,'" Alberto explained.

With the lights on in the garage, Matt looked around and could see that Alberto had in fact created the experience with duct tape and Band-Aids.

"So, we started the shows here in our garage," Alberto continued. "We started three months ago, and we've been mostly sold out for the last few weeks. This garage is our little experiment. We are testing the concept to see if it works, and we'll figure out the bigger opportunity later. In the meantime, though, we have spent $3,400 while generating $9,200 in tips and tickets, not to mention that we are taking a tax deduction on our garage as a business expense." Alberto smiled and chuckled a bit at the surprising success that had ensued these last several weeks.

"The reality," he continued, "is people *like* that the experience is in our garage. It's sort of silly, different and original. People like feeling they know about something that's a little underground. We got a story in the *Chicago Reader* last week highlighting us and this pop-up concept. So, interest has increased quite a bit and we are starting to get a lot of calls. Last week, we got asked if we would host this experience at a company holiday party this winter, which is something we're thinking of doing."

"That's awesome," Matt replied. "The show is strangely enthralling."

"See," Alberto continued, switching to teacher and mentor to Matt, "it's easy to focus on the wrong stuff. So, let me ask you, what do you want to do?"

"Well, it's interesting that you ask," Matt replied, "because I've been having conversations about that. What I want to do is to help business owners, small business owners, figure out their strategic business challenges. I want to do it in the context in which we can share a passion for physical health and the outdoors: climbing, hiking, and being out in nature. Things like that. I don't know what this audience needs, but I believe other people like me are out there who would want that as well. I'm not sure if that makes sense yet, but that's what I'm leaning toward."

Alberto jumped in, "Regis would tell you to solve that problem now. It's not about some fancy business yet or anything other than you, Matt, solving the problem. You see, in the industry I'm competing in, some guy is running around with a perfect PowerPoint presentation pitching Disney about some big idea of an experiential entertainment concept he wants to create, and he wants to convince them he knows how to create it, how great it will be, and all this other stuff. Meanwhile, I'm over here, and 16 people just left my garage and *actually* had an incredible experience, and I made—," Alberto pulled cash out of his pocket and looked in the tip jar, "about $400."

Alberto put the cash back in the tip jar. "Can I tell you the best advice I ever got? It's this: *Doing* is the new résumé. It's one of the things we say often to each other. I thought I wasn't qualified, at least based on my résumé, to do any of this stuff. My wife and I don't have anything that someone else, based on our past experience, would examine and say, 'Oh. Hire these guys. They'll be perfect.' No. We don't have that, but it turns out you don't need that. The person who *does* it *is* the person who is qualified.

"So, we have become the experts on how to hold pop-up experiences in a garage, and it's not because we majored in it, wrote articles about it, or raised money to do it. It's because we actually did it. Some people think you need expertise to start doing the thing, but that's backward. You need to do the thing in order to earn the expertise. So, for you, go out there and show a passion for helping those business owners facing big strategic challenges, or whatever, who also love being connected to the outdoors, and I'm sure they will reveal their

145

Proof It Works

needs and how you can best serve them. You can't think your way to the answer. You have to get involved and start something. Thinking about your own needs is a great place to start. It sounds as if, and don't take this the wrong way, that you're a decently successful management consultant who likes what he does, wants to do it on his own terms, doesn't get outside enough, misses the camaraderie with other like-minded outdoorsy types and wants to enjoy more adventures like hiking and camping. If you solve that need for yourself, other people will likely have that same need and you'll be solving it for them, too."

Matt nodded slowly. "That makes sense. At least, I hope so. I'm nowhere near where you are with what you have done here."

"Well, don't compare what you are doing to what I am doing," Alberto said. "You work in professional services. It's probably going to look different for you. For me, it's a whole production, and for Chad, it's the salon series to sell maps. For Yisel, it's the coffee, but for you it might be demonstrating, through conversations, your passion for supporting executives working in an area about which you are passionate."

"Well, I'm starting by organizing a climbing club as an excuse to bring people together to climb for free and to build some relationships," Matt said, realizing he had put a stake in the ground for what he was planning to do next even if he hadn't figured out how it would be monetized or if it could be a real business.

"Well, there you go. That's acting like a Third Shift Entrepreneur. You're out there taking action, bringing people together to go climbing, and the needs will be determined in time. Your customers will co-create that with you. Once you're up close and personal with them, you'll know. In a sense, you've already started."

Alberto's words meant a lot to Matt. In another context, he might have dismissed him as a goofy guy running some illegal entertainment operation. But standing with him in his garage, having witnessed an exceptional performance in which he made a few hundred dollars, Matt had this deep admiration. *This guy is the definition of a real entrepreneur.*

"Listen," Alberto abruptly cut the conversation short, "I gotta go. Maribel is gonna kill me if I'm not in for dinner and the kids' bath time, which is sacred in our house, but I do have to share one more thing: Feel free to ask for what you want or need to be successful. When this thing started, between this and my day job, there weren't enough hours in the day. I was thinking about quitting my job and going all in, which is what I assumed you should do if you are starting a business, but the Third Shift crew jumped in and told me that would be a dumb idea." Matt understood and nodded.

"You'll need the money you earn in your day job to keep the side hustle going, right? But I looked at it and said I could get by on less, particularly if the Apocalypse Experience started generating revenue. I figured I could, temporarily, get by on 60 percent of my income. So, I did something the group encouraged me to do, which I didn't think was even an option: I asked my boss if I could work 60 percent of my current hours or be moved to an independent contractor status. I would let her pick the hours, which gave her flexibility. I felt weird asking for it, but she approved it, and it allowed her to manage the team schedule more easily. I can go back full-time later, but this has been a good solution. Don't be afraid to think about *what you want*, first of all, and then *ask for it*. I'm glad these guys saved me from myself. I would have likely quit a job, gone broke, and be sitting with a 12-month lease in some strip mall somewhere."

"Matt, is he talking your ear off?" Alberto's wife, Maribel, called from the back window. "Alberto, let the poor guy go. Dinner's ready."

Alberto turned to Matt. "Hey, I appreciate your coming out. See you Wednesday with the group. Text me if you need something. Oh, and I want to ask if you can commit to getting 12 more people to come to the show?"

Matt was surprised by the specific request. Getting 12 more people seemed a little ambitious but given how much Alberto had shared and that he had given him two free tickets, one of which he didn't use, he felt compelled yet also pleased to do it.

"Done," Matt said. "Maybe I'll bring the new consultants at the firm over for this experience. Regardless, I'm good for it."

They shook hands on the deal as Alberto sprinted inside. Matt wandered away thinking about what he had experienced. He had seen these alley garages thousands of times but had never envisioned one could become a theater. What else was he not seeing in the world around him?

Chapter 15

Observing the Pull

"Good morning, everybody," Regis said, calling the Third Shift Entrepreneurs meeting to order at 6:00 a.m. on Wednesday morning. "Let's get started."

Each of the entrepreneurs grabbed their coffee and found their seats. Regis began. "Let's open with a check-in: One thing I learned, one strategy I employed, and one area where I'm holding myself back."

Matt observed how punchy and direct the meetings were and how precise the instructions from Regis always were. He wondered how he could bring some of this entrepreneurial efficiency and discipline into his corporate environment. They sat quietly for a few moments, writing in their journals, contemplating what they would share with the group. Yisel then spoke up. "I'll go first."

Regis turned to her. "Thanks, Yisel. Go ahead."

"One thing I learned is that upscale South American-themed or Central American-themed restaurants are interested in carrying a brand of coffee that is otherwise unavailable to the public. I brought a sample by this new restaurant in the River North neighborhood even though I didn't know anybody there and ended up chatting with the chef. He was far more interested in the 'story' of the coffee and where it was sourced from than the price point, so I will focus on high-end restaurants for the near future. One strategy I employed was to lower the risk of saying 'yes.'"

Matt had not heard of this strategy of lowering the risk of saying "yes." He was taking notes.

"One restaurant's chef had concerns about changing up his coffee without knowing the demand, so I suggested we make it a featured coffee for the month in addition to their regular selections, and I would only charge them for the coffee they used. No need to pre-purchase a bunch of bags until we know the demand. That moved the chef from a 'maybe' to a 'yes.' I preferred having it as a featured coffee because it meant more promotion for my product and more waiters and waitresses talking about it as opposed to it just sitting on the menu."

Yisel thumbed through her notes. "Oh, and one thing holding me back is my marketing. It's okay, but I keep making excuses for why it's good enough or why I can't afford better branding, but it needs to be stronger, not according to what I think, but according to what my customers think. They need to 'love' it, and they don't. I know because I've asked them. I think the problem is the packaging. It looks cheap, and if I want to be in expensive restaurants where there is interest, I need a compelling brand and packaging. So, I need to acknowledge that and work on it."

Yisel sat for a moment and then exhaled. "I feel better saying it!"

Chad signaled to Regis he would go next. "Thanks, Yisel. Over to you, Chad," Regis said.

"One thing I learned this week is that people will purchase a map for less than $500 on the spot. For anything more than $500, they tend to want more time to deliberate. I discovered that selling maps for a couple thousand dollars, which I consider a mid-tier price point, is hard. It seems easier to sell maps at the market's top end, meaning $10,000 or more, or the lower end of less than $500, than at the market's mid-point, which was interesting. One of the strategies I have employed is to create an experience that keeps people inside of a community that I curate and support, which in turn keeps customers wanting to come back for more. In the past, I might sell some old chart, but that would have been the end of it. I want a reason to continue my relationship with my customers and cultivate repeat sales, so I've been doing that with these wine-and-cheese pop-up parties like the one that Matt, Kenneth, and Regis attended this week."

Chad acknowledged each of them with a nod of appreciation. "I'm thinking about creating some sort of a first-look club, which is invitation-only, for showing new pieces on the market exclusively to people who have bought within the last 12 months. One area in which I am holding myself back is in my sales approach. I try too hard to sell a given map to people as opposed to listening to their preferences and being more consultative in my approach. I've seen people decline to buy and not share why, but I suspect it's because they felt I was pressuring them to buy something they didn't want as opposed to asking them what they did want." Chad paused and consulted his notes.

"I need to adjust my sales process, so coming to an event like the one I had this week is the beginning of a sales

151

Observing the Pull

process, which ideally is followed up with an in-home visit where I bring maps over for a consultative discussion. I did that once, and after an evening of discussing cartography, they will at least consider buying something."

"Good self-reflection," Regis said. "Yes, the hard thing is that customers, when they don't buy, won't tell us why, mostly because they don't want to hurt our feelings. So, we must be vigilant and observant and must ask them what we could do differently."

Heads were nodding in agreement.

"I'll go," Kim chimed in. Matt had not spent time with her. They were planning to do so this week, and because they had served in the Army, he suspected they would have an easy conversation. Each of the Third Shift Entrepreneurs, including Kim, seemed focused, determined and even a bit competitive, though not with each other but, rather, with themselves. None of them had ever mentioned competition in the marketplace, as if it didn't exist. They seemed clear-eyed that if they could build something that served a specific audience need, they could succeed, which had nothing to do with competition per se.

"You are going to think I sound like a broken record, but here it goes. Focus, focus, focus. That is what you are constantly telling me, and what I'm learning," Kim explained.

"I'm working on helping young women coming out of the foster care system to transition to independence. So, what I learned this week is that being really focused on who I am serving is essential. I am serving 16-to-20-year-old women, which is progress because before, it was men and women up to the age of 21. Being more specific, I'm going to be providing housing as opposed to those other services I have mentioned in the past. I met with a woman who could be a funder, and she told me I lost her when I started talking about employment services, food, psychological counseling and so on. I said the women have these needs, but she told me that if I try to do all of it to start, then I won't be doing any of it well. She would rather see me focus and do one thing better than anybody, and then build partnerships for the rest of the services."

Kim looked at her notes and continued, "So, the strategy I am working on is to solve *specific* problems so I can be *specifically* referred. I keep thinking about what Regis said about the babysitter who was wanting more business and said, 'Oh, and by the way, I can mow the grass as well. I can cook as well. I'm great at household repairs as well.' By the end of it, she had weakened her case for getting hired, and the family doubted she was good at what she claimed, including babysitting. She would have been better by saying, 'I'm the best babysitter you can find, especially with babies up to two years old.' Boom, that's it. That would have been the stronger sales message because it is focused. So, for me, I'm tightening the message, the demographic I'm serving, and the support I'm offering in terms of transitional housing. That's also the thing holding me back. I want to do everything for these women, but I know if I try to run in a hundred directions, I won't be successful."

"Thanks, Kim," Regis said. "I appreciate your progress here, and I want to make a point for Matt's benefit." Regis turned to Matt. "What Kim is doing in terms of starting a not-for-profit has its own unique challenges. She is the right

Observing the Pull

person to start this mission-driven organization, but some people think starting a not-for-profit is easier because you don't need customers, per se. In fact, it's actually harder because you have two sets of customers: those you serve and those who fund it. You need both of those customers to be happy for the organization to be sustainable and effective. For good-hearted entrepreneurs, like Kim, saying 'no' to programs and services can be challenging even though that is often the strategic right thing to do." Regis turned back to Kim, thanked her, and deferred to Alberto.

"Mine is quick," Alberto started his report. "I learned that people are interested in converting their garages for other uses. They've seen us be successful, and they have their own ideas. It's pretty wild. I got three calls this week about people wanting to use their garages for everything from antique clothing boutiques, to tarot card readings, to selling fresh vegetables. People like the experience of walking into an alley as if it were some kind of pop-up bazaar. So, I'm not sure what to do with that." Alberto paused and looked at his notes.

"The strategy I used was based on something Yisel shared, which was that if you want your customers to share information about you on social media, you have to give them something to brag about for themselves. So, I was thinking about what that could be, and my wife and I printed out these fake citizenship papers for this foreign planet. Matt got one when he came this week. And it worked. Almost everyone took a selfie with this citizenship paperwork, put it on social media, and tagged us as well. We had tried other things like discounts for future experiences if they posted or even asking people to share on social media, but giving them this fake citizenship certificate seemed to work the best. So, thanks for the tip, Yisel." She smiled at him.

"The thing holding me back," Alberto continued, "is thinking bigger. I need to think bigger about where this will head. We are getting good at running the shows, and it's a good little business, but we need to reach out to bigger partners and get them to come and experience this. In other words, we need to remember that what we have built thus far is not the end product but just the proof of a concept that allows us to go bigger. That's hard to remember, though, especially when you have some early success. Not to mention, there are days when Maribel and I are exhausted, so pulling back and assessing the bigger picture can be hard because we're putting on these experiences every night. I don't want to be running these experiences out of my garage in five years. I want to take what I've done and use it to ladder up the business. I need to figure out what that is."

Regis jumped in. "That's an important point. The term for that is *success complacency*. It's the idea that you get some small wins and confuse that for the big win or the vision of what you want to achieve. The early successes are information for how you can proceed to build a bigger, more viable business. It's good to pull up once in a while and remind yourself about the ultimate destination."

"Got it," Alberto said, while he and the other Third Shift Entrepreneurs were taking notes, including Matt, who was soaking in the updates and insights from the group.

"Okay, Kenneth, over to you," Regis directed. "One thing you learned, one strategy you employed, and one area where you're holding yourself back."

Kenneth gathered his thoughts and started. "This week was interesting. I learned a lot. I discovered that if my wife and I live at the retreat property, we might be able to qualify for a residential mortgage. That would make this financially more reasonable than a commercial loan and allow us to get things moving sooner. So, that was interesting, and we are talking to different mortgage brokers about our options. We also identified a property that fits our criteria for what we need in a retreat center. When we started, we would look at a property and make the case as to why it could work, but this group helped us flip that approach and define our needs first in terms of the number of bedrooms and acres, proximity to Chicago, aesthetic appeal, and all of the other things we determined were important before we look at properties and fall in love with them. So, it slowed the search process because we were more targeted, but we think we have a property target that fits our needs." Kenneth looked at his notes.

"One strategy we have employed is to make partners into investors. This was something Kim shared a while ago. For a time, we thought we would need angel investors or venture capitalists that we didn't yet know to come in and invest capital. That felt daunting and not the kind of business they would be interested in. Kim pushed us to find people who are already involved in our effort and would have a vested interest in this being successful, such as a clinical partner who would host rehabilitation retreats, and offer them the chance to invest." Everyone nodded.

"As part of that thinking, we have talked to this one boutique mortgage lender about giving us preferred terms if we let their employees use the facility for free. It spends about

156

Third Shift Entrepreneur

$80,000 a year in training, and a lot of that is overnight lodging and meals. If we host them for free, they would save that money. So, it's potentially a win-win for all parties and not something that they would have thought of if we didn't think of it first and propose it."

Regis commented enthusiastically about Kenneth's approach to a creative partnership. "Excellent. That's great and the sort of idea to compel people to support your vision financially."

"What's holding me back. Hmm," Kenneth thought. "Well, if I'm being honest, me. I'm not communicating as I need to with my wife, and I become defensive when she has suggestions. I tend to treat suggestions to improve the business as personal insults, and that is a no-go. Regis, you've called me out on that as have some of you as well, and I appreciate that. Fortunately, my wife has *no* problem reminding me I can be my own worst enemy."

The group laughed heartily as though contemplating ways in which they, too, could be their own worst enemy and have heard similar things from their spouses and friends.

Matt was the only one left. He'd been way too busy taking notes and soaking in the stories to capture his thoughts completely.

"Okay, Matt," Regis prompted, "let's hear from you. What you have learned, what strategies you are employing, and what's holding you back."

"What I'm learning. Well, everything. Since last week, I've been in this discovery process, thanks to each of you, learning things I never would have known. So, I guess the thing I have learned is that I can't do it alone. I need a—," Matt paused to find the words, "I'm not sure of the word, but a team to do this work. I would never be where I am today without each of you, based on that first meeting with Kenneth. And my world is very different for me today than it was a week ago."

"Well," Regis interrupted, "in entrepreneurship, as in life, you need to find your people, as they say, and stick with those people who will hold you accountable and keep you moving forward. We can't do this without support."

Everyone in the group nodded and acknowledged the truth in that sentiment.

"The strategy I used was to be smart enough to realize how little I knew and to listen to each of you instead," Matt continued. "Yisel told me to reach out to someone in the industry which I'm interested in impacting. Chad told me to go public with my expertise or idea and get to know these customers. Kenneth made sure that whatever actions I needed to take, I didn't delay and did them right then and there. Regis told me to put it on paper. He said it won't matter if I don't, and people can't get behind it if it isn't defined somewhere and given a name. So, I have done the homework you guys have given me for the most part, and the results have been immediate. Kim, I'm waiting for your homework assignment, though." Matt smiled at Kim.

Alberto interrupted, "Speaking of taking advice, I realized that I didn't give you any homework after the show. Your homework is this: Brainstorm at least 10 possible options about how you could move forward. The more creative, the better. Creating a volume of ideas forces creativity and possibility thinking. Our brains are wired to give us two options, so create 10 and see which you like. When you know what it is you want to do, ask for it from the people who can make it happen. Like when I asked if I could go 60 percent part-time. I had brainstormed a bunch of options including this part-time option, which I asked for. You need to do that. Don't assume the answer is no without asking for it. We tend to limit our options before we actually know what they are."

"Got it." Matt smiled and wrote himself a note. "I'll brainstorm some possible outcomes. I guess the thing holding me back is not knowing what I don't know. If you told me last week I was going to start a business, I would have thought I knew most of what I needed to know, or at least I would not have thought that what I needed to learn would have come by way of you all with these different businesses unrelated to the one I am thinking of starting."

Kenneth acknowledged him, "Yup. I know that feeling."

"But I feel I'm getting closer to knowing what business to start and how and when to start it. I'm starting this climbing club with other people who work in finance, and that will be a stake in the ground to go public, in a sense, and bring people together to give them something beneficial, as well as being beneficial for the gym, so that feels like progress. I have a renewed humility to say that I don't know what I don't know, but for now I'm trusting in the micro-movements and this community's support to get me to where I am going."

"I believe that's right," Regis responded. "And let me underscore something here. You need to fall passionately in love with the problem but not in love with the solution. It's better to desire to get connected with your customers and learn about them, ask them what they want, before you build

159

Observing the Pull

some solution they may or may not need. Some entrepreneurs think the key to being successful is never taking no for an answer and being persistent. That's partly true. You need to be persistent, but only toward finding a solution to a real problem that exists. If you focus on one solution no one wants and just keep trying to sell it, you might miss the larger opportunity. You need to present options as to what could be and see where the market *pulls* you." Matt wrote more in his notebook.

"So, for you, Matt, it's better to offer this networking and learn what these folks need before you commit to a solution you're not sure they want. Does that make sense? Too many entrepreneurs sell solutions no one wants and think they are being persistent, but that's the wrong kind of persistence. Smart persistence stays focused on the problem, but it is a little agnostic about the solution. Being dogged in starting a business requires that you don't hold on to any sacred cows for the way in which you think it needs to end up. Let your customers tell you that."

The Third Shift Entrepreneurs were nodding as they listened to Regis and one of his more repeated refrains.

"Okay, one more strategy, and then we'll break for the morning. Matt, I'll pick on you. Let's say I said to you, 'Go make a movie that gets everyone talking.' What would you do?"

Matt knew this could be a setup for an answer he was unlikely to produce on his own, but nonetheless, he jumped in.

"Well, I suppose I would get some big-name movie stars, get a great script, probably make some action shots that people want to see, and get a big producer to help finance the whole thing. Essentially, to understand how Hollywood makes blockbusters and borrow some of that secret sauce."

"Okay," Regis said, "you're not wrong to be thinking like that, but let me give you a different paradigm as a Third Shift Entrepreneur. Everything you described to me is about making a better movie, but it's within the constraints you currently think about movie making. You haven't changed the fundamental format of making a movie. Instead, you've played with the content of it and within the existing boundaries, as it were. Creative entrepreneurs play with the actual format or the very boundaries of the thing as well. So, let me answer the question I asked you, which was what could you do to make a movie that gets everyone talking? I want each of you to brainstorm for a couple minutes and answer this in terms of the *format,* not just the content, of a movie."

Yisel was keen to share because this strategy was something she had been working on. "I would maybe make the movie 24 hours long, or 30 seconds short. Or maybe have the whole thing shot from iPhones, which would get people talking. Kind of like the *Blair Witch Project* did."

"Good thoughts. Kim, what about you?"

Kim jumped in, "Okay, I don't know if this makes sense, but I would maybe cast only former professional athletes to star in roles, or maybe reality TV stars. Famous people who aren't actors. Could be funny."

"Clever. Thank you, Kim," Regis offered. "Alberto, what about you?"

Alberto, always thinking about experiences, offered that he would want to make a cult movie where everyone is supposed to wear a specific outfit or costume to watch it, like all black or with specialty goggles or some other technology differentiator. "I would insist on it being an experience unlike any other."

"Great, yes. And finally, you, Chad. What would you do?"

Chad, thinking about his current model, offered, "I might release a film that could only be viewed in homes by people who have been granted some special privilege. Make it a salon series. I might disrupt the distribution channel for a film, like maybe release it from my Facebook page or through LinkedIn to mix it up and build some anticipation."

"Great, all good ideas. So, that's the lesson today. Consider disrupting not just the content and making a better product or service, but think about building a whole new mousetrap as well. You might find a quicker path to a disruptive win in doing so." Regis closed his notebook and, as always, was keeping his eye on the time to bring a punctual end to the meeting.

Regis turned to Matt. "Okay, Matt. Because you're the new guy here, you get the final word."

Matt was caught off guard but looked over his notes. "Creativity. I've been lacking creativity in thinking about the various paths available and that came through in this last exercise. And that piece on the format versus the content. It's ironic because the less I talk about being an entrepreneur, which feels intimidating, and the more I tell myself I am here to solve a problem for an audience I'm building, the closer I think I am to starting a business."

Chapter 16

Packaged and Productized

Matt became consumed with fleshing out the concept he and Cory had discussed. He was channeling the wisdom of the Third Shift Entrepreneurs: define what you are offering your customers, put it on paper, remove barriers to lower the risk of saying yes, create value before you charge money, start small and think in terms of micro-movements as well as other lessons.

The concept emerged for a networking group called "The Climbers," as a play on people working their way up corporate ladders as well as climbing walls. Matt and Cory primarily focused on inviting people with the title of VP, or equivalent positions, who were in their 30s and 40s working in roles where they might be hiring outside consultants. They would get together once a month to climb and network and once a year to go on a more adventurous camping trip in a national park for a week in which they would bring a bigger-name person to join them, such as a CEO for a large company or a senior partner of a larger consulting firm who had an interest in camping and hiking and being physically active.

Matt and Cory emailed back and forth their ideas. Cory seemed to have equal enthusiasm for this concept as it was coming together. Maybe he was bored at work, maybe he wanted to do something bigger, or maybe he wanted to change up his career, which is something he acknowledged at their first meeting at the climbing gym. For whatever reason, something had sparked in him, and the two of them found themselves as partners on this journey of creating something, brainstorming ideas and crafting potential solutions for themselves and for other finance professionals.

Matt, as it turns out, had reached out to a few other senior executives, including the one from Adventures Unplugged, whom he found during his customer research, and had received an enthusiastic response from him. Matt found that, as his roster grew from two names to four names and to six names, the asks became easier and the yeses came more quickly. People were interested in being a part of this group, no matter how it was shaping up.

Matt and Cory created a logo online and set up a private LinkedIn group for The Climbers. They built a Power-Point to generate increasingly specific details about the group and shared it with new members, fielding their questions and suggestions and then filling in the gaps wherever they existed. As they worked to define their offering, giving it a name and packaging it accordingly, Matt was getting better at making decisions on the fly. Where no answer existed, such as whether or not to charge for The Climbers, Matt used the document they were assembling as a way to experiment with an answer and change it if they got specific feedback.

Matt and Cory found that by including other new members in some of these strategic questions about the direction of the group, it solidified their participation and ownership over the whole idea. Allowing others to feel some sense of co-authorship was part of how this group came together in the first place.

Amid this flurry of activity with Cory, life seemed to come into focus in other ways as well. Even though the group had not fully launched and wasn't close to being a business, something had shifted in Matt. He no longer felt this lingering discontent and uneasiness that life was somehow passing him by. He knew he was taking action, and with that knowledge, Sabina saw his self-esteem and self-efficacy being restored. Ironically, even in his day job at the firm, new opportunities seemed to be emerging. Saul noticed this and mentioned this newfound enthusiasm that Matt seemed to carry with him.

As part of this new change, Matt decided that fully recognizing Sabina's role in his turnaround was long overdue. She had been a faithful supporter of this process over the past several weeks. Matt left work a little early and didn't have any Third Shift commitments for the moment, so he could take the time to go shopping and prepare dinner for her.

When Sabina walked in the door, threw her coat down, and was about to go through the mail, she did a double take at the scene around her: candlelight, the aroma of a homemade meal and music floating throughout the house. Matt brought her a glass of wine, gave her a soft kiss and a long hug, and whispered to her, "Welcome home."

Sabina, not one for surprises, wasn't sure if this was meant to be sincere or a setup for something else. "What has gotten into you? This looks nice."

"I wanted to do something special for you. You've always been there for me, especially in the last few weeks. I have been all over the place, taking meetings at all hours, bringing you to meet strangers for dinner, and hardly being available."

Sabina turned to him and pulled back to look him in the eyes. "Matt, the version of you I've seen the last few weeks reminds me of the man I married. I'd rather have you be happy and enthusiastic about doing something in the world, even if it means we spend a little less time together."

He held on to her. This was what being supported and growing together was like. The journey he was on, whatever the destination, had made him a different and better person.

Over dinner, he shared more about The Climbers, the growing interest, other ideas that might ensue once the group was successful and what he was learning from the homework assignments. Matt began to ask more pointed questions about Sabina's career, her clients, what made her distinctive, what she loved about her work and other things that gave him a fresh appreciation for her talents as a professional, something he had always been proud of but had not fully appreciated.

Matt was ready to discuss another topic as well. As they moved to the third course, he looked at Sabina. "There's something else that seems to be coming into focus for me as well. It seems to be a season of possibilities."

"Oh, really? What's that?" Sabina asked. She was enjoying this whimsical side of her husband and, even if unsure how long it was going to last, was committed to enjoying it for the moment.

"So about our family," he said, smiling, as he held her hand.

Chapter 17

Leading from Passion

The visit with Kim occurred later than the meetings with the other Third Shift Entrepreneurs. For some reason, Kim insisted that Matt needed to visit her on this particular Sunday night. *Would he be doing more visits with each of them?* He certainly hoped so. He had many unanswered questions about this group and how they operated.

The address Kim provided was a third-floor apartment on a residential street in the Humboldt Park neighborhood. Matt stood outside on the street thinking that he had been to more neighborhoods in the last few weeks than he had in all of his time living in Chicago. He contemplated how staying in his immediate neighborhood and visiting the same familiar spots was an easy default that had deprived him of the richness and diversity of all of the neighborhoods, people and places available in a city like Chicago.

He rang the call button from downstairs. The line answered with Kim's voice, "Hellooo!"

Matt could hear laughing and active conversations in the background. "Hi, it's Matt from the Third Shift Entrepreneurs."

"Yep. Hi Matt, I'll buzz you in. 3A."

The buzzer sounded and Matt pushed through the front door and up the stairs where Kim swung the door open and gave him a hug. "Welcome. Come on in. Let me introduce you to everyone."

The tidy apartment had a small living room that flowed into a dining area and then into the kitchen. Six young women who looked to be in their late teens were in the living room. Here, in Kim's apartment, among this small assembly of young women, he felt a strong sense of being in a cozy and welcoming home, even if he felt like the outsider.

Off to the side, Matt noticed another woman, older than Kim, who sat upright with a sweater draped across her shoulders. She had close-cropped gray hair and a set of tasteful but noticeably large diamond ring bands.

Kim escorted him around the room, holding his shoulder as he reached out and shook each young woman's hand as Kim shared their names. Each offered a polite, if sometimes shy, smile in return.

"And Matt, this is Ginny Holcomb." Kim said as she placed a warm maternal hand on the older woman's shoulder as Matt reached out and shook her hand. "Nice to meet you, Ginny."

"And you as well," the older woman replied, without much explanation from her or Kim regarding her role in this whole thing. Then again, Matt didn't know anyone's role.

Matt scanned the walls at the displays from Kim's time in the Army: an American flag, encased folded into a triangle and ribbons, signed photos from former commanders, and lots of pictures from bases around the world of Kim in uniform, with a beaming smile. A display sat on a side table with coins, pins, and other active duty paraphernalia. Matt had trouble reconciling the world of experience the walls showed with Kim's age. She was still only in her mid-40s.

"Okay, ladies," Kim called the room to order, "and you, Matt." Kim had a unique way of cutting through formality to make strangers into friends.

Kim darted in and out of the kitchen, where she was busy pouring chili, bringing them out two at a time to hand to each of the women. After a few sprints, she brought two final bowls, one for Ginny, who had still remained silent on the perimeter, and for Matt.

Kim threw her apron off and returned to the circle of women and Matt. "Come close. Squeeze in everybody. You, too, Ginny, come on and squeeze in."

"Okay," Kim started, "rather than me doing the talking, let's hear from one of our young ladies here. Brianna," Kim turned to one of the women, "Why don't you explain to our guests what we are doing here."

The young woman began, "This is what we call 'Supper Club' here at Kim's. We do it every couple of weeks on Sunday. Kim makes chili, we get together and talk about life and stuff, and Kim helps us with things we need. We also help each other. Each of us," Brianna went on, pointing to the other young women in the circle, "has spent time in foster care, so we just talk about challenges in life and elsewhere. Kim shares her experiences of having grown up in foster care, too. Kim calls us a family."

"Thank you, Brianna." Kim reassumed control of the group. "So that's right, and tonight is a little unusual because we have two guests: my friends Ginny and Matt." Kim smiled and motioned to the two outsiders. "But we are going to do as we always do. And you're right, Brianna, we are a family, and this is how we support each other and show up for each other. And let me say this. People are people, so Matt and Ginny, you are expected to share as well."

Kim proceeded to facilitate a check-in, in which each woman shared what was going on with her. The conversation had a structure that reminded Matt of the Third Shift Entrepreneurs check-in, only here, each woman answered the questions: "How's my body, my mind and my heart, and what do I need from my family here?"

The stories were, for Matt, heart-wrenching, inspiring, and mundane, too. Everything from figuring out where to stay to acceptances to colleges, to boyfriends, to new clothes, to new jobs and the need for transit passes. Kim's natural gift for convening and leading this "family" was evident. Kim validated each of the stories she heard and the challenges the young women faced with her own stories of being at different times in the care of foster parents, and the disappointment disorientation, as well as gratitude, of experiencing adults coming in and out of her own life. There was also much discussion about planning for the future. That week, one of the women had chosen to enlist in the U.S. Navy, a decision for which she gave credit to Kim for the inspiration. That and other small triumphs were causes for celebration.

After the young women had shared, Kim insisted on pulling Ginny and Matt into the conversation as well. Kim was resolute as she explained to everyone that they were a human family and no one was exempt from the feelings, dreams and challenges that come from living their lives. Kim said it plainly, and with a loving laugh to Ginny and Matt: "You don't get a pass. My house, my rules." Ginny and Matt shared vulnerable things.

For Ginny, it was the death of her husband and that he was an alcoholic and had been, at times, emotionally abusive to her. She had never felt she could share this among their friends, but by hearing the honesty of these young women, she felt called to share with them. She talked about how many people attended her late husband's funeral, given that he was a prominent and successful businessman, but privately she had mixed emotions about him, their marriage and the damage he inflicted on her and her children. Kim, seated on one side, put her arm around Ginny and pulled her close while Brianna, seated on the other side, offered her tissues.

Matt then shared how he had felt stuck, lacking purpose, with dreams of being an entrepreneur. He was excited about shaking up his life, disrupting some routines and doing some soul searching. He paused for a moment, then pushed himself to go deeper and be more vulnerable. He shared that had felt too insecure to start a family until he had become the person he wanted to be. He feared he would end up like his unhappy father, who struggled with addiction and never found his purpose in his life.

He shared how all of this accumulated inside him and made him anxious and depressed and then shared in detail how that anxiety and depression shows up for him. He shared how he felt gratitude for Sabina but shame for not being something more. Exactly what, he didn't know. He paused again, feeling the relief from having shared vulnerable things with strangers who affirmed him in the process.

The conversation and dinner went on for two hours, and Kim concluded with a prayer over the women to protect them and to ensure their gifts would flourish in the world. When Kim stood up, she hugged each one, and came to hug Ginny and Matt.

Ginny took Kim's hand. "What you have done here is extraordinary," she told Kim. "I see it. It affected these young women here, and it certainly me. I'm all in. Let's meet next week to talk about where we go from here."

Kim was visibly excited. "Ginny, I'm glad. Thank you for showing up tonight – physically but also spiritually. I hope you can see how my vision comes to life. Imagine tonight with four times as many women living under one roof in the safety of a permanent home."

Ginny broke a smile, her first of the night. "I see it. I see it, Kim." Ginny gathered her things and slipped out.

After Ginny slipped out the front door, Kim turned to Matt, visibly excited. "This is *big*. I've known Ginny for about a year. I was volunteering at a gala for a different organization that supports foster care families. She was one of the sponsors of the event, and I made it a point to meet her and share a little bit about my heart for helping women in foster care. We've emailed here and there over the last year, and I know she has some *serious* money." Kim grabbed Matt's hand, slowed down and lowered her voice to convey the point again. "The kind of money that can bring this whole vision to life, Matt. I didn't want to make the wrong ask, though. Regis and the Third Shift group told me to be smart. Don't just ask for financial support. First, show her what you're doing and the magic in it all, they told me. So, I've been building toward tonight for some time, and it was a success." Kim took a breath, relieved and grateful the night had gone as she hoped it would, if not better.

"In the past, and even with Ginny, I was all over the map about what I wanted to do. I mean, I love these young women, so that has never been the issue. The question was how to take that love and turn it into a plan that makes sense. I thought because I wanted to start a not-for-profit that people would help because it's charitable. Not true, my mentors told me. The same rules apply whether you're launching a business or a not-for-profit. You still need to sell this vision to a customer, in this case a funder, as well as prove you have the capacity to deliver this mission by getting the right people in the room. So, the Third Shift group has been forcing me to focus." Matt knew the group had been doing the same to him.

"Today, I've settled on housing, meaning creating a house where we host weekly dinners and where some women live for free and others pay, so it's a differentiated pricing model. Basically, I will do what we did here." Kim panned her arm across the living room. "But I will take it up a notch. Six bedrooms serving as a refuge for the entire community, like being an adult and dropping in on your parents' house. There needs to be a place to show up and regroup. We need that in life. I've got a building that would be perfect, and I shared this with Ginny. I sent her the link, asked her what she thought and asked her if she would be willing to tour it together, which she has agreed to. I shared my vision for dinners every night with the residents or bigger dinners once a week for the broader community of young women coming out of foster care. I've been saying this for a while, but I wanted Ginny to see it because I know what it is in my head and heart, but I have a hard time explaining it."

Kim paused and exhaled. "She saw it tonight and gets it."

Matt agreed. "She is definitely sold on you, more than anything, as well as on your vision for the home you want to create. Who wouldn't be? You've given me a gift tonight. Thank you."

"So, listen," Kim moved from reflecting on the night and focused. "Before you go, I have some homework for you. Have a brave conversation with someone who could help you. It doesn't need to be perfect, but it needs to be specific and needs to show your passion coming through. Ginny wouldn't have magically appeared in my living room if I hadn't reached out and invited her. I didn't have to pitch her or put together some presentation to get her to become an investor. She just needed to *see* the impact with her own eyes. And she did tonight. She can see that the only thing missing is some financial support which she knows she can provide to actually bring this to life."

"That makes sense, Kim," Matt said as he nodded.

"When you have your vision, and it looks clear, you need to bring in other people alongside you. I'm not talking about posting on LinkedIn. You might have to do that, too, because it is important to publicly commit yourself to the task at hand. But you need to have a specific and personal conversation with someone who can help move the needle for you. You'll be surprised at how helpful people will want to be when they believe your heart is pure and your plan is clear. We all need something to believe in and some place to belong."

As he prepared to leave, it was Matt this time who initiated the hug, thanking Kim for including him and being able to not only witness the evening but for feeling restored himself.

Chapter 18

Binary Thinking

Saturday morning, Cory and Matt met at the gym to climb for a couple of hours and then met up for brunch with Jesse and Sabina, where he would use the time together to, among other things, brainstorm some ideas. Cory had been talking to other strategy consultants in his network, which was more developed than Matt's for people working with public parks, nature preserves and camping facilities. They had put the finishing touches on The Climbers group, and they felt good about that as an initial start. They had identified 12 people for who had committed to participate. Even before this group had fully launched, though, Matt knew something bigger was possible.

The waiter took their orders and Matt and Cory pulled out their notebooks. "Okay," Matt started, "thank you guys for offering to give us some ideas here."

"Free breakfast and time with Sabina. That's an easy sell," Jesse replied with his dry humor.

Matt continued, "So, Cory and I want to do more. We're launching The Climbers, which will largely be social and have a networking component. We've got the week-long camping trip confirmed for early November when we will go to

Yosemite. I got the CEO of Adventures Unplugged confirmed as our guest for that one. That all feels good, but we want to plan for more. Cory, what would you add?"

"Yeah, that sounds right," Cory said. "Putting this group together will unlock possibilities. I'm ready for a career change, but I don't want to just fall into a good opportunity that gets presented to me. I want this move to be more intentional; I want to feel like I'm choosing a path forward that's aligned with who I am and the work I want to be doing. So, part of the homework here for Matt, or I guess for us, is to define 10 possible outcomes for what could follow out of this networking group. This brainstorming assignment is intended to expand our mental model for what could be possible and not to fall prey to a simple win-or-lose mindset that ignores other possibilities."

Jesse looked at Sabina. "Happy to help here, but we don't know anything about this industry, so I'm not sure what I could offer—."

"That's the beauty of it," Cory said, jumping in. "You guys aren't close to this, so you might see opportunities we can't. Just try. All ideas are possible."

"Okay, I'll start," Sabina said. "Three ideas off the top of my head. One is this climbing group continues to grow, and you have, say, 50 members or so. Maybe, at that level, you start charging for participation, and it becomes its own little business." Matt and Cory nodded approvingly but careful not to say anything so as to not stifle her brainstorming.

"Second idea," Sabina continued, "is you start this group and then people look to you for help with their business or organizational strategic challenges. In essence, you have started your own boutique consulting firm to serve the relationships you've built. It could grow out of this whole thing. And the third idea, and maybe you guys don't want to hear this, is you decide this climbing club is enough of an outlet for your creativity and you like your jobs enough to stay at them. Maybe this puts this all into perspective."

Matt nodded and took notes. "That last one is a possibility and something I have thought of and others have expressed, which is somewhat ironic. Once you take action, others have said, and I think I am feeling this, the pressure on your day job to be the answer for your happiness seems to get lighter. You stop feeling stuck and start to feel empowered, so everything you thought was broken, like your job, isn't necessarily doomed. But that's not going to happen in this case," Matt added emphatically and with a laugh. "I'm ready to start something and go out on my own."

"Okay, great start. Thank you, Sabina. Jesse, your turn," Cory said, turning to his partner.

"Sabina took two of my ideas. I won't say which ones, but okay. A fourth idea is that people love the Yosemite camping trip, and you end up starting an adventure camping business where you just focus on these bigger trips. A fifth idea is you create a not-for-profit out of this to engage the private sector, which would pull on Matt's background, to support public sector initiatives, which would lean on Cory's background. So, some sort of program or effort that gets corporate audiences outside to support the mission of the Forest Preserves and other types of organizations like that. I'm not sure."

"That's great. Keep going, this is good stuff," Matt encouraged him.

"Okay, another idea is that you partner with the gym to expand the concept of The Climbers to other groups of people beyond management consultants, like designers, lawyers, or whoever. You build this networking juggernaut that's like a chamber of commerce but for younger, more active people. Oh, now I'm on a roll." Jesse clapped his hands, now that his creativity was flowing. "A seventh idea is you buy the gym and expand it through franchising, or partner with the woman who owns it to build the franchising model, pull in the right investors, and do whatever else needs to happen from a corporate standpoint."

Matt and Cory were busy scribbling notes.

Sabina jumped back in. "Okay, I have another idea. Somehow through doing this, you grow your network and get job offers for the perfect job you think blends a commitment to nature or the outdoors with your expertise in finance. I wouldn't be surprised if people come to you to interview for some roles each of you would find interesting.

"Maybe the inverse of that is you start a head-hunting business where you place management consultants in roles relevant to their passion for the outdoors. You become a sort of niche agency for identifying top strategy talent with a passion for camping, the outdoors, or whatever and for placing them at companies who see this as being mission-aligned for them."

"Oh, I can see that," Jesse enthusiastically affirmed. Sabina laughed at his enthusiasm in return and continued, "Okay, I've got one more. Somehow, other people find this interesting and you film the whole thing or write a book about two middle-aged guys finding themselves and it becomes a reality show. *The Cory and Matt Show*, where you find other middle-aged guys with MBAs who are unhappy, and you help them find their path in life. Personally, I'm not sure I'd watch, but hey, people love *Shark Tank*, so maybe there is something there."

Matt and Cory both laughed. "That might be the best idea yet," Matt said.

"Well, I'm no expert," Sabina said, "but two people as smart as you two with as much context and expertise can figure this out." She thought for a moment. "Maybe you should chat with Saul. He's smart, and I bet he could provide a good perspective on all this."

"I don't know," Matt said. "That seems a little weird. I mean, it was only a couple weeks ago that I even acknowledged I had an interest in realigning my work and getting reconnected to this outdoor passion of mine. If I come in with a full plan to my boss about starting a business, he might wonder what I've been doing with my time, or assume I'm halfway out the door."

"Okay, it was a thought, but maybe you don't give Saul enough credit. I mean, you and Cory have committed to talking to people, so I'm not sure whom you had in mind."

Matt suddenly remembered the homework from Kim. This was it. You have to talk about it with someone who can help you advance the idea. How quickly he had forgotten, and how ironic Sabina would remind him of it. "You're right," he said to Sabina, "You're right. Saul is someone I should obviously talk to."

Sabina blinked, confused by the sudden change of heart. Then Matt recalled how Chad had leveraged the chairman of his law firm to host an event that helped get him started. He also recalled Regis's story of starting the safety software company that he spun out with the company's support and capital. Or Yisel's partnership with the coffee roaster. Many of the entrepreneurship stories he had heard these past few weeks involved co-opting people with whom they worked to help build their future. Matt grabbed his notepad and scribbled a note. "I'll talk to Saul first thing Monday morning."

Chapter 19

Finding Co-Authors

Monday morning, Matt went through the usual question-and-answer period with Saul standing at the door to Matt's office: *How was your weekend? How is Sabina?* As Saul was about to leave and pop his head into the next office, Matt made his move. "Hey, Saul, you have another minute? I wanted to run something by you."

"For you, of course," Saul said as he stepped back into the office and took a seat across from Matt. "What's up?"

"I had this random thought. Well, maybe not so random. Remember how I asked you about whether we ever had clients that worked in the outdoor space or something along those lines?"

"Right. I remember."

"Right. So, I met with this new friend who is the CFO over at the Forest Preserves, and we got to talking."

Matt tiptoed into the conversation and shared some of what they discussed, slowly revealing he had thought more about his emerging business idea and had begun to make plans.

Saul sat with his hands clasped together, relaxed in the chair, taking in the picture Matt was painting.

Matt kept talking, wondering what Saul might be thinking. Not knowing made Matt nervous, which in turn made him talk faster and in increasing levels of detail.

"This is interesting," Saul said slowly, when Matt paused.

A read of Saul's facial expression told Matt he was on safe terrain. He relaxed a little.

"It sounds as if you have put a lot of thought into this. Can I ask? Do you have something you can share with me that lays all of this out?"

Should he share the PowerPoint that he and Cory had developed? Matt paused, nervous he had already potentially shared too much. "Yes," he said, recalling the counsel of Kim and the other Third Shift Entrepreneurs, and feeling their emotional encouragement as well. "Yes, I do."

Matt pulled up the PowerPoint that provided an overview of the concept of The Climbers, the problem it solved, which was getting people in specific strategy roles at larger companies connected and their plan to meet every few weeks and do an annual outing. He walked through the basic financials. Saul seemed interested, nodding approvingly as the level of detail was shared. *None of this*, Matt thought, *would be controversial yet. Heck, Saul might see this as a business development opportunity that benefits Coopers & Tompkins.* Matt knew the punchline of this PowerPoint, which was growth and business opportunity, could be pursued because of this mostly volunteer effort.

After explaining the full concept of The Climbers and seeing Saul's approval, Matt held his breath and advanced to the next slide, which showed the potential to grow this networking group into his own consulting firm which he and Cory would lead.

Saul inhaled through his nose, put his arms behind his head, leaned back and let out a deep breath. Matt felt his stomach sink.

Saul smiled and leaned into Matt.

"So, you're leaving me," Saul said with a loving smile.

"No," Matt replied. "I mean, honestly, we don't know where this is headed. We're focusing on getting this networking group going, and we did brainstorm where it could lead and—"

"Matt," Saul said, gently interrupting him. He sat for a moment looking reflective, and continued. "You know, before I started my company, I had a similar conversation with my boss. I talked about a different way to service small businesses from all these personal relationships I had built. I had a way of helping them, which wasn't what my first employer was doing, or at least they weren't doing well. I thought I might be writing my own termination as I sat there and shared with him what was in my heart and in my head. And this guy had been so good to me, which made it all the harder. He was my mentor and someone without whom I never would have gotten my start. In the moment, I felt devastated."

Matt looked at Saul. "What happened?"

Saul laughed. "He looked at me and said, 'Go build it,' and not in a 'You're fired' kind of way, but with the thought that he wanted to see me go out, be successful. He believed that goodwill would help the firm I was leaving. Which it did, by the way. Over the years, I sent dozens of clients that didn't fit our mold back to my old boss until he passed away 15 years ago. What a wonderful guy he was."

Matt took this in. He had never thought of Saul as the younger professional beginning his career, and he had never heard the story about how he left to start his own business.

"Look, I don't have a lot of years left doing this," Saul continued. "Some people think I'm past my expiration date here, but the reality is I love seeing guys like you come up in the world. That's the real privilege for me. That's why I get up and continue to come to work. Not to mention, Sharon doesn't want me home all day bothering her."

They sat in silence, recognizing the special nature of their mentor-mentee relationship.

"What do you think you need?" Saul asked.

"What do I need?" Matt didn't understand the question.

Saul sat up a little and leaned in. "This business, this idea of yours. What do you think you need? Look, it's not rocket science. You take the kind of work we do here at the firm, but you focus it on a client segment that cares about the outdoors and create some market expertise with clients in camping, national parks, whatever and do it with a good marketing strategy and you're on your way. You take your strong credentials and create a niche for yourself. This is a playbook, not to deflate you, that lots of people before you have executed on. I can see it could work when it's off the ground, but you might need some runway to get yourself in the air."

Matt didn't want to admit they had thought through and talked about this. He and Cory had a rough answer: about $100,000. The funding would create the operating runway for Matt and Cory to quit their jobs and pursue this full time, but they weren't sure they needed the money. They thought they could build this slowly and organically. But why was Saul asking? Did he have that kind of money lying around? He had been successful with the business, but he and his wife lived frugally. Maybe he knew other potential investors? Matt decided to answer the question. "We'd need $100,000 for an operating runway to pay ourselves until we get a few clients. We want to launch a charitable foundation committed to conservation that supports local protected wildlife areas. But again, Saul, I'm not even saying this is happening for sure, and I'm not sure we need the money or are even—."

Saul interrupted him again, smiling as he did it. "Matt. Listen to me. I wouldn't ask if I didn't believe in you and think you could be successful. I've actually wondered when you would make your move. This doesn't really surprise me."

Matt sat back in his chair, soaking it all in.

"I might have a better idea," Saul said. "You could incubate here. We're set up for it. It might seem a little unconventional, but I'll talk to the other partners. I think it's a strong signal to current consultants that we help our top talent like you launch their futures from here. To the extent you are pursuing smaller clients, which we aren't working with anyway, I don't see an issue. Keeping you attached to the firm, in some way, could be a strategic move for us. Selfishly, I want you around. Bring that Cory guy in and let me meet him."

Saul paused, looking Matt in the eye. "The reality is I don't think you will need that kind of money to get started. You're talking about your time. Maybe you can go part-time, and we can have some agreement about which clients you can't compete for. Of course, you realize this likely takes becoming a partner off the table."

Matt thought about what Saul was sharing, which felt exciting. It was as if a path forward had been opened that felt safer for him to explore, even if Matt knew he would be walking away from making partner and the known financial rewards associated with that. Saul's willingness to broaden the aperture of the professional relationship with Matt was surprising as well. Saul was pushing him closer to the reality of starting his own business than he had pushed himself.

"Saul, this sounds surprising in some ways, but really great. I've struggled with leaving, especially at this point in my career so close to making partner. I've always appreciated you and everything you've done for me. I feel I need to pursue this, and I need to know if I can build my own business and create this niche for myself around my passion. If a path forward to doing that exists while keeping one foot in the firm, that's a dream scenario for me."

Saul smiled, "I'm sure a path forward exists somehow that we all feel good about. It might be difficult to figure out, but it's been done before. If we do it right, it could be a strategic opportunity for the firm. And, listen, about this charitable effort you want to launch alongside. That's a good angle because it will open up conversations you wouldn't have been able to access otherwise. Not to mention, you'll be doing some good things in the process. Count me in for a donation. Let's say somewhere around $5,000 once I see the details."

Matt listened with shock at the commitment to a generous donation to an effort Matt had not fully defined. "Saul, I don't know what to say. That's generous of you."

"Listen. Sharon and I donate to these things, including conservation causes, a lot, and we want to do more the older we get. Knowing someone as competent as you will be part of creating a philanthropic strategy makes this easy for me. Believe it or not, finding a not-for-profit organization that not only excites you but also gives you confidence is difficult. I know whatever you decide to do will be well thought out and impactful, so I'm grateful for that. Remember, you didn't get lucky; you spent years earning my trust. I've watched you up close and personal, so supporting you and this endeavor feels easy."

Saul could tell Matt was still surprised at the offer of seed donation of $5,000 for his nascent not-for-profit effort.

"Plus, Matt, to put you at ease," Saul said, leaning in closer, "a young guy was a client of mine once. A wonderful guy like you. He had a good heart and wanted to do well by others in the world. He wanted to solve problems and create a better life for people, not some guy wanting to make a lot of money. I became something of a mentor to him. He had come to this country as a kid not speaking a word of English and worked harder than hell. He needed an additional $80,000 to start his own manufacturing plant, and we worked out a deal where I gave him the money he needed over time as an investment."

Matt nodded. He didn't know Saul had ever invested in his clients before.

"I didn't know much about manufacturing, but every time we talked, he told me he knew from his existing customers a need for a certain kind of precision manufacturing existed, and if he bought the right equipment, he knew he could sell an expanded product line," Saul continued. "It's funny looking back on it. That was a lot of money for me to invest at the time, but I told him it was an investment in him, and I trusted him. We didn't have any legal agreements. We probably should have. We sketched out the deal on a piece of paper and we signed it. Well, it worked. That plant got to full capacity selling high-margin, precision-manufactured parts, and he parlayed that into a whole bunch of other lines of parts manufacturing."

Saul paused. "So, I recouped that money and more, but I treasured the friendship. We get together and have breakfast at this diner where you can't spend more than $25 for two people, and we call it our 'shareholder's meeting.' I kept that agreement, which we pull out and laugh about. It's just money, Matt. If you can't spend it on the things that matter to you, then what's the point?" Saul smiled. Matt thought about Saul's success in this investment and of growing and selling his own firm, and how, in spite of those things, he stayed focused on the human relationships he treasured.

"So, come back to me when you have that foundation piece set up," Saul continued, "and I'll be honored to make that investment. And use your time here to get this new business going. But I have one condition that won't be anywhere in the investment agreement: Just pay it forward. Be generous with your time and resources, especially for the people who have less than you. Do we have a deal?"

Matt looked at the man in his 60s with his gentle eyes and reached out his hand. "Yes, Saul, we have a deal."

Chapter 20

Repeatability

A s Matt was finishing listening to his weekend edition of Kara Jones's podcast, thumbing through the paper and sipping coffee, Cory knocked on the door to his office. "Hey partner, how was the weekend?"

"Hey, it was great. Sabina and I knocked out that training run Saturday and laid low yesterday. I'm feeling it today. What about you guys?" Matt asked.

"Real good. We went over to the gym and climbed last night with Jodie, and we started the conversation about expansion," Cory answered.

It had been six months since Cory and Matt had first convened The Climbers, which had grown to 22 people meeting every two weeks at 7:00 a.m. to climb and network. Jodie, the owner of the climbing gym, was happy to continue offering the space for free because six of the people in the group had already purchased memberships. Jodie had become a member of The Climbers herself because she was exploring how to scale out the business through franchising and she figured she could use some expert advice.

"Fantastic," Matt said. "Yeah, I want to get that PowerPoint finalized that lays out specifically our process for helping organizations scale. I'm hoping Jodie will be the first client and a great use-case for future ones."

Once Matt and Cory had secured their first client, whom they met through The Climbers, Cory built a budget and determined he was in a strong position to leave his job to start the new business, Carney & Schneider, a boutique management consulting firm. He had thought about taking a few weeks off in between to decompress and maybe take an extended trip with Jesse, but the prospect of getting to work felt more exciting. Their first consulting project was in the public sector, which Cory would focus on leading, while Matt was concentrating on building relationships and offering management consulting services to private sector companies and private foundations. Their early branding drew on environmental themes, and the first edition of their newsletter would tell inspiring stories about the positive difference that companies and public agencies were making to protect open lands. They were also looking at putting together a quarterly lunch series with guest speakers.

Saul popped into the office to check on his protégés. "How's the office working out, gents?"

"Saul, the office is great. Thank you," Cory answered. "I can't believe that only a couple months have passed. I'm amazed at how quickly everything has begun to unfold."

"Oh, trust me," Saul said, "it gets faster. Don't forget to slow down and appreciate the journey. By the way, I was talking with an old friend of mine. She's on the board of an open land organization in Montana, where they have a summer home. They're about to receive an estate gift and need some help figuring out how to structure it. Mind if I make the introduction?"

Matt smiled. "That would be great. Thanks, Saul." As it turned out, they had not asked for nor needed the $100,000 in operating runway given Matt's ability to continue to serve his existing clients while carving out time for the new prospective clients under the business Cory and he had created. Cory had sent a few referrals to Coopers & Tompkins when he knew that both Matt and himself didn't have the capability to do the client work. Cory supported a thoughtful transition for his successor at the Forest Preserves and continued to maintain strong relationships with his public sector contacts.

"And how is the business?" Saul asked.

"Really good," Matt explained. "We took your advice to serve as a provisional or part-time chief strategy officer for smaller clients that have ongoing needs and want us at the table on an ongoing basis. We've developed that as a retainer model and think we will fill up quickly in addition to selling some of the more traditional strategy projects clients occasionally need. How is it working for you?" Matt asked, sensitive to the changing nature of his employment relationship.

Saul gathered his thoughts. "You know, I think it's fine. Financially, the firm continues to make money on the engagements you are working on, not to mention the referrals you and Cory have sent, and this has created a sort of interesting example about how we get into other niche markets. So yes, even though this arrangement is creative in some ways, it all makes sense. The alternative is you would have stayed here and been unhappy, and then, at some point, you would quit and have posed more of a competition risk for us. In my mind, this is smarter."

"Well, we're grateful for how this has worked out. Saul, I wanted to remind you," Matt continued, "that we're headed to Yosemite next week for our hiking outing with about 15 people, including that woman, Monique, you sent our way. The forecast is perfect fall weather."

"Oh, I won't need you. On the other hand," Saul responded, with sarcasm, "Who leaves a pregnant wife? Maybe Sharon and I will invite her over one night. We've got something for her."

"I'm sure she would love that." Matt smiled back.

Chapter 21

Creating Leverage

Matt and Sabina were a few minutes late in arriving. Matt still couldn't believe almost three years had passed since he co-launched Carney & Schneider. He loved the opportunities to connect with the Third Shift Entrepreneurs, though those opportunities had become less frequent as everyone's lives and professional pursuits had taken flight. The drive out to Eldridge House was about two hours outside the city, beyond the suburbs and into a rural community. They waited a bit to leave so that Ella could take her afternoon nap in the car.

Pulling up to the house, it was in fact, better than Kenneth had described it to be and even far better than the photos on Instagram showed it to be. A wide, set-back driveway passed lush and varied trees throughout the property, with up-lighting across the yard that led to a house with a dramatic black paint job accentuated by white window frames and a set of double doors to welcome you in atop the slate stairs. Originally an old farmhouse, the previous owners had expanded it and built eight additional bedrooms and bathrooms to make the full conversion to a bed and breakfast while preserving the facade. This significant home and estate were unlike anything within miles, which was otherwise a sparsely populated rural area with working farms. Driving for an hour without seeing much of anything and arriving at this majestic retreat property made it all the more exceptional.

With Ella still asleep in his arms, Matt rang the doorbell. Kenneth answered the door. "Welcome to Eldridge House," he said and smiled, as Sabina handed him a bottle of celebratory champagne while they exchanged hugs and greetings.

There was laughter, many conversations, and music coming from inside as Matt and Sabina made their way through the porch and saw all of the Third Shift Entrepreneurs assembled.

"You made it," exclaimed Yisel who, along with the others, came over to greet Matt and Sabina and to take an adoring look at Ella.

"And this must be Ella." Kim immediately went to hug the two-year-old, who had since woken up. "Look at her. Those eyes are all you, Sabina. I haven't seen her since the baby shower."

The opening of Kenneth's retreat center, along with his wife and business partner, Janelle, had been cause for celebration and a reason to reconvene. Though in-person gatherings had become more difficult to coordinate, the group nonetheless remained close and regularly emailed, checked in with each other, and texted the group for input. At some point, however, the flywheel of success had begun to kick in for each person's aspirations and the hard work of creating something from nothing was replaced by the hard work of supporting customers, pursuing new opportunities and growing their respective businesses. The desire for simply the friendships and support had replaced the need for account-ability as everyone's businesses began to take hold.

Regis called the group together. "Friends, I want to invite you to gather around."

"It wouldn't be a Third Shift Entrepreneur get-together if Regis didn't have us share *something* with the group," Alberto observed as others laughed, having thought the same thing.

"Now, I don't want to stop the fun here, but I know we have a lot to share, and I would be remiss not to ask everyone to tell us what you have been up to, and more importantly, what you have learned. I can't think of a better place to have this conversation than the newly revealed Eldridge House." Regis swept his arm across the room as if to reveal the house.

The small group offered a round of applause as Kenneth grabbed his wife Janelle's hand.

"Well, yes. It's open!" Kenneth began. "It's been a journey. We opened a year later than we expected, but it's here now. As you all know, we had another property in mind, and we were under contract to close on that place, an interesting, historic property that needed some work, but we had a vision for it. Three nights before we were set to close, I was up late at night scrolling through properties for sale and I saw this one pop up, newly on the market. I sat up in bed and couldn't believe what I was seeing. I had this unbelievable anxiety, sensing we had to change course. I woke Janelle up and said, 'Babe, you've got to see this.'"

Janelle laughed. "That's true."

"So, we ran the numbers for eight bedrooms instead of six, looked at the marketing plan, maintenance costs, remod-eling estimates, and other factors, and we decided we had to go with this place. Getting it right, even if being late, for a business like this seemed to be the right course of action." He and Janelle smiled at each other.

"The best part is that even though we have finally and formally opened, we have hosted three preview events with event planners and influencers. We built up our brand by hosting actual retreats at places that we would rent, including boutique hotels as well as this house, which we rented for a week from the previous owners before we made an offer. Doing that validated we had an audience, that this space worked for us, and we could generate business. We have secured six events for the summer, which gets us to our breakeven point. If we can get 12 events for the summer and fall, which I think we can, we get back to our previous income levels. If we do a lot more than that, well, that would be great. Mostly, we are living our dream and the life that we want for ourselves. So, yeah, it's all happening."

The group offered a chorus of congratulations while Janelle turned and passed out postcards to share with any friends and colleagues looking for a small group retreat.

"And what I've learned? Patience," Kenneth continued. "Had we moved on the wrong property because it fit our timeline better, we would have missed the mark. We had the patience to host retreats at other properties to validate the business model even though we didn't own our own property. That was invaluable. So, here we are."

"And we all couldn't be happier for you," Regis cut in. "I think we can all commit to bringing one group here at some point, don't you?" Regis checked the group for affirmation and found it. "And that would get you to at least six more events."

"I'll go next," Yisel chimed in. "Well, it's been crazy to say the least. I kept roasting and selling small batches for a whole year before I perfected what I thought was the right blend and brand. I landed a few boutique hotels, including Eldridge House," Yisel said, pausing to smile at Kenneth and Janelle. "About six months ago, I met a woman, through one of our hotel clients, who was a sourcing consultant for the hotel industry. I had no idea that job existed, but I am in a trial with a major hotel chain and have the potential to expand globally across its properties if it goes well. I am also talking to people that work for larger food brands about scaling up my operations and brand."

"Awesome," Alberto said aloud, echoing the group's excitement.

"So," Yisel continued, "what I've learned is you need partners to grow. When I started this whole thing, I assumed I would be in charge of growing my company at each stage. What I've learned is that if you get the right channel partner, you can go from zero to a hundred in a few months. But you need partners for distribution, sourcing, and sales."

"Partners, yes. That's great. Thanks, Yisel." Regis nodded to Chad to go next.

Chad gathered his thoughts. "I've learned that even though what I am technically doing is selling maps, I am actually selling a certain lifestyle and the ability to belong to a community. I've grown the brand and have stayed with the pop-up event format for how to build my community and sell the maps, and I have added an extensive online presence that's generating a lot of interest as well. What I didn't realize was how strong a community I have been building and how attractive that community is to other people. Realtors, travel agents, jewelers and other lifestyle experts who sell luxury products and services are coming to me asking to participate in my salon series. I even do a Facebook Live show that took me a while to get comfortable with, but people love the segments as I offer sort of a blended history lesson in cartography and present antique artifacts for sale." Chad paused to consider his path forward.

"I'm exploring organizing a trip where we will go to Portugal and explore some of the history of mapmaking. It would be top dollar, and people have shown a lot of interest in additional curated experiences like that. If you told me I would not have a storefront and instead have a Facebook show and might be planning a luxury vacation back when I started, I would have thought that was crazy. Instead, I'm profitable and growing, and I've been able to accomplish that without a lot of overhead."

Kim offered, "Yea, Chad" and gave him a high five, which he awkwardly returned, garnering laughter.

Kim continued, "Next week will mark the one-year anniversary of Kim's House. I can't believe it's all come together. I focused on what I was doing to create a living environment for these young women, and with the seed grant I secured, I purchased a historic home in the neighborhood with seven bedrooms. Not as fancy as this place, Kenneth, but nice nonetheless. We are fully occupied. So, some women just turning 18 are living there for free while other women who have stable employment are paying about $400 a month. Among the rents, government housing voucher reimbursements and some private donors, this model works. Everyone must contribute to the house in other ways as well. And we have built this beautiful, supportive community. Sunday is open dinner night, where we might get 20 to 30 of these extraordinary young women who show up and get access to this family-by-choice, as I call it. I was doing my day job for the first several months to keep my income source, but two months ago, I shifted to doing Kim's House full-time. All of you, and I mean this, need to come visit if you have not done so."

"Kim, that is extraordinary," Regis said.

Chad added, "I've been there. It's awesome."

"What I learned," Kim continued, "was to stay focused and do one thing well. I got really good at those chili dinners and focused on finding a house to accommodate up to 12 other women. I had to get good at fundraising and developing a model for sponsorship, but that's working as well. I have established partnerships in the community for other services that the residents may need beyond housing. I've also launched a board of directors, and I'm leaning on them to bring expertise for areas that are new to me. So yeah, it's hard, but I will tell you, every morning I wake up and never, ever question whether or not this is what I should be doing with my life."

The group affirmed Kim's sentiment about the hard days they had experienced and the lack of regret in the choices they made. Regis turned to Alberto, "So, tell us Alberto. How is the business?"

"Well, like everyone else, it's been interesting, wonderful and not exactly what I expected." Alberto received approving nods from the group. "We ran The Apocalypse Experience for about a year, got all of this great press and people were excited by it. Of course, this labor of love was a lot of work for Maribel and me. We were thinking about our next move, how to scale the concept, and we got lots of interest from people wanting us to come create experiences for them, almost as consultants, if you want to think of it that way," Alberto explained.

"It turns out companies and other organizations, even cities, want to host their own experiential events. So, we shifted the business to doing that. The money has been bigger as a business-to-business offering, rather than selling tickets for the individual experiences. And working as an event company for other businesses, we get bigger budgets to design cool experiences." Alberto paused for a moment, reflecting on all that had changed and was coming.

"We just created this experience called Into the Future, where we envisioned what life on another planet could look like in 1,000 years, and we put it together for a leading tech conference in Silicon Valley that brings over 20,000 attendees each year. It's sort of a must-attend for people in technology and venture capital, and I had one guy who works with Disney ask me if I would be open to a partnership. So, those conversations are taking place, and I don't know where they will lead. In the meantime, Maribel and I are running our business full-time, making good money, and are having more fun than ever."

The group mirrored the excitement and joy that Alberto expressed. His success was their success.

"I've learned so much, but most important is to listen to the opportunities coming to you. I never could have imagined that by running these experiences out of our garage we would ultimately be creating the experiences for other organizations or tech conferences, but those were the calls that came, so that's the direction we took."

"That's exactly how this goes oftentimes, isn't it?" Regis reflected. "All we can do is step forward, do our best work, and showcase our capabilities. Then we hope the market comes to us with the opportunities. It's almost this faith we need to have, first the willingness to work hard to bring something to life and then that the market will respond and show us the way. Not to mention, you and Maribel are great at what you do, Alberto. That can't be dismissed."

The group turned to Matt and Sabina. Sabina held Ella's hand while she patiently listened to the stories.

"I'm inspired by you guys. Amazing," Matt said. "Well, the ride has been wild for us as well. I met a wonderful guy along the way, Cory, whom I've mentioned, and he and I launched our own management consulting firm to focus on clients who share our passion for the outdoors. After some soul searching and watching us in action together, I realized he would be the better leader to run our business. Therefore, I'm a co-founder, but I consider him the boss and the visionary to lead the business and scale it. The firm is doing well and, honestly, the discontent I felt about needing to do something with my professional life has vanished. I've been hiking and camping more in the last two years than I have in the previous 20 years, and that has been the greatest gift. The irony is, every camping trip is considered business development, so I don't have any guilt about being out there with friends and clients doing the things I love most, which is enjoying beautiful national parks and having conversations about strategic decisions for the organizations I'm supporting.

"Saul, my old boss and mentor, continues to be a huge supporter of mine and a business advisor. We gave him a small equity stake for all he has given us, mostly because we want his advice and involvement. He is a longtime believer in entrepreneurship," Matt said, looking at Regis, knowing the deep value of the mentorship that Regis and Saul, as well as the other Third Shift Entrepreneurs, had provided him.

"Now I'm thinking about what could be next, but the unease around that has shifted. I have no more anxiety, just curiosity. I wake up every day grateful to be surrounded by all of this possibility. I will say, I'm thinking about doing more active volunteer service. I have showed up to support organizations I'm interested in and am using the Third Shift Entrepreneur strategies again. It turns out that it works in the volunteering world, too."

Matt picked up Ella and put her on his hip. "To be honest, what I'm most enjoying right now is this growing project in my life, this two-year-old right here."

The group smiled, seeing Ella and the obvious joy that she brought Matt and Sabina.

"Oh, but I would be remiss if I didn't acknowledge the newest entrepreneur in our family," Matt said, looking up. "You see, after seeing all my crazy activity, Sabina thought about her own career. She had always been a successful therapist working for another practice with a number of loyal clients. The practice she worked for was more of a general practice, but her passion is kids, so," Matt looked at Sabina, "I encouraged her to start her own practice specializing in child development and parent-child issues. In short order, it has grown into the go-to practice for her specific practice area. She took on three additional therapists, rented new office space, and started a podcast that gets a lot of recognition. So, it turns out, she's the real entrepreneurial star and success story in the family. But you all already knew that."

Matt looked at Ella, then at Sabina. "I think I'm actually a better cheerleader and a strong number two for the real talents in the world. Maybe that's my real calling."

"Perhaps that is, Matt," Regis said, smiling. "Perhaps that is."

Part II

The 12 Observations

The second part of the *Third Shift Entrepreneur* shifts us from fiction to nonfiction, in which I present 12 Observations to guide you in starting a business, and tell real stories of Third Shift Entrepreneurs who are applying this thinking to start and grow businesses. I know the people that I highlight here, and I admire them. They're starting businesses and it isn't easy, but it's working. They share their stories as an act in vulnerability and as a gift to you, that you might see how starting something actually works. Unlike traditional work, where effort and input are paid for and rewarded, entrepreneurship rewards value that is created for people who need it. If you create a lot of value (even without a lot of effort), you can be successful. If you aren't creating value (no matter the amount of effort), you will not be. So, the task is not about what you need to do, per se, but rather what needs to be demonstrated, evidenced, or observed. Said differently, if you came to me and said, "My business isn't working," I would revert to these 12 Observations and ask you a question related to each one. "Are you really committed to this?," "Does it actually work?," "Do people want this from you?" and so on. With those questions, you will get closer to diagnosing what works and what doesn't (yet) with your approach.

My bias is that you keep your job, or have an established financial platform for yourself, while pursuing this process of bringing a business to life. The idea of starting a business while keeping your job is not novel. I simply hope to make it popularly understood and popular again. Phil Knight spent five years selling his athletic shoes before leaving his full-time job in accounting to start Nike. Sara Blakely developed her idea for Spanx over years and kept her full-time job selling fax machines in the meantime. Markus Persson was a programmer who built video games on the side. He first launched Minecraft, unfinished, on a gaming portal. He kept his day job for a full year before committing to Minecraft full-time, eventually selling it to Microsoft for $2.5B. Daymond John worked at Red Lobster while sewing clothes in his mom's basement during his off-hours as he built his clothing brand FUBU. The timelines here are important: All of these successful entrepreneurs spent not weeks or months at their day job but years before they were fully employed by the businesses they were building.

The entrepreneurs I have seen successfully start things had executed most of these 12 Observations. In some cases, you can achieve these observations without a lot of work. In other cases, you'll need to be thoughtful in doing things to produce the evidence. Presenting a framework centered on you, the entrepreneur, versus the business, represents an innate challenge given that each business is different and the context for how you apply this is going to look different. My hope is that the entrepreneur profiles that follow in Part III provide more of a picture of what this might look like for you and the business you are starting.

Third Shift Entrepreneur

These 12 Observations are the building blocks for what I have seen when people's full potential takes flight and businesses are launched. This is also the moment in which I believe you offer your greatest gifts to the world. Starting a business, stepping into your professional fulfillment, and bringing something to life does not only serve you; it's something the rest of us need from you as well.

1: Obsession

Matt Merjavy had been a management consultant for six years following his time in the U.S. Marine Corps. He was 35, on a good professional track, but felt that something was missing. "In fact, I felt nothing. If I had an involuntary thought of a different career, it just seemed rational to dismiss it. I was in a highly selective career that not only guaranteed financial security but also helped me avoid boredom and monotony, the plagues of so many other careers. Consulting gave me a constant feed of new people to meet, new technology to learn, and new cities to explore. Transitioning out seemed highly irrational, so if that thought ever popped up, it was only rational to squash it. I told myself, 'Be grateful and appreciate what you have,' and it worked well until it didn't."

So often, the dreams that are ignored, the monotony that is suppressed, and the anguish that is felt represent the beginning of what is possible. Entrepreneurship begins with identity: who we are, what matters to us, and what we want to create in the world. Sometimes, we are so compelled that we must proceed. Other times, we live in the anguish of convincing ourselves that what we have should be enough, until one day it isn't. Still other times, the life we have assumed ceases to be recognizable to who we know ourselves to be internally. Yet, in other cases, it is an invitation to do something, a simple curiosity we follow, or an accidental act of creation of which others demand more that begins the journey into entrepreneurship.

"After two years of a self-imposed ban from considering an alternative career, random thoughts of having one did not fade," Matt explained. "To avoid going insane, I had to figure out why the extremely fuzzy idea of 'doing something else' had such abundantly clear appeal.

"I thought the answer was some complicated riddle, one that would require some psychedelic experience during an expedition in the Amazon or months of prolonged practice in mindfulness to reach the deepest of meditative states. Eventually, I said screw all that and went with the simplest approach I could think of. I decided to ask myself the basic question of, 'What do I want to do when I wake up in the morning?' and observed my actions over the course of one to two months for the answer. The answer: 'Make stuff.' I knew it was hilariously vague, but I was proud of it because it was truly honest."

Our journey into entrepreneurship demands this level of honesty about who we are and what matters to us. It cannot simply be an intellectually engineered set of activities. We must see something of ourselves at stake. For Matt, this kernel of truth that "making stuff" mattered to him and had been missing opened up a world.

"So, when I stumbled upon some beautiful ash wood from a fallen tree in my backyard, this very natural almost boyish wave of excitement took over. Aside from using an old power drill to hang a few shelves and curtain rods, I owned zero tools and had no carpentry experience to lean on. What I did have, though, was an unmistakable craving to use my hands for something other than typing and swiping."

And so it began with Matt: this curiosity to create things, first working with the fallen ash tree, which in turn led to him making other things out of wood. In time and with practice, he made a coffee table, a dining room table, and a handful of custom wood furniture pieces. He had another discovery along the way: Mastery of one craft was not as life-giving as the process of learning new crafts. He began to work with metal and brick, and he began to garden. He made a four-foot-wide brick pizza oven, built an outdoor kitchen, and hosted movie nights where people would pick fresh basil from his garden, make their own wood-fired pizza and then gather for community and movies.

"With all that, now there was an experience. What I didn't know is how many strangers our backyard would attract. On an almost weekly basis that summer, someone who lived in the area would drop by to inquire and introduce themselves. Due to the simple redesign of a small 900-square-foot backyard, dozens of new friendships were formed and dozens more got the social experience they needed," Matt explained. Though this passion was not yet a fully formed business, Matt had several people who asked him to re-create their backyards into places that brought similar experiences. People were asking him to teach them how to build things, and Matt saw a generational need and a larger purpose.

"The first intrinsic need is this desire and reward of making something yourself, which is built into our human DNA, even though our modern economy has disincentivized us from ever learning how. The second intrinsic need is for community. You know that weird realization which all city dwellers have about not knowing their neighbors even though they see them every day? I think it's the defining paradox of our time: the fact we live so close together yet are so far apart. We don't have easy access to communal activities nor the spaces to support them. Yes, there are plenty of common areas, but none are communal areas. If there's a market to redesign space that turns strangers into friends through learning and making stuff together, the way my backyard and pizza oven did on my block, I want to help it thrive."

Matt is on the path. There is something here: a passion that has been explored, something real that has been created, and a noticeable reaction by people curious and wanting more of it, including some wanting to pay for it. Though you can contract people to redesign outdoor spaces, what Matt is doing is unique in terms of the totality of his vision. He is so connected to his passion and the intersection of making things with his hands and designing for experiences, that people will want what he offers. It is not yet a business; that will come. But for Matt, the willingness to step into his own curiosity changed things, "I became more conscious of, more grateful for, and more fascinated by the world around me. As tacky as it sounds, I became happier."

The mind is where this negotiation and preparation for bold action takes place. We come to resolution in our minds first, and the decisions that come later are something of a lagging indicator for the work that has been taking place internally. My journey follows similarly to Matt's and many others. My professional life, in most instances, has followed the 12 Observations of the Third Shift Entrepreneurs with some clear violations along the way, such as quitting and moving to a city without a job, which cumulatively has been the foundation for my professional life. I have run businesses and organizations I have started, pursued ideas that never culminated in anything, and have had jobs working for others. Throughout all of it, I felt free to pursue the things that mattered to me. This is the fundamental crux of this book: to find professional and personal fulfillment through starting things. Freedom from obligation is not the goal; freedom to pursue the things that matter to you is.

Accordingly, the first observation required is that you have a deep passion, or even *obsession*, with an idea. This isn't meant as a feel-good mantra but rather as a question of sustainability. An idea in which you do not have some deep and abiding interest will not command your attention long enough to bring it to fruition. The passion for an idea is what allows longevity and persistence amid inevitable setbacks. For Matt, it was making things. For me, it was coaching people toward professional fulfillment. What is it for you?

Nancy Preston, CEO of Milk Money Kitchens (www. milkmoneykitchens.com) expresses it perfectly. "Obsession looks more like a hole that I must fill by trying and continually moving forward even after I get my ass kicked all over the city. There have been times when I would have loved to have gotten off this ride and go back to my more comfortable, safer lifestyle. But I had to know how this would end. I had to take this all the way, or the 'not knowing' would haunt me."

Some find this level of commitment in the product itself, others in the desire to prove something to themselves and still others in a commitment to a higher-order virtue, such as a family legacy, a societal wrong, or an improvement in a given market. The entrepreneurs we talk to often see their businesses in the context of these deeper values with expressions, such as "People deserve financial freedom," "I was not going to let this fail," "Everyone has a right to own their home" and "This was about my daughter as much as anything." Still, others are intellectually committed, as expressed with comments like, "This totally makes sense," "This would be such a better way of doing things" and "She offered me this opportunity and I keep getting excited every time I think about it."

Tools are available to gain this clarity in your life, the first among them being journaling and self-reflection. What patterns are you noticing? What do you find yourself daydreaming about? What are the images and the scenarios taking shape in your imagination? What parts of those images are ego-centered, and which parts of those are service-centered? Assessment tools can inform a portrait of your talents and unique contributions. Talking to other people, including those personally close to us as well as professional colleagues, can inform this picture. Ultimately, wanting to be an entrepreneur is not enough; we need to attach ourselves to some solution or some problem driving us forward. In and of itself, wanting to be an entrepreneur is simply an identity statement that will prove insufficient in sustaining you. Rather, you need a problem or an idea you cannot seem to let go of.

This is the language of obsession in which turning back is not an option or one in which the idea continues to pull you in, occupying your mind. This is not, to be clear, the language of doing something reckless, quitting your job and taking a financial risk; this is where the faulty narrative as to what it means to be an entrepreneur comes into play. Having discovered something you care deeply or are excited about is necessary, but it's nowhere near sufficient. You will need both the passion as well as the plan. More on that to follow.

Observation: I keep coming back to this idea I have.

2: Your Internship

A myth about entrepreneurship is that it starts with a moment of brilliant insight or an idea, often beyond the scope of our daily lives and professional expertise. It's as if we have found a golden egg, the idea is good in and of itself, and it's only a question of who claims it. We might even scramble to create legal protections through NDAs to prevent the theft of this idea. People can hold the false notion that the speed of pursuing the idea, like quickly cashing in a lottery ticket before someone else finds it, is how you win. The idea stands alone, this thinking goes, and you are the lucky person who thought of it.

This, however, is flawed thinking. In a study by Capshare of 100 unicorn businesses in 2016, 6 percent of new businesses started as the result of a brainstorm or new idea. The most significant place of origin for these businesses was among the 27 percent of founders who had deep industry expertise. Another 19 percent wanted to scratch their own itch to address a problem they had experienced or an opportunity they saw personally. Beyond that, 20 percent either copied an existing business but with a twist or grew something out of an existing business. People rarely build a business doing something in which they are not an expert.[1]

Tanikka Dennison spent years accruing the right networks, industry context, and building her professional reputation before she launched CrossTech Consulting Group (www.crosstechcg.com), which provides IT staffing and workforce solutions for enterprise clients. Having previously worked over the past decade in various roles that live at the intersection of technology, HR, and account management for companies like Cisco, ManpowerGroup, Verizon, and Staples, Tanikka understood the landscape for IT staffing needs. "I've always been entrepreneurial and enterprising. As a matter of fact, all of the corporations that I have worked for have hired me because of my entrepreneurial spirit. I knew this was the business I was meant to start because I love working with and helping people, and staffing allows me to do that. Additionally, with my IT background, I knew that component would work well in the IT staffing industry."

She continued: "I had expertise in understanding IT and some expertise with staffing, as I had run recruiting programs and had done RPO recruiting. However, I did not have

---

[1] discover.shareworks.com/a-private-company/startup-ideas-how-the-best-founders-get-them-and-why-novelty-is-overrated

experience working in an agency environment. I built a team of current and former IT staffing agency mentors to help fill the gap in areas that I was unfamiliar with. Additionally, I joined trade organizations in which I could connect with other IT staffing business owners. Finally, I read a ton of books and took training classes to help fill the gaps in the areas where I lacked knowledge." Tanikka's "internship" had been the last several years of her professional life gaining deep industry expertise, so when it was time to launch her business there were few unknowns. She knew the pricing model, decision-makers IT staffing needs, which markets experienced staffing shortages and who key partners could be.

For Tanikka, as it is for so many entrepreneurs, cultivating the networks and expertise are years in the making before launching the business you are meant to launch. Particularly in professional services, businesses are most often built from the place of expertise and from where you sit. Having this understanding removes the unknowns from the business you want to start. Designing your internship is about getting you closer to that place of expertise and understanding.

To be clear, I do not mean you should get an internship at a company. Rather, this is a call to get close to the environment where you will learn what you need before you start a business. You can have an interesting idea that comes to you, but your mission before you pursue it is to get closer to the industry, people and networks that can help bring you greater clarity. That may be within your company, how you spend your time outside of work, what projects you choose, what you read or consume, or it may involve a career change.

This is simple advice, but a surprising many miss the step. If you want to open a restaurant, get a job working various shifts at other restaurants. If you want to open up a day care facility, work in a day care facility or at an afterschool program. If you want to become an executive coach, consider a shift to working in HR and focus on opportunities to do executive coaching. If you want to launch a nonprofit that helps military veterans transition out of the military, volunteer for another nonprofit doing similar work. If you want to build a SaaS platform, work on managing or implementing a SaaS platform similar to the one you're thinking of building.

A key question for you might be, "What could I be doing today that moves me toward being the person who, logically, would be in a position to start this?" For your idea, what unknowns can you make known by orienting your professional life and your extra hours toward filling in the knowledge gaps? Designing your internship is about giving you proximity to the idea and creating a certain inevitability that, because of where you sit, you are closest to understanding what the business and the opportunity could be. Businesses that represent a total and clean departure from your current reality face intrinsic challenges. Stepping into a self-assigned internship will help inform what steps you will take next and help resolve the emotional condition of feeling stuck or defeated. You're not stuck. You're taking action. You've begun the process of learning what could be.

Internships, in this context, prioritize learning more than career advancement. We do not put ourselves in this proverbial internship for the material rewards; we are there to learn what we need to learn. For us adults, it's a self-imposed internship not measured in semesters as a college student would but in terms of what we are learning and who we are meeting with our time. If what you hope to build is unrelated to what you do professionally today, consider a career change to get closer to your idea. If it is related to what you do today, then shift your projects and time closer toward gaining more expertise and strengthening your network. Often, it involves what we do on our nights and weekends: starting a blog if we want to be a writer, joining the board of a nonprofit if we want to start our own someday, joining a community-based organization if we think we will run for office, or attending a Health IT conference if we want to start our own Health IT company someday.

Internships help us gain context for the industry, competition and people involved, whether our idea has any merit and whether we even find it interesting over time. Creative entrepreneurs, as the stories in this book reveal, often find ways to create internships from their place of current employment, or they do things in addition to their day job that also pay them. No one else will necessarily know we have put ourselves into a self-assigned internship. They don't need to. As entrepreneurs, we are cultivating our ability to lead ourselves, which includes putting ourselves into the right environments for us to discover and learn what we need to.

Observation: I am doing things at work and in my free time that will naturally build my expertise, networks and credibility for the thing I want to start.

3: Personal Readiness

When LeAnn Darland started TALEA Beer Company (www.taleabeer.com), nothing looked inevitable, yet something compelled her to proceed. She had a love for craft beer and was continually surprised how the male-dominated industry didn't speak to her or other female beer drinkers. In her own words, it was "the voice in the back of my head always asking, 'what if?' What if I could make beer on my own? What if I could be a trailblazer in the beer industry? No matter which corporate job I had or how happy I was with my daily grind, I was always hungry to have something of my own."

That instinct grew, and LeAnn met her co-founder, Tara, who could perfectly compliment the gaps that LeAnn had, including experience in marketing, hospitality and navigating small business legal issues. That LeAnn and Tara were co-workers also helped. "We were working at the same company, so we tried to keep it under wraps until we knew we were leaving. That meant lots of meetings at night and on weekends although we would sneak away about once a day during working hours to discuss our to-do list. We each had a pink notebook we used for our startup . . . if we walked by one another with the pink notebook in hand, we knew it was time for a quick, secret meeting." Your personal readiness is built by finding the time and insisting on it as LeAnn and Tara did.

By the time LeAnn left her job, she had evidence this idea was working and a path for TALEA existed. With her husband's support and her partnership with Tara, pursuing this passion felt right. Founders will never fully abdicate themselves from the risks associated with starting something, but partnerships, keeping their day jobs while exploring the idea, create powerful safety nets, both financial as well as emotional, that mitigate those risks. "Having a brewery was my dream job and meeting my co-founder, Tara, was the catalyst I needed to make it a reality," LeAnn said. "We balance each other emotionally as our business goes through highs and lows, which is as important as the tactical business skills." Fortunately for LeAnn, Tara brought the technical and emotional contributions to allow her to fully pursue TALEA Beer Company.

They made other strategic choices along the way, such as outsourcing the brewing of the beer to another brewery while getting traction to prove there was a market for their brand. They picked up some wonderful press, including from the *New York Times* critic Florence Fabricant, who described TALEA's beers as "easy-drinking beers, perhaps to replace that glass of rosé." They deployed creative marketing strategies to reach their target markets as well. "We hosted beer tastings at places that typically wouldn't attract a beer company," LeAnn explains. "Soul Cycle, The Wing, Chief, *Elle Magazine* and other venues, and sure enough, people who said they didn't drink beer loved our products."

Today, LeAnn and Tara are building their first brewery and taproom in Williamsburg, Brooklyn, which will open after they have been in business for three years, achieved retail distribution, and weathered the COVID-19 pandemic. When asked what aspiring entrepreneurs get wrong, LeAnn offers, "That you have to quit your job to start your business or to lay the foundation of the business." That's prescient advice from a woman whom I first met while she was hosting pop-up tastings with her small-batch brews.

When it comes to personal readiness, the question is how will you support yourself financially and emotionally? Most people frame the conversation about whether or not to start a business as a question of how much risk they are willing to take. This assumes a winning or losing scenario. Instead, the right question to ask is what is the worst-case scenario? What have you established as the financial and emotional floor of your life that you can fall back on? When asked that way, most people confront that they are back to where they started and usually at the job they never left. The risk is reputational more than financial. The fear is not bankruptcy but embarrassment.

As a thought experiment, assuming you have created a financial floor for yourself as LeAnn and Tara did by keeping their jobs, consider the possible outcomes that could emerge that are different from the simple win or lose scenarios. Binary thinking, which our brains are prone to do, can limit us to thinking of only two scenarios, "success" or "failure," when dozens of scenarios are positive but not the the clean "success" nor "failure" narrative we construct for ourselves.

For example, in LeAnn's case, any number of large beer brands could see her vision for reaching an underserved market and would want to hire her. Perhaps LeAnn and Tara discovered that retail sales are easier than opening a brewery, or perhaps other brands would want to hire them to develop their own differentiated branding in male-dominated markets, given the effectiveness and sophistication of the TALEA brand. Perhaps an acquisition comes earlier than expected, or someone wants to film a documentary about their relationship as they start this business. Or "worst case," they return to their jobs having demonstrated an enormous entrepreneurial capacity that has them stand out from their peers. These are not outlandish scenarios. These are among the "failing upward" wins I regularly see aspiring entrepreneurs achieve beyond the goal of their business.

Is securing the financing to build a brewery and taproom easy? No. But they are not bootstrapping that part, and the financing comes after they have validated the market and their position in it. They have built a business, and from that place, have established the credibility to bring in outside investors and lenders to use their capital to scale. The alternative is putting your own money forward to build a brewery and taproom, which most of us do not have. Or we spend time endlessly pitching investors to invest the capital required before we've proven we can build a business. That investment never materializes.

An assessment of your floor, how far could you fall, and a brainstorm about your ceiling, how high could you go, are relevant for considering how and when to start a business. My argument has been that entrepreneurship at its best minimizes risks by taking evidence-based and incremental steps toward bigger investments after smaller moves have been validated. The financial floor of your life is determined by the cost structure of your life, the income you have, your ability to pay your bills and some consideration for who else, such as a spouse, friend, roommate, or parent can step in and help. When we start a business while keeping our jobs or at least piecing together a few gigs, our floor remains intact and at the place of our current lifestyle. When we quit a job to start a business, we remove that floor and the pressure intensifies.

Our ceiling is determined by what is possible by taking action, which we tend to underestimate. Psychology here again has a lot to say on this. The psychological phenomenon of loss aversion, for example, demonstrates we strongly prefer avoiding losses over acquiring equivalent gains. In other words, we are far more concerned with losing five dollars than earning an additional five dollars. That kind of thinking can keep us stuck. The time horizon over which we consider the risk is also relevant: decisions made with the consequences of the next three months keep us stuck, but decisions made with the consequences of the next 50 years might invite some bolder action.

For the purposes of becoming a Third Shift Entrepreneur, I would offer this: Define your floor and then protect it. If your floor is weak, then starting a business will prove problematic. If your floor is strong, you can proceed with building the community of potential customers, running strategic experiments to determine opportunities and building a business from there. Knowing you can return home to your established floor, as it were, after failed experiments gives you the capacity and the confidence to proceed on.

The floor can be established in other ways: commitments that we can return to a job after a leave of absence, moving into that paid "internship" to get closer to your business, secondary income streams, a spouse who can provide, a small retirement income, or reducing your cost of living while reducing hours to create more space to build the next business. LeAnn built TALEA Beer Company from a strong floor: a job, a supportive spouse and the perfect business partner. She was ready. She mitigated the risks, and the opportunities for her and the business became numerous.

Observation: I have a strong floor established for my life. I am in a good position to pursue this.

4: The Space to Discover

Kit Lancaster is undeniably passionate about helping people find stability and freedom through sound financial management of their assets. Kit's studious demeanor and gentle disposition might belie his previous service in the U.S. Army for four years, where he learned the fundamentals of leadership and management that served him well in working for larger financial services companies. Today, he is the founder and CEO of Sterling Edge Financial (www.sterlingedgefinancial. com), which he started three years ago.

His nascent business turned profitable in short order, but that does not tell the whole story of how he was cultivating future clients and partners for years prior to starting his own business. In Kit's own words, "I spent a lot of time with other business owners and engaging other financial planning firms in Chicago. I also spent time with business owners I could network within and around Bunker Labs. Within the first 90 days of launching Sterling Edge Financial, anyone who knew me or remembered me from connecting over the years, reached out and was super excited. Way more excited than I thought, and they reached out to learn more about my business and to see if or how they could help. The marketplace had a lot of confidence in me and saw my move as a sign of strength." Kit then added with characteristic sincerity, "It was humbling, as I didn't anticipate the response."

The businesses we start, when we are well-positioned, come as a natural extension of the networks we have built and the conversations we have been having. Launching cold-start into a new industry in which we have not built up some credibility or expertise presents significant structural challenges toward building a successful business. Kit's story, presented as a natural set of activities centered around what he is passionate about in an area he has been working in, underscores a key consideration for how to build a successful business.

This fourth observation here calls for you to have created the space in which you have direct connection with those who could become your customers someday. If old thinking suggests you'll meet your customers once you open the business, Third Shift Entrepreneur thinking demands that you know your customers and are having an active conversation with them before you start the business. Though I refer to this as having the "space" to discover, it could be a channel you've opened through a podcast or LinkedIn Live segment, a set of conversations you've committed to having over coffee, a position that you have assumed within an industry association that gets you closer to your customers, a monthly potluck dinner that you organize, or a weekly email that you send. The space to discover will look different depending on the business, but having that forum established is a specific but often overlooked activity that allows us to present our offerings to potential customers. Even before we know what the offering will be, we know we will need the relationship with our potential customers and the mechanism through which to offer our solutions.

In Kit's case, it was the network he was building from his existing job (in Third Shift parlance: his internship) and the commitment he made to having coffee with his existing relationships. He also began producing thought leadership through emails he would periodically send. His passion, as he explains, is in listening to his clients, "I try to constantly learn. Good meetings, bad meetings, networking, reading, professional development and conferences. I have always wanted to be a financial planner. I started investing in stocks when I was 17 with a little bit of money I made working two jobs over the summer and a part-time job in high school. I love learning new ways to drive value and create value for specific problems, strategies, people and their goals in finance."

Kit continues in his theory about what makes a great financial advisor, noting that only 8 percent of financial advisors in his industry are younger than 40 years old, "What I have learned about being a financial advisor is that the technical work is the easy part. The human element is everything. Anyone can work hard and do the technical work. What most people don't want to do is figure out how to engage, communicate and care about their clients and market on a deeply human level. How to create a human experience that is hyper dialed into the client, that the client can emotionally digest and evolve within. A guided journey, of sorts. I have learned to be a master listener and I am obsessed about how I communicate to my clients and how people communicate. What they say, how they say it, what is the specific language they use? Why do they use that language? How can I best position an engagement, which is a series of conversations, to create the most value as it relates to the purpose that drives my clients?"

It's never been easier to open up a direct channel with your audience than it is today. One of my favorite examples comes by way of Heather Cox Richardson, a professor of American history at Boston College and the author of several books. Beyond her impressive and credentialed career, she started hosting Facebook Live sessions in September 2019 in a longer, usually one hour, format to help people digest the pace of current events and to learn more about what is happening in the context of American history. One year later, she had over 600,000 devoted followers to her Facebook feed and thousands tuning in to each of her live sessions.

Professor Cox Richardson has been an expert in American history for some time, but she democratized her work by leveraging Facebook and inviting people into the conversation. She's adored by her viewers for her notably unsensationalized approach to talking about history and the implications for today's current events. What's important here is not her expertise, though she is an expert, but her willingness to go live, be public, and offer something in the public domain. She's opened up a space with her consumers.

She could not have known she would amass an audience as big as she has, who choose to tune into her longer form content beyond watching, say, the nightly news. She is, in my view, an entrepreneur exercising the steps outlined here to evidence something that is met with an enthusiastic market response. Her decision to choose Facebook, a longer format, and the frequency and nature of her broadcasts are all decisions she made to create the space to discover. Focusing on her content as the differentiator is easy, but without those decisions about the platform, frequency of broadcasts and length of broadcasts, the audience will not receive her content. She was choosing her "channel" or the "space" through which to create these interactions and build this customer relationship (my language, not hers). She has chosen other spaces in the past, including in front of the classroom, in academic journals and through published books.

Another friend of mine owns a boutique public affairs firm where he consults with various politicians and companies to help them shape their messaging and reputational concerns. He's a pro at what he does, but beyond that, he's been strategic in building his space to discover what his clients, and those who can impact his clients, care most about. For years, he has been hosting a monthly lunch series where he convenes journalists, elected officials, lobbyists, clients and other public officials for off-the-record conversations. He holds the luncheon at the storied and iconic Gene & Georgetti's Italian Restaurant on Chicago's Near North Side where politicians of all moral and political persuasions have gathered for decades in its dimly lit dining rooms to converse on the day's issues.

My friend is in his element hosting and playing master of ceremonies during these sessions where passions occasionally flare amid family-style platters of chicken piccata, meatballs, and mostaccioli being passed. For him and the guests, the monthly lunch represents a sort of political communion.

Though as I view it from the lens of the Third Shift Entrepreneur, it serves a highly strategic purpose to create that sort of standing proximity to the relevant people who can advance your business. Out of those lunches come opportunities to serve his existing clients, meet new clients and elevate his work as the head of his public affairs firm.

Each of us, in pursuing our aspirations toward starting something, must create proximity with the customers, partners and other people who can meet us halfway, endorse our efforts and advance the thing. If we have not established a way of reaching them, then we have nowhere to bring our ideas or solutions for reaction. Before we build the minimum viable product, we must build the place in which we meet these people, get to know them and earn the privilege of asking for their opinion, reaction, support, or business. The strategic entrepreneur would do well to deliberate and be strategic in choosing the mechanism by which they will create that proximity. Will it be something you do one-on-one? Will you create a community event? Will you create an environment online? Will you publish something? Choosing an authentic environment allows you to be consistent, and capture the eyeballs and the hearts of those you want to serve.

Thinking of opening a kennel? Start a Saturday dog walking club. Considering becoming your own investment advisor? Start a weekly newsletter with investment tips, and feature people who could be clients someday. Considering starting a nonprofit? Commit to organizing fundraisers for other related causes to build relationships with potential donors. Wanting to start your own real estate investing business? Hold free seminars online to teach what you are learning or to interview other experts. Thinking of making artisanal leather goods? Create a video series or a free public workshop on how to work with leather.

Creating the space is having an answer to the question, "Where will I bring the thing I'm considering building for a reaction?" In some instances, it's as simple as an individual relationship, and in other instances, it's akin to building an entire organization or network that gives you the necessary environment to pursue what you want to pursue. To be clear, creating this space where you can engage with your potential customers and partners is not simply broadcasting something on social media. The space requires a two-way dialogue. It requires gathering the evidence that the right people are showing up, are engaged and can exchange ideas with you. You may have a podcast, but if the right and relevant people for the business that you want to build aren't tuning in, then you haven't evidenced this step yet. The best environments are those where people can show up without fear of hearing a sales pitch.

Building a relationship, gaining trust with people and earning credibility can take time. Rather than chasing social media followers or networking for networking's sake, this step is about building a professional community to earn the privilege of solving the community's challenges. This work of creating communities requires a generosity ethos, offering to solve their challenges and add value to their lives, and it is predicated on helping expand their networks as well. The politico lunches, Kit's one-on-one coffee meetings and Professor Cox Richardson's Facebook Live segments demonstrate this. This form of community building represents the foundation through which our businesses can come to life. After all, a customer that says, "I've known her, she's been relevant to me, she's cared about this issue for some time, I've seen her expertise and other people like me follow and trust her" will be the customer who says, "Given all of that, of course I'll be interested in what else she can offer me."

> **Observation:** I'm actively and personally engaged with the people who could want what I'm building.

5: The Team

Entrepreneurship implies a lonely pursuit, but this is rarely the case. Of course, there are entrepreneurs who shepherd the idea amid the odds and deserve rightful credit for what they bring to life, but the ecosystem of support and supporters often looms alongside. Collectively, it offers the web of support without which the business would struggle. We need people alongside us to bring our businesses to life. The team includes your prospective customers, which we have just articulated, but it also includes those people who will help you with a range of technical topics, connect you to relevant networks and support you as mentors and guides as you begin to build.

Ian Folau is managing director of LMI Ventures (www.lmi.org/ventures) and previously the co-founder of GitLinks (www.gitlinks.com), which helped enterprise clients govern their use of open source technologies, ensuring security and legal compliance. He knows the importance of having a team and that the team is often an informal one beyond the confines of your company. He built his company while attending Cornell University's Johnson Graduate School of Business, where his "floor" was established. His leadership style, as is true of many whom I have met and have been successful, is empathic, inclusive, focused and receptive to the needs of his multidisciplinary team. His humility and curiosity bring people into the story of what he is building, and he has a way of enlisting them as cheerleaders for his business' success.

When I asked Ian about the team he had built, and why he was the right person to start this business, he answers bluntly, "I wasn't. I neither possessed the technical capabilities to build the product nor the ability to talk about the solution intelligently. But the opportunity was so glaring, having interviewed dozens of executives at large corporations in New York City, that I figured 'Why not me?'"

Entrepreneurs are not necessarily those who bring the technical expertise to bear. LeAnn understood that women were underserved by the beer market even if she did not know how to brew beer. Kit understood people's financial anxieties and what they needed beyond the technical craft of investing. Tanikka knew her future clients and IT staffing needs even though she had not run or worked for a staffing agency. Those individuals can do the pattern recognition because of the networks they have created, the conversations and spaces they have opened up and the strategic experiments they have run that makes them positioned to start the business. The technical skills can be borrowed, but the entrepreneur must drive the vision of the solution.

The 12 Observations

Knowing that gaps in his technical capabilities existed, Ian has created a philosophy about how to build his team. "I believe in building a network and gaining public equity through being involved in volunteer events or just taking the time to attend meetups. I share a little about what I do at all these events, and it has paid off multiple times with introductions to people who could help progress my company."

He acknowledges a lot of the right people show up along the way, particularly driven by his inclusive leadership style. "Once you uncover the root of the [customer's] problem that nobody else has cared to talk to them about, you start to gain a lot of cheerleaders for the development of your solution." This theme emerges among other entrepreneurs, which is that when you initiate a solution, others seem to show up to carry it forward. These co-conspirators, as I call them, may not even identify as being on your team, but they can help in big and small ways. His power, in part, is in sitting at the nexus of these networks and creating the environment in which people develop a shared vision toward what is possible.

Conceptually, the idea that people will show up and provide value through introductions, contribute their time and technical expertise and offer mentorship can be hard to grasp for people who are not conditioned to operating with a give-first leadership model. It can be tempting at times to operate with a scarcity mindset or to assume that someone will steal your idea. This can be especially true if that is how you've been conditioned through corporate employment, but it yields the wrong results as an entrepreneur. The risks of sharing your idea widely rarely outweigh the benefits of bringing people alongside. We need people involved, paying attention and helping us, and this requires an openness on our part. We will not know who needs to be on our team as we start; several members of our team may come to us in-flight. Once you have declared what you are seeking to build and what you think you will need along the way to make that possible, people will begin to engage with you.

Emily Drake, whom I acknowledged at the start of this book, runs the Collective Academy (www.thecollective-academy.com), where she designs and implements leadership development programs. She is a licensed therapist and executive coach who works with a number of entrepreneurs. She articulates her life's work as being on a mission to "end loneliness." Even though many of her interactions as a coach and therapist are one-on-one, she always operates with a team to support her. She advises people to consider creating Personal Advisory Boards, which can be a fully identified roster of people whom you can lean on for support. These are not folks you need to hire, per se, but rather have on speed dial or text for support. Some categories she suggests include the following:

Personal Support

- Someone who will encourage me no matter what
- Someone who will push back and play the skeptic
- A guide who is three years ahead of me doing the same thing I am working toward
- Someone who can remind me why I started and whom I am serving

- Someone who asks the brilliant question
- Someone who asks the obvious question
- Someone who represents the customer at all times

Network Support

- Customers
- Channel Partners or those who are Super-Connectors to your Customers
- Fellow Entrepreneurs
- Competitors
- Entrepreneur Support Organizations
- Technical Support
- Website and Brand
- Data and Digital
- Budget and Finance
- Sales
- Product Development

This list is not exhaustive nor is it necessarily relevant to your business. In fact, the job for the entrepreneur is to sit and deliberately build the list of who will be needed alongside you and proactively recruit that team. For most support, it may simply be a phone call or a text to ask a quick question, and for others, it might look like more sustained support and a more formal acknowledgment of the role they are playing in your startup venture as a co-founder, employee, or board member. Too many entrepreneurs waste time becoming expert or competent at something they should outsource, such as therapists building their own websites, technology entrepreneurs learning how to make customer contracts, real estate investors learning marketing and so on. Technical expertise, particularly at the business ideation stage when you should not be building something expensive without a demonstrated market, should be borrowed to the greatest extent possible.

Your identity plays a role in this notion of building the team. In 1989, Wendy Kopp founded Teach for America (www.teachforamerica.org) to address a national teacher shortage and dire academic challenges for under-resourced student populations whose academic performance had not improved in decades. Though she was not an expert in education, she understood how to reach and recruit the young people graduating college, as she was herself graduating from Princeton, who could be deployed to serve as teachers. So, she gathered 100 part-time student recruiters from 100 different universities to begin Teach for America's first recruiting season.

As for Teach for America, Wendy Kopp was in some ways an unlikely founder at the age of 22 and not being then an expert in education. In other ways, as a new Princeton graduate, proposing a program that would engage other new graduates like her, she was the perfect founder. Ian Folau was not an obvious founder in his own mind of GitLinks, yet with the depth of customer interviews he had done and being in business school with access to other ambitious talent and university resources and building a new technology where customer-centric ideas (more than technology-centric ideas) were needed, he looks instead like the inevitable founder. We can see the deficiencies in the technical capabilities of these founders, of which there were many, and understand that what makes them successful is their proximity to the people they are working to engage.

The founder of a business most often becomes not just the leader who puts the business together, but also the symbolic representative of the effort. We cannot possibly have all of the technical expertise we need to launch and sustain a business, but we don't need to. We must be the right person to tell the right story and cast the right vision at the right time. That requires this observation being demonstrated and that we can bring the right people in to help us along the way.

Observation: I have the right networks and right people alongside me to bring this to life.

6: The Hypothesis

Nancy Preston grew up watching her mom work a number of jobs in the food service industry after her father had passed away. She put in 10,000 hours of working in kitchens before she was 18 years old. Nancy Preston, also an Army veteran who attended the prestigious U.S. Military Academy at West Point, is not afraid of hard work. She exudes passion and warmth, particularly when it comes to the role food businesses can play in changing the trajectory of people's lives. Her business, Milk Money Kitchens (www.milkmoneykitchens. com), provides commercially licensed kitchen spaces on-demand as well as wraparound services that help food entrepreneurs launch and scale with little capital and far less risk. It's co-working, in a sense, for food entrepreneurs, but for Nancy, the mission is much bigger.

Reflecting on her own challenges launching other food businesses, Nancy said, "If it was this difficult for us, what chance did other hard-working people have to use food to change their lives? [My mom] had no chance of ever getting from the 'back of house' to the 'front of house.' Now, with Milk Money Kitchens, we help people make that transition unlike any other opportunity out there."

Nancy comes to this point having evidenced the previous five observations:

1. She's been obsessed with seeing how food businesses can transform lives, having watched her mom's experience and countless others working, surviving and thriving in the industry. She keeps coming back to this idea.

2. She put 10,000 hours into her internship before the age of 18, not to mention what she has done subsequently in talking to other aspiring food entrepreneurs.

3. She is personally ready. In spite of a lot happening in her life, she is pouring herself into this emerging idea.

4. She is creating the space to connect with potential customers through networks in which she is involved, the Bunker Labs community, the events she is attending and the mentoring in which she's engaged voluntarily for other aspiring food entrepreneurs.

5. She has the support of her husband and a strong network of other entrepreneurs, and she is growing a number of contacts in the food industry in New York.

With that, she had a strong hypothesis emerge: There is too much personal and financial risk for aspiring food entrepreneurs to start businesses, but if they remove that barrier of the infrastructure investment costs, more would start food businesses, in turn creating a positive socio-economic impact in their communities. Nancy believes in, and is quick to share, the potential for food businesses to transform lives, families and communities.

To take what might have been a passing assumption about the challenge for food entrepreneurs and frame that as a specific hypothesis, Nancy and her team had work to do. "We took data. Lots and lots of data," Nancy explained. "We made the assumption that food businesses needed on-demand kitchen spaces and services, but how do I know for sure without having a kitchen? So, we did interviews, bought data, and scraped open sources to see who would pay for this and how much. A difficult aspect of having something that you think is really innovative is finding a [comparable]. So, we came up with the assumption first: If we can secure and operate a kitchen space for $20 per hour, then we can break even in 24 months by selling that hour for $35 an hour. When I looked for a comp, I thought about SoulCycle. They rent a bike for an hour for about $40, and all you get is an hour to sweat. So, would a person who wanted to start a business spend $40 an hour? We started taking surveys of our market and found that the sweet spot is $45/hr. But the assumption came first."

Developing a hypothesis allows us to move forward with curiosity to discover, rather than to sell, the right solution to the problem we have identified. In Nancy's case, her desire to help more people start food businesses by lowering their barriers to launching became the genesis of the problem she wanted to solve. That is the thing for which she has had a deep, intrinsic passion. How she has done that, though, can and should evolve based on what she had discovered along the way. In Nancy's case, it was testing the various pricing scenarios with potential customers to discover what would get them to sign up. As it turns out, she discovered that in some ways, she had over-delivered for $45 an hour what her customers expected, and that given the scarcity of options, they were happy at that price point even with a slimmed-down offering.

Entrepreneurs have to be passionately in love with the *problem* they are working to solve but be agnostic as to how the *solution* comes together. This can be a difficult balance for entrepreneurs to strike because popular culture tells us we need to keep selling until we get the yes. Committing to the wrong solution, and continuing to sell it, ignores what your customers need. Committing to solving the problem while being adaptive to the solution allows you to get to the right solution and business model. Nancy was committed to the problem of wanting to help more food entrepreneurs, and she had a hypothesis that shared kitchen space, community and other collective resources to help them become entrepreneurs could be the solution. What exactly was in that mix that they were needing, she would find out subsequently through experiments.

Dr. Tendayi Viki, author and innovation consultant, argues that a strong hypothesis needs to be testable, precise and discrete. For the Third Shift Entrepreneurs, this may seem overwhelming amid other priorities, but a good plan and well-articulated hypothesis will save time and effort. In Nancy's case, the hypothesis for a kitchen sharing offerings for food entrepreneurs might look something like this:

Testable: Idea can be proven true or false based on evidence.

Ok Hypothesis: Food entrepreneurs need on-demand kitchen spaces and services.

Stronger Hypothesis: Aspiring home-delivery food entrepreneurs who are pre-revenue would sign up for a shared kitchen space for $45 an hour in the East Village.

Precise: When you know what success looks like and it describes the precise who, what and when of your assumptions.

Ok Hypothesis: Food entrepreneurs can't afford the set-up costs of a kitchen and, therefore, don't start businesses.

Stronger Hypothesis: 30 percent of first-time food entrepreneurs in Manhattan, when presented with the option, would rather rent kitchen space by the hour than build their own kitchen until they have earned $100K in organic revenues.

Discrete: Your hypothesis is discrete when you have isolated one variable to test.

Ok Hypothesis: Food entrepreneurs, who would initially sign up for hourly rentals, will convert into monthly rentals.

Stronger Hypothesis: 50 percent of new customers, who have signed up for at least 40 hours of hourly kitchen rentals, will convert to monthly members in a six-month contract for $500 a month.

In each case, we are seeking to take the things we believe to be true and are assigning the words and numbers against those beliefs to validate what we think is true is, in fact, true. Though we are passionate about our ideas, we want to be deliberate, detached and scientific in our approach to validating a hypothesis. If the conversion rates are not what we expect, then we can ask customers why. If the retention rates are not what we expect, we can adjust our proposal and present it differently. Perhaps it is the price, the location, or the wrong target customer, or perhaps what's driving membership is different, like a desire to be a part of a food community and has nothing to do with opening restaurants. Therein lies the richness of a well-crafted hypothesis and the observed results.

As with so many aspects of entrepreneurship, simplicity and speed are virtues. Entire books are written on hypothesis testing, and many experts have examined this topic. For simplicity sake, I would just say that as a Third Shift Entrepreneur, you must have a point of view that defines what you expect to happen and then compare that to what happened. That's it. Many entrepreneurs do this instinctively, but others require a more rigorous approach. Finding false indicators of success or false indicators of failure early on is easy. Your job is to have a clear picture about what is working and what isn't and then adjust accordingly.

Nancy adjusted her pricing model based on what she learned and again adjusted her community support model based on what the food entrepreneurs she was serving told her. She was finding traction and meeting her customers' needs with a profitable business. She experienced a major disruption when COVID-19 hit, but Nancy adjusted course and developed new hypotheses about what she thought would be needed. Never one to let an obstacle deter her, Nancy reaffirmed her guiding belief, which is that food business can be catalysts for stronger communities. She launched an initiative, along with other veteran, minority, or woman-owned businesses, called FOOD FOR IMPACT+ to provide healthful meals prepared by Milk Money Kitchens Members to healthcare teams and first responders. Within a few months, they had secured sponsors and delivered 8,000 meals across all five boroughs and, in turn, kept their employees, vendors, and their businesses alive. She had validated her latest thesis about what was needed.

Hypothesis development and testing is a dynamic process. As the circumstances change, customers are better understood, the business matures and new opportunities emerge, the entrepreneur continues to develop hypotheses and deploy them for validation. As an entrepreneur, you need to love the problem you are committed to addressing while staying curious and open about the solution you're developing. Though other entrepreneurs understandably struggled amid COVID-19 and could not imagine a business beyond what they had built, Nancy reimagined it quickly, captured the moment and continued to live her purpose through empowering food entrepreneurs.

Observation: I have a theory as to who wants what I'm building and what they would be willing to spend on it, and I have a few key metrics that will tell me if the theory is true.

7: Running Experiments

When you have developed a theory about the impact you might have or the need you might fulfill, it is time to act and run the experiments to validate your assumptions. Emily Drake, previously mentioned, talks about this as the required tension between action and uncertainty: "Something I've had to cultivate is a tolerance for uncertainty. So many fields get this right in an explicit way. Science and creative arts come to mind, in particular. But here's the thing: the only way to get closer, better and stronger is to take action. Within our organization, one of our values is action. Experimentation is action versus spending too long hypothesizing. What makes all of this more palatable is a strategy, a plan, a vision for where you're going beyond the time horizon of the experiment in front of you."

As an entrepreneur, Emily is constantly running experiments to grow her business and pursue other projects that matter to her. Her over-arching desire to help individuals and organizations realize their full potential has not changed, but how she pursues those things has changed based on her environment and current events. Following the murder of George Floyd, she felt compelled to make a contribution to social justice action, and as an experiment, she started a group called the Justice Marathon. The idea was simple: she would invite people to sign up for the newsletter and then give people three actions they could take each week: to learn something, to invest in something and to show up somewhere and volunteer through "footwork." The hypothesis she held was that some people were outraged but didn't know where to place their energy, and that in launching Justice Marathon a structure for action would appear.

"To be honest, I started the Justice Marathon out of fear," Emily explains, "of what it would mean for me to stay in a thinking status and, while donating to end racial injustice, never move into action. To never put myself out there. To this day, I still grapple with the question of 'Why am I doing this?' Is it so I can be a 'different white person'? Is it to contribute to change? Over time, it became something bigger than me and even still my ego is in play. I think my goal now, as a founder, is to slowly extract the 'me' out of the organization and have it supplanted with the 'we.' I'll do that by inviting others into the vision and co-create events with me, asking the Justice Marathoners what they want and finding a partner who can envision how this grows and sustains. Because we can't ever stop the fight."

Emily's hypothesis was that people want to take action toward racial justice but need guidance and structure on how to do that. The experiment was to launch a newsletter, a website, and then present three specific things for people to take action on each week that she curated related to learning, investing or donating, and volunteering. Emily has raised several thousand dollars for different organizations, activated over 40 volunteers and has directed over a hundred people to learning about issues affecting race, identity, privilege and social justice. Is it a full-time job or a fully functioning organization yet? No. But this represents the iterative work of an organization in progress. This is the place where entrepreneurs must live in a state of experimentation to learn what customers need, how many customers need it, whether she, as founder, wants to push forward, and the potential that exists. It may be a volunteer effort she and others sustain. It could sunset, having made an impact for the duration of its existence, or it could emerge as a 501(c)(3) nonprofit organization with staff, a budget and a bigger platform.

If our instinct as an entrepreneur is only to put things out there which we know will be large successes, then we stay paralyzed by the uncertainty. Emily is uncertain as to the outcome of her efforts but taking action anyway. She is running this experiment for the Justice Marathon to see what it yields and is doing so while running her therapy practice and The Collective Academy. She demonstrates this portfolio approach of managing the now while cultivating the next. She did not ask people what they needed before she launched the Justice Marathon. She started it as an experiment to cause a reaction and to gauge true intent for people to participate. Focus groups, surveys and pre-commitments cannot fully indicate what will happen as if we start something and ask people to participate. It's the difference between speculating what people might do versus observing what they did do. This is the difference between simply having a hypothesis and running an experiment to learn what is true.

Kirby Atwell, who built a real estate business called Green Vet Homes (www.greenvethomes.com) that buys, renovates and rents homes to homeless veterans through a subsidy program, understands the value of a good experiment. "I talked to and studied other landlords who were doing what I wanted to do, which was to rent to veterans through a HUD voucher program. I also met with the director of the HUD voucher program, went to a 'how-to' briefing put on by the housing authority, and learned all the details and ins and outs of the program itself and where it would make the most sense financially," Kirby explained.

"I had a theory about how to proceed and tested this program on the smallest deal that I could find that seemed to have the most margin built in. I passed on a lot of deals initially to find a $26,000 house that needed minimal work that I could start with. By doing this, I figured it minimized my risk while I test the idea." For Kirby, the experiment was in purchasing a property he could afford to test the fundamental assumptions of his business model.

"I took all the lessons learned from that first house, and that's when I put the stake in the ground and said this is how the business will do future deals going forward. I followed that for the next few years before pivoting to the state of Indiana where the short-term model made a lot more sense."

Running experiments is all about bringing forth what you have to offer in a specific way and allowing the market to respond by saying, "Yes, but actually this would be better." At Emerson House, a B&B and retreat space my husband and I own, we hosted the local Chamber of Commerce members and pitched three specific but different concepts to ask them what they liked. We found a boutique marketing firm that worked on commission for booked events that did split testing for "corporate retreats," "family reunions" and "weddings." Weddings was the winner for what people wanted.

Then, we hosted open houses with prospective brides, asked them what they liked about the venue, what other venues they were considering, and poked into what they were willing to spend on venues. We took what we learned and packaged our offering specifically around a Do-It-Yourself-Weekend for a fixed fee and three nights. The experiment was asking people to buy this package, which they did. This option for boutique and outdoor weddings proved to be particularly popular during COVID-19. Had there not been this kind of a reaction for something we were offering, we would still be experimenting with other models and offerings.

My vision for this property is not for it to be a wedding venue. Rather, my vision is to host leadership retreats and experiences for aspiring Third Shift Entrepreneurs. However, with COVID-19 and other challenges, that larger vision is not what the market wants right now. I learned that through running experiments. I will make turns toward my vision in time, but I don't want my stubborn vision getting in the way of what the market is telling me it needs. Running experiments requires you to approach your market with curiosity.

You have a talent, a vision, or in my case a physical asset, and your goal is to run and present scenarios for how it could be used, listen to the feedback and the reactions to the offering and adjust accordingly. Some entrepreneurs can be defensive about the feedback, but holding on to humility and curiosity while taking action will allow for the path forward to emerge.

Have you envisioned the experiments you'll need to run? Once we have articulated a scenario that might work, we have to find small ways of testing to see if our hypothesis is correct. This could be a Google Adword campaign, an invitation to join a volunteer effort, a pitch presentation for potential customers, or an email or set of text messages you send to your friends. Running experiments requires getting out of your head and, as Silicon Valley entrepreneur Steve Blank says, "getting out of the building and bringing it to the doorstep of your customers for reaction." Though there is much literature and celebration for businesses that scale, I encourage people to stay focused on the small idea, the small start, the small shift, the small experiment from which bigger things will emerge. If conventional thinking is that I build something impressive to finally reveal it, the Third Shift Entrepreneur invites you to reveal something small and specific to the people who need it to discover whether you should continue to pursue it.

> **Observation:** I'm running an experiment that involves my customers to determine whether my thing is needed, my hypothesis was correct and if the demand is great enough.

8: Proof It Works

Developing a hypothesis and running the experiment is great, but the thing you are building also has to work as promised. Courage to put it out there can only get you started. Your customers must validate that what you are offering is exceptional, unique, hilarious, helpful, interesting or highly recommended. This standard of care, knowing you've captured people's attention, identified their needs and are offering them the solution, really matters. Some entrepreneurs miss the cutover into this consideration, instead focusing on growing audiences, engaging in brand building, or fixating on non-essential tasks like technology investments, pitch decks, and hiring people before they have demonstrated a capacity to deliver against the promise they have made.

If you have to err, it's preferable to err on the side of having something extraordinary where you need to discover the business model than it is to have a great business plan or business model but not the demonstrated ability that what you have built is extraordinary. Daymond John and Sara Blakely, mentioned earlier as Third Shift Entrepreneurs who kept their day jobs while creating their respective clothing lines, are great examples of this.

Sara Blakely first got the idea for Spanx by cutting the feet off of pantyhose and wearing them out (www.inc.com/sara-blakely/how-sara-blakley-started-spanx). In her words, "So, I had this idea . . . I spent all my hard-earned money on this one pair of cream pants that hung there, and I decided to cut the feet out of control top pantyhose one day, and I threw them on under my white pants, and went to the party. I looked fabulous, I felt great, I had no panty lines, I looked thinner and smoother, but they rolled up my legs all night. And I remember thinking, 'This should exist for women.'" She did not set out to launch a clothing line; instead, she simply solved a problem she had personally experienced.

The 12 Observations

She cautions on the trap of seeking affirmation, "Don't solicit feedback on your product, idea, or your business just for validation purposes. You want to tell the people who can help move your idea forward, but if you're just looking to your friend, co-worker, husband, or wife for validation, be careful. It can stop a lot of multimillion-dollar ideas in their tracks in the beginning."[2]

Proof that it works has to be demonstrated by people wanting to wear your clothing, for example, wear it again and tell their friends about it. It has to work. Simple enough, but we can create a blind spot for ourselves by not wanting to hear the truth or only seeking affirmation. Feedback, particularly critical feedback, is a gift because it helps us get better, and it is an act of generosity on the part of the person giving it. Unless entrepreneurs push for it, most people will only offer a gracious, passing encouragement but privately have doubts.

Daymond John also focused on making clothes people wanted even as he walked away from and returned to FUBU several times. He was smart in staying small and focused as he went. "The important point is that I took affordable steps. I ran out of $1,000, $2,000, $5,000," John said in an interview with Business Insider in 2018,[3] "And every time I'd run out of money, let's say, the six months that I wasn't doing FUBU anymore, somebody would say, 'Man, what's going on with those shirts?' or 'I bought that shirt from you at an expo. I been looking for you all year!' And I'd always go, 'All right. I'll make a couple more.' I'll wear them and they'll go, 'Hey.

[2]www.fundable.com/learn/startup-stories/spanx
[3]www.businessinsider.com/daymond-john-fubu-founder-shark-tank-star-2018-1

Where you get that shirt?'" Metaphorically speaking in terms of you and your idea, people need to love the clothes you're making, and you better love wearing them as well.

Jessica Dalka, the founder of Chicago Planner Magazine, is no stranger to hospitality, having been an event planner and having worked in the industry in varying capacities most of her professional life. As the pandemic hit, she saw the devastation firsthand of so many businesses, but she saw an opportunity. "A friend of mine was getting cocktails delivered from a bartender. Having been to our house for parties, she knew my boyfriend Zach made really good cocktails and encouraged us to start our own business."

Jessica explains, "There's not a person we know who doesn't love Zach's food and beverage creations. My mom actually said she would pay $200 for his turtle cheesecake, where he makes the caramel from scratch. His catering experience means he had come up with clever ways to make cocktails you'd normally get at a high-end cocktail bar but on a large scale. I worked in venue management roles where I was helping to design menus and packages and selling events, so I understood price points and what experience people are looking to have." Between Jessica and Zach's experience, they figured they could sell a packaged craft-cocktail offering delivered to people's homes.

I thought to order some cocktails to welcome some new tenants who were moving into a building we own in Chicago. Having worked with Jessica in the past, I wanted to give her new business, BadCat Cocktails, a shot.[4] Her website was clean, intuitive, and it allowed

---

[4]www.badcatcocktails.com

me to offer personalized instructions as to whether there was a special occasion. I shared that these were intended as a move-in gift for new tenants who had traveled across the country. The cocktail kit cost $25, and I decided to get three: one for each of the tenants in our three-unit building. I provided their names, addresses, and the suggested delivery time. I placed the order and did not think much of it. A few days later, I received a text message from one new tenant with a picture of the cocktail kit and a handwritten note from Jessica welcoming them to Chicago; I also received text messages from our existing tenants who were similarly appreciative of the thoughtful touch.

Our tenants were blown away, as was I. She made my husband and I look like better landlords than we probably were. That loyalty and appreciation, expressed for only $75, was a steal. Jessica and her team had delivered and then some. Ultimately, the cocktails were beautifully presented in mason jars with seasonally appropriate ribbons, along with the thoughtful (and unexpected) handwritten notes. The feedback from the tenants, one of whom was a real cocktail connoisseur, was that the cocktails themselves were outstanding. Like Daymond John and Sara Blakely, Jessica Dalka has an exceptional product. I'll go to her every time for welcome gifts of any sort because what she has done with BadCat Cocktails. It would have been easy to cut corners, but she didn't, and it showed.

This eighth observation for the Third Shift Entrepreneur is as critical as it is obvious: Whatever you do, your customers should rave about it. Like the other steps, if you don't get this validation, it will be hard to move forward. I'm a willing first customer for lots of entrepreneurs with whom I work. I will place the purchase, put some money into a crowdfunding campaign and be a first adopter if allowed. I am occasionally disappointed, having made it that far, that the actual product or service has fallen short. It's important, and I'll argue ethical, to stay in this step until the product you have built is ready for prime time and you can be proud of it.

In so many ways, you've done the harder part, which is to organize your life for entrepreneurship, take that thing you've been interested in and developed the hypothesis for a solution, opened up a community or conversations with your potential customers and put it out there for sale. And, importantly, people want what you are offering. To do all of that hard work, to have people get what you have built and to be disappointed because it wasn't good enough is a travesty but a solvable one.

I think Jessica could and should charge more for her cocktail kits, which I told her, but that is a good problem to have, and it will be fixed in subsequent observations. Having a great product with a known audience is a wonderful place from which to grow. The inverse scenario is a product that doesn't work, which is a worse place to be. Do people get this wrong? They do. I was talking with a marketing entrepreneur who was frustrated his growth strategy was not working. I asked him to show me his client portfolio, and truth be told, I didn't think the work he had done for his clients looked particularly compelling. I asked him what he thought and, more importantly, what the client thought. He hedged a bit, acknowledging it could have been better. I asked if his client was interested in renewing, and he had not asked because he assumed the client would not be. This friend of mine did not have a marketing or growth strategy problem; he had a performance problem.

How do you know it's working? You, the entrepreneur, cannot answer this question. It is observed as something apart from you by other people sharing it with people you don't know, other people talking about how helpful it is (when you're not around), or sharing it on their social media feeds (and not caring if you notice; they are sharing because they want to). Sometimes this shows up as validation through online evaluations, but often it shows up by word of mouth mentions.

For an executive coach, it might be, "I know Anastasia, and she mentioned how specifically helpful you were in helping her prepare for a conversation with her CEO." For the inventor of the Hangover Helmet, a real product that allows you to put ice packs into a trapper hat to cool your headache, forged in irony and humor that quickly sold out, it is people buying the helmet, wearing the helmet and posting it on social media (www.hangoverhelmet.co).

For a marketing entrepreneur who helps food brands develop customer loyalty programs, it would be measured by retention in customers. For the contracts attorney, it's the ability to deliver legally airtight contracts on time and on budget for a client who is happy with the result. For the aspiring nonprofit social impact entrepreneur who wants to help third graders attain literacy, it would be the proof that third graders are attaining literacy and funders are choosing to renew their investment. Though entrepreneurs must be the chief salesperson for their idea, at some point, others should be joining them in acknowledging the impact, beauty, or effectiveness of what they have built. If not, entrepreneurs must ask themselves honestly whether what they have built is working, needed, or desired.

> **Observation:** I'm offering something other people have said is great (or unique, distinctive, convenient, needed, valuable, helpful, delightful, hilarious, choose-your-differentiator).

9: Observing the Pull

If the COVID-19 shelter-in-place periods have an upside, it may be in observing some of the creative initiatives that people have freely launched to create some levity in the world. Though it all quickly seems like ancient history, we saw images of Italians singing on their balconies, which was mirrored in other cities and public places, to create a sense of community and inspiration. Comedians, performers and satirists found big audiences online through TikTok, Instagram and Facebook by creatively engaging in current events. Campaigns and moving tributes went viral to support front-line healthcare workers facing COVID-19. These events have a common denominator, which is the initiative of the people behind them and that they became "viral."

Virality in my definition is people sharing with other people besides the person who initiated it. Your babysitting business has gone viral if parents you don't know call you and ask for your services without you having called them first. As marketing professionals will tell you, engineering virality is fraught with peril and futility. You can try, and some attempts are better than others, but virality often happens because of the authentic resonance people feel with what has been brought forward. If you can't engineer virality, then what can you do? The answer is to get good at starting things, get good at meeting your customer's needs and give them the tools to spread the word beyond you. I don't know the Italians who sang on their balconies, but I do know some of the Americans who followed suit, and they are the same people who are willing to put themselves out there. They lead experimental lives, willing to try things and be public in their pursuits, knowing their ideas may not catch fire but understand this is part of the creation process.

I call this learning to observe the pull. We cannot simply push our businesses or ourselves into success, but we can bring our ideas forward for consideration. The good ideas, the ones that people need, will get pulled from there. Entrepreneurship requires a dance of sorts with the marketplace, and though we entrepreneurs must bring our ideas forward, the market must give us the invitation to proceed based on other people wanting our idea and for that pull to be exhibited. Some entrepreneurs misinterpret not seeing that pull as a failure on their part, that they didn't try hard enough. Maybe. Maybe no market for what you've created exists. That's OK, too. Now you know. The only thing worse than not observing that pull for the thing you've built is not building it in the first place or continuing to push it even though no demand exists.

Curtez Riggs has experienced that virality, or pull, having created a popular conferencing series titled the Military Influencer Conference (militaryinfluencer.com/). For him, it all began with fulfilling his own need: "I was looking for a program that essentially allowed us nobodies, who were content creators, to get together and teach each other foundational things that we needed to know to start a business. I didn't find it, so my idea was to create this forum where other content creators got together. So, what started as a small event for 80 people where we were talking about digital content and growing our blogs and individual brands ended up becoming a much bigger marketplace for brands to come to find influencers."

When asked what continues to drive the growth of the Military Influencer Conference, Curtez is fixated on his customer's needs, what he calls "the community." He explains, "We build it from the bottom up every time. I'm constantly asking the community what they want to see. And so, what brings people to the event is that they know they will have an experience that they helped to craft and design. It isn't just Curtez sitting on a throne and basically saying this is what we're going to do next year. Literally, I have a core group of influential people who helped me shape and design the next iteration based on their needs."

When so many other conferences feel like an annualized rinse-and-repeat cycle or the conference is about displaying the expertise of the organizer, Curtez understands that his job is to be in the background and play host, explicitly meeting the needs of the community he serves. They come not to see him, but each other. And it works. Reflecting on his agnostic approach toward the events, other than it needs to serve the community, Curtez says, "You have these individuals who are inflexible. Maybe they thought they identified the problem and they developed what they thought was the solution.

They bring that solution to the market and the market rejects it because the market didn't have input. Right? And because they are so rigid that they are not willing or able to take that either deconstructive or constructive criticism and flow with it, it loses its momentum. And then we wonder why our products or services aren't growing as a result."

Humility in the design process, according to Curtez, is key. The Military Influencer Conference continues to grow in popularity because of Curtez's leadership and because of the strong ownership that the community feels over the events he hosts and the platform he has created. At this point, he could not stop this community even if he wanted to because it has transcended him as the founder. This is the pull we are seeking: when we finally have a product or service that works, that has found its market, that our customers insist on and that shows signs of virality.

Marc Andreessen describes recognizing the pull, or finding product-market fit, this way: "You can always feel product-market fit when it's happening. The customers are buying the product just as fast as you can make it, or usage is growing just as fast as you can add more servers. Money from customers is piling up in your company checking account. You're hiring sales and customer support staff as fast as you can. Reporters are calling because they've heard about your hot new thing and they want to talk to you about it. You start getting entrepreneur of the year awards from Harvard Business School. Investment bankers are staking out your house. You could eat free for a year at Buck's."[5]

---

[5] a16z.com/2017/02/18/12-things-about-product-market-fit/

In other words, you'll know it when you see it. If you aren't observing a pull for what you've offered, it's time to revisit the earlier observations: Is it valuable? Does it work? Have you presented it to the right people and in places where they can find it? Was the hypothesis correct, or do we need a new one? Do you have the right team around you, and is this something you have the capacity to do? If the answer to any of these questions is "No," then despair not. You can choose to receive that emotionally as a failure, or you can choose instead to receive it with curiosity, like a scientist, and begin the diagnostic analysis as to what variables you can adjust to keep moving forward.

I asked Curtez where he sees the pull for his next business or mission. Not surprisingly, like so many entrepreneurs who curate a portfolio of professional interests, he is constantly scanning the landscape and doing that pattern recognition to assess future opportunities. He is always building his now and his next. "A lot of it has to do with, you know, the political aspects and what's going on in America right now. Our community wants to see more diversity, more diverse spaces, more diverse founders, and so I'm stepping out of my comfort zone, and we're literally focused on growing and elevating a lifestyle brand that's meant to highlight Black and Brown service members." He has more to say on his emerging lifestyle brand. He will no doubt find a market for it given his proximity to the audience he seeks to serve, the people who can help bring that business to life and the discipline and humility with which he focuses on meeting his customer's needs. Like any difficult endeavor, he argues that entrepreneurship and the art of starting things gets easier the more you do it.

The 12 Observations

Observation: Managing the flow of inbound demand has taken over my need to generate new experiments.

10: Packaged and Productized

Charlynda Scales was leading a busy life serving as an active duty officer in the U.S. Air Force stationed at Wright-Patterson Air Force Base outside Dayton, Ohio, when she discovered that her grandfather, Charlie "Mutt" Ferrell, Jr., had left her the coveted recipe to his all-purpose specialty sauce, which he had created in 1956. Earning his nickname "Mutt" for his ability to blend into any situation, he too had served in the U.S. Air Force for over 20 years, enjoyed a 50-year marriage to the love of his life and lived his life believing that laughter, food and friendship were the common elements to breaking down cultural barriers. Mutt had never turned his sauce into a company before his death in 2005.

Upon his passing, the family wondered what happened to the original recipe. He was the only one who knew every detail of the complicated recipe until, in 2013, Charlynda's mother revealed the recipe and Mutt's desire that Charlynda take custody of it. Not sure what to do, Charlynda decided the only thing she could do was to bottle and share it with the world with the love and determination of Mutt's legacy.

I love Charlynda's story, not to mention the sauce, which is available in four flavors, including one that is gluten-free. The sauce works for any and every meal, with its unique flavor profile that is both sweet and tangy with a little bit of heat. When Charlynda developed Mutt's Sauce into a business, it was still just an idea (www.muttssauce.com). She was focused on her career in the U.S. Air Force. Charlynda became more serious about bottling Mutt's Sauce and producing it at scale after encouragement from a mentor she met through the Small Business Administration's SCORE mentoring program. "The first production was December 2013. I have a habit of 'planning backwards.' I planned a big event at the Beavercreek, Ohio Chamber of Commerce, before I even had the product. I promoted it and everything. This way, I pressured myself to get all the bottles made and production done on schedule. I had to create my own system of accountability." And create a system of accountability she did. "When we had the first event, we sold all 700 bottles. And they liked it! I remember taking the money and asking my mentor what I should do with all the money. He laughed and said, 'Make more sauce. And sell it.'"

Charlynda, having successfully produced and sold 700 bottles at her first event, decided to continue making the product and growing the business. "All of my free time was spent doing something to grow the business. I was on active duty in 2013 when I started the company, so serving in uniform was my number one priority. When the day was done, I'd go home and research everything: barcodes, nutrition facts, bottling options, etc. On weekends, after first production, I'd do farmers markets or tradeshows. Every extra moment was an opportunity to sell."

The rest is not yet history, but rather it is unfolding as Charlynda continues to serve in the Air Force, grow her business and look at other partnerships to help her scale. She has crossed a significant threshold, though, which is that the product is available for purchase. The focus has shifted from the entrepreneur having an idea or product challenge to having a sales and growth challenge.

Every entrepreneur needs to package and productize what they are offering. This is obvious when it comes to selling a sauce. Of course, you may be thinking, it needs to be productized, packaged, labeled, priced and presented somewhere for sale. It is also true, however, for all businesses, including professional services and nonprofit organizations. In constructing the 12 Observations, and observing hundreds of aspiring entrepreneurs, this turns out to be an important challenge. I've seen podcasters building enthusiastic audiences but without anything to sell or convert them toward. I've seen compelling pitches by experts who can solve a specific problem but who also don't have a way to convert that "yes" into a sale. I've seen people explain compelling ideas but have nothing to send as a follow-up. Often with professional services, such as management consultants, wellness experts, accountants, or executive coaches, people are unsure of their pricing model or how to package and sell their expertise. Worse, some of them defer to the customer to define what they want to purchase.

Aspiring nonprofit entrepreneurs can produce the observations up until this point: a clear problem they are addressing, an effective solution, an audience who shares a commitment to solving this challenge and even a ready donor base with the financial resources to support it. At this point, some entrepreneurs expect that goodwill to convert magically into donations, but a framework, a packaging of some sort, or a product must be created. If people say, "I'm in," what do you send them? What does being "in" mean? If it's a sauce, it means the purchase of a bottle, but what is it if you're in professional services, have a technology solution, or want a donation to your nascent nonprofit? You too need something to present for them to buy. People cannot say yes unless they have something specific to say yes to.

Andrew Andrews-Ramirez co-founded his firm, VargasAndrews (www.vargasandrews.com), to "help businesses achieve the highest valuation by implementing our framework and simple set of practical tools to transform their business into something that is scalable, repeatable, and most profitable." Like many people who have started professional services firms, the question of how to package and productize your expertise can be challenging, particularly when what you are most passionate about is doing the work. You may not have thought as much about how to price and package your offering. "We tried different types of fee structures dependent on the stage of a business," Andrew explained. "For the earlystage companies where we believed in their team and mission, we severely discounted our rates in exchange for equity. We are now moving toward our messaging being focused on results so that hours are not a part of the equation. If we don't deliver, we don't get paid, but we would never not deliver," he adds, "and so this is a non-issue in our book."

He discovered the Entrepreneurial Operating System (EOS) developed by Gino Wickman, which is explained in the book *Traction: Get a Grip on Your Business* (BenBella Books, 2012). He began using this system for his own business, and then with his clients as well. Much of the magic of that system is it has explicitly productized the relationship between the business coach and the company you are serving with a fixed daily fee, an explicit meeting cadence of one quarterly all-day meeting and an exacting transformation process that follows. It takes what is otherwise a set of good ideas and turns it into a turnkey and airtight system for a fixed annual price. Clients like buying it because they know what they are getting and can see the tangible results.

For other advisory services they offer, Andrew explains, "We are in the process of creating a front-end offering by using a Learning Management System (LMS) to educate our prospects on business transformation, at a nominal cost, which will inform them of what they need to do in order to get the results they want and create a more consistent process for us." Though Andrew and his partners will continue to push for ways to productize the services that his firm offers, he continues to grow with some clients paying him on a retainer basis, others using the EOS fixed-fee system and others in which they take an equity stake in exchange for advisory services. "I don't consider what I do work," Andrew explains, "It's a passion, and I love what I do. Every day is different because all my clients are facing different issues in their business at different magnitudes and different stages of maturity. I knew there wasn't anything else I would rather be doing than working with business owners and their leadership teams to solve the toughest problems and to have fun while doing it."

The entrepreneurs' job is to define what can be bought once your client or customer has told you they want it. Often with nonprofits, you will see galas; table sponsorships; gold, silver, and bronze levels identified; a campaign to have names placed on bricks; sponsorships for one person for one year; or inclusion of some kind of published "honor roll." All of those things are attempts at productizing contributions. Donors need a structure through which to donate. They have to be asked, and then presented with the options for how to donate. Professional services entrepreneurs need to know whether they are pricing by the hour, for a given project or deliverable, as a retainer model or perhaps through some sort of a membership model.

There is a lot to be read on these different options and specific models, but the point for the Third Shift Entrepreneur is that what you are selling has to be defined on paper with the ability to purchase, receive payment, produce a receipt and deliver the product or service. If you're at this point, then you're winning. I don't recommend investing a lot of time determining these specific details until you've proven you can solve a relevant problem for people with whom you've established proximity. Once you've proven that, however, you do need to package the thing so other people can share it around and provide a model for how they purchase what you are offering.

> **Observation:** What I am offering stands on its own without my needing to explain it or sell it for people to purchase it.

11: Repeatability

If you ask most people who invented the hot dog, they will usually offer one of two answers. The first answer is that Nathan Handwerker, a Polish immigrant, brought America the hot dog and the brand now known as "Nathan's Famous." The second answer is, "I don't know." If you had asked any of the Quinn brothers, Jimmy, Joe and Michael, growing up in south Brooklyn and visiting Coney Island in the summers, they would have immediately known the rightful inventor of the hot dog was not Nathan Handwerker; rather, it was Charles Feltman. Their uncles and grandfather would regularly tell them the story. Nathan Handwerker once worked for Charles Feltman as a hot dog bun slicer before opening up his own competitive restaurant next door and offering hot dogs for 5 cents compared to Feltman's 10 cents.

Reflecting on this story of the origin of an entrepreneur, Joe shares, "I think people think that innovation and entrepreneurship has to be some social media app or technology or fintech startup, whereas Charles Feltman was watching beachgoers fumble around trying to eat food to go, with plates and silverware, on the beach in Coney Island. He was a German immigrant and was actually a baker, and he had this idea of making an elongated bun and putting a German sausage in the middle of it. It took off like wildfire because that's what New Yorkers do; we like to be quick and always on the move. So, he turned this small pie cart with this small innovation of an elongated bun to eat on the go and ended up building the world's largest restaurant on Coney Island until it shuttered in 1954."

The legend here is fascinating to me but equally so is the passion that Joe displays for the importance of family when he tells the Charles Feltman and Coney Island hot dog story. Joe leads with family and stories: his uncles and grandfather who shared about Charles Feltman as the rightful inventor of the hot dog; the time he and his two brothers Michael and Jimmy would spend in Coney Island together. Joe reflects on the dreams they all shared, and some that were different. Joe, as the athlete, had a desire to join the military or become a police officer like his father, while his brother Michael possessed creative entrepreneurial instincts, and his other brother Jimmy had the business acumen given his bourgeoning early professional career working on Wall Street for Cantor Fitzgerald.

Tragically, Jimmy was killed on 9/11 in the World Trade Center at the age of 23. Though Michael and Joe went on to do other things, the desire to honor Jimmy's memory loomed. Though Feltman's closed in 1954, brothers Joe and Michael brought back the boardwalk favorite, Feltman's Original Hot Dog, in honor of their brother Jimmy (www.feltmansofconey island.com). To listen to Joe talk about the business is to know that Jimmy is present every day in the heart and soul of the operation. As is so often the case for entrepreneurs, particularly for the Quinn brothers, this business is far more than hot dogs: the business honors family, community, the history of a place and service to others.

In asking Joe how it's going after five years, to say that it's working would be an understatement, "So, in 2015 we sold one pack of hot dogs at Brenman's, a local butcher in Brooklyn that did it as a favor to my mother. Today, we are in over 3,000 supermarkets across the country including Publix and Whole Foods. We are also selling online through e-commerce. I think our first year we sold maybe a couple hundred hot dogs, and this year we will sell between four to five million hot dogs. So yeah, it's just been wild."

Growing from concept to this level of scale in five years is an extraordinary thing, and it's something exciting in and of itself for an entrepreneur. Though Joe shares extensively about the story of Feltman's and the Quinn brothers, he has this to say on designing for scale, "There are all these off-the-shelf things that are perfectly fine to get started, like making a Facebook page, getting legal documents through LegalZoom, using Gmail for your business, or building your first website on Wix. There are so many of these great tools that I can't even picture being around in the 1970s trying to do all this stuff. I can't even wrap my head around it."

I always remind entrepreneurs that the first dollar is the hardest sale, and that future sales get easier. The first dollar requires figuring out how to create and package the product, determine who wants the product and make all sorts of as-you-go decisions about pricing, marketing, customer experience and product delivery. With your first several customers, your goal as a startup is to learn, improve and pursue systematizing everything you are doing so each subsequent sale has less friction, greater impact or consistency, and more profitability. Some use the term scale, but I think for the Third Shift Entrepreneur, thinking about *repeatability* gets us to the same place.

The question for you is this: If you've sold your first package of hot dogs, your first 100 bottles of hot sauce, your first management consulting project, your first gold-level sponsorship, or your first hosted pop-up women's fashion event, do you know what needs to happen next for you to support twice the demand, three times the demand, or 10 times the demand? And what are the specific tasks that need to happen to produce this product and deliver it with great, consistent results to make this process repeatable? Some entrepreneurs prematurely spend time in this step of designing for scale and thinking about systems without ever having validated the earlier observations or produced the evidence that people love what they are building. To be at this place of needing to design for repeatability is great news; you have demonstrated you have something customers want "as fast as you can make it" to quote Marc Andreessen again.

As to what has driven the success of Feltman's of Coney Island, Joe has a clear perspective for aspiring entrepreneurs: "I think you can compete either on differentiation or price, but I think for entrepreneurs just getting started, it's impossible to compete on price, so you have to be differentiated." For them, being all-natural, sticking to the original old-world recipe, making it an all-natural and uncured hot dog, and telling the story of Feltman's and the Quinn brothers are what differentiate them in serving their mission to "inspire families to eat natural food, one hot dog at a time."

Interestingly, the core processes of how they operate as a business have not changed much since their founding. As Joe explains, "I remember I built the first website on Wix, and then we connected to Shopify, and then my brother would fulfill hot dogs in his 300-square foot apartment in Manhattan. That model just has not changed. It's just improving with more distribution centers, better websites, and moving the operation out of his apartment. But the thought process hasn't changed, just the execution has."

Repeatability is about understanding that your business or any business is a specific set of tasks that get completed to produce the same result. It calls for creating standard operating procedures, templated answers, checklists and operating metrics and calls for solving any issues as they come and solving the issue "forever" for the business. Repeatability also allows us to have a strong predictive view of what we need to do from a marketing, number-of-conversations, or number-of-farmer's-markets standpoint to forecast outcomes, such as the sales, revenues, costs and customer retention rates.

Sometimes, we get lucky up until this point: We didn't know that our initiative to host a park clean-up, conduct a Facebook Live cooking class or do a pro bono project to help build a personal wealth forecast would be so popular. Others are now asking for it. We've captured some magic. In some cases, we've been working methodically toward the 12 Observations, and something has finally clicked. In either case, we need to pause, assess the situation and ask ourselves what has happened to create magic and how we re-create those conditions, repeatedly and predictably so this alchemy doesn't happen by chance but rather by design.

If you are at this place of having validated the desire for what you are building, you may be ready to graduate beyond the Third Shift Entrepreneur framework and pick up other books and methodologies that can carry you forward in thinking about designing for scale. My intention for the Third Shift Entrepreneur framework is to be the catalyst to get you started, but that you will grab hold of other frameworks to be followed, experts to be considered and systems to be implemented when building out your organization from this point forward.

Choosing a strong operating system is key for growing startups and something many entrepreneurs do not sufficiently consider. An operating system is how you choose to organize your team, the systems you create to address issues, your internal meeting rhythms, the accountabilities you set, the metrics to which you hold yourselves accountable, the quarterly, annual, and three-year forecast and the goal setting, among other things. This step calls for knowing when your business has emerged from childhood and is stepping into adolescence. What got you here, won't get you there.

Again, I endorse the Entrepreneurial Operating System (EOS). I've used this system to grow and manage different organizations and have seen extraordinary results. Like a diet, several systems can work but only if you stick with one and stay disciplined in following it. The EOS includes elements that will seem familiar to the avid business strategy reader, including those evangelized by John Doerr, renowned Silicon Valley investor, in *Objectives & Key Results* (Vahlen Franz GmbH, 2018) and *Measure What Matters* (Portfolio, 2018), a powerful meeting format with some elements advocated by Leigh Espy, et al., in *Bad Meetings Happen to Good People* (Blue Room Press, 2017) and a hiring and performance management system that honors philosophies and strategies espoused by Geoff Smart and Randy Street in their book *Who: The A Method for Hiring* (Ballantine Books, 2008).

A good operating system sets up how you will operate and manage the business, not simply lead the business, to create transparency, accountability and repeatability for the benefit of your customers, your employees and your own well-being. It also dictates how you manage the business today while building the business for tomorrow. A good system should include how organizational values are created and sustained, the core processes that you run as a company, what metrics you follow and how you operate through meetings, technology and culture. This observation calls for you to take a moment to work *"on"* the business and not just *"in"* the business.

As the entrepreneur, your job is to know which phase of the business you are in. Are you still looking for that pull from the marketplace? Have you found it and need to design for repeatability? Is the business not working because you have the wrong solution, the wrong market, or the wrong people on board? Lacking an operating system, which many businesses do, is akin to wanting to lose weight but only talking about the number of pounds you want to shed and not the daily, weekly and monthly rituals which will get you to that outcome. James Clear, author of *Atomic Habits* (Avery, 2018), reminds us that we do not rise to the level of our goals but rather we fall to the level of our systems. At this point in your journey, you need to have a conversation and make decisions about the systems that will constitute how you operate your business.

A myriad of questions need to be asked and answered, and more will emerge. You won't have answers to all of the questions (let alone know what the questions will be), and you will not need to as you get started, but a strong operating framework gives you the scaffolding to take them as they come. A strong operating framework reduces politics and drama, allows for fast decision making, lets you know if you are on track or off track and reveals specific issues quickly. Building this scaffolding too soon takes you off task from finding the pull from your market; building it too late will cause friction, result in missed opportunities to scale and create customer experience and quality issues.

Observation: I have processes and systems in place to ensure future customers have a similar or better experience than earlier ones.

12: Create Leverage

Dr. Brené Brown, a household name as a researcher, author, and expert on such topics as shame, courage and vulnerability got her start as so many of us do as a Third Shift Entrepreneur. "People look at the success of *Daring Greatly* [Avery, 2012] or *The Gifts of Imperfection* [Random House, 2020] and think 'Oh man, this has worked out really well,'" she explained in an interview with *Time* magazine in 2015:[6] "But I self-published my first book. I could wallpaper this building with 'As sexy as a book about shame sounds, we're going to pass' letters. I borrowed money from my parents and sold copies out of my trunk. And then I got a book deal, and that book failed."

I remind people and myself that all great and big things start small. It's in those small beginnings where the idea is

---

[6]time.com/4029029/10-questions-with-brene-brown/

forged, pressure tested and run through the gauntlet, with us alongside it, to discover what can be. Momentum, if caught, is something magical that cannot be fabricated. Brené Brown's trajectory is extraordinary, but I've seen it with lots of entrepreneurs, although not to that scale. In my language, she was deploying the 12 Observations, running experiments that involved putting herself out there in courageous ways, and making her talents available in the event the *pull* would come, which of course it did.

Hiring Brené Brown personally is difficult, but her thought leadership has scaled far beyond herself by her having productizing and packaging her various efforts, designing for repeatability and willingness to create leverage. She is CEO of The Daring Way, which is a professional training and certification program. She has created leverage by taking the principles she's articulated and created the Daring Leadership Assessment, a trainer certification program and a series of training resources for companies. Selling books out of the trunk of your car is no longer required and in-person public speaking bears with it an innate limit as to what is possible, but building an organization that can scale, empower trainers, host podcasts and continue to develop content (now with the help of teams of people) allows more organizational leverage for what she hopes to achieve.

As your business succeeds, it should create leverage for yourself, which is more capacity returned to you through the organizational capacity that you build. Entrepreneurs who do not create leverage for themselves, in turn, create the upper bound for the growth of the business or cause themselves to burn out by not changing the way they work in spite of the growth and demand for their business. Leverage can be returned to you through increasing the pricing to toggle demand, outsourcing various tasks, hiring additional staff, implementing technology and productizing what you offer. If your old intake process involved an hour of your time, perhaps the new intake process (once you've evidenced the pull and external validation for what you are offering) can be an online survey instead, a video exchange in place of an in-person exchange, or a virtual assistant to manage your schedule instead of you scheduling yourself.

Kirby Atwell, the real estate developer mentioned earlier, talked about the flywheel effect that begins to take place when you have identified that the market wants what you are offering and you have built a business to support this niche. "When I was primarily flipping houses, I searched for any house that I could turn into a deal throughout the Chicagoland area. After testing my first $26,000 deal with Green Vet Homes and seeing that this model works and was repeatable, I got super specific about the three towns that I wanted to buy houses in, in the south suburbs, the price range, the house attributes, the projected equity and cash flow numbers that needed to exist to make the deal worth it.

"I shared this information with wholesalers, agents, and birddogs, and although it was substantially more refined than my previous search parameters, my deal flow actually picked up. This is counter-intuitive because you would think with the search aperture wider you would get more deals, but because I tried to be all things, I wasn't thought of for anything specifically. Once I got super specific, then the agents, wholesalers, birddogs and sellers thought of me first when the specific type of deal I was looking for popped up on their radar because they knew I was the [subject matter expert] and I would ultimately close the deal."

As Kirby matured his business and focused his market, more opportunities began to come his way, in turn creating leverage for himself and the business. Early success in identifying your market should lead to increasingly specific and impactful ways to narrow in and serve that market, which requires saying no to unnecessary new experiments or ideas that do not yield results. Businesses can become more valuable by doing less, particularly if the early entrepreneur's instinct was to cast a wide net and run a wide array of experiments, which served them well initially. Kirby took that additional leverage and made more strategic decisions in how to focus his business strategy.

As Kirby explained, "I determined the financial outcome that needed to exist for this to be a sustainable model and built a financial projection of income and expenses and based the type of deals and flow of deals off of this. This is where I identified what 'opportunities' I would have to say no to. I realized with a fixed amount of hours in the day and limited access to capital, I was actually hurting my business by saying yes to low hanging fruit (or lower ROI deals) because they took time, attention and money away from the much better deals that were out there. It was hard to develop the discipline to pass on good deals in order to be able to pull the trigger on great deals."

Entrepreneurs up until this point are used to wearing all the hats and knowing all the details, as it should be. I sometimes see entrepreneurs hire virtual assistants or even staff before they are generating revenue and, in my opinion, it's money wasted and may be a signal the entrepreneur does not have the right priorities. We should be scrappy. We should, proverbially speaking, be comfortable with self-publishing and selling books out of the trunks of our cars on nights and weekends. There is honor and important learning in that. I would not want a virtual assistant getting in the way of learning what I need to learn at this stage, even if I can afford to hire one. However, there comes a time, a fortunate time if you realize it, in which the business works, customers demand more, it's repeatable and you have built something exciting. The choices you now confront are to let go of good opportunities to pursue the great opportunities, as Kirby explained. At this time, entrepreneurs can tighten their market focus, outsource or staff core functions of the business and further look at the processes you have created to achieve predictable and exceptional results.

The entrepreneur must learn to "let go" to allow the business to scale. All founders have habits they don't want to let go of, yet every step along the way if you are growing (again, the best problem to have) requires letting go of certain details to other staff and processes to meet the moment. This is how I think about leverage. It's the assessment of your time, pricing and organizational position to allow for growth. Creating leverage is not something that happens accidentally. You need to design for it, talk about it and make decisions accordingly.

Not every entrepreneur wants to scale and hire a team. I'll argue, perhaps as a contrarian, that hiring people, scaling an organization and adding complexity to your life can come with stress, time and more emotional labor. In the worst-case scenario, you may work more, make less money and feel beholden to a business that no longer expresses your aspirations and creativity. There are "solopreneurs" who want to work for themselves as therapists, leadership consultants, charter boat operators, magicians, or real estate developers. You can still create leverage, reclaim time, and rationalize the demand for what you offer by charging more. Of course, if scaling your business is your aspiration, that is great, too.

Edward Tufte is a pioneer in the field of data visualization and information design. He has amassed an enormous following and has published several books related to data visualization. Though he holds a Ph.D. in political science and started his academic career there, it's really in the field of data visualization where he found the *pull*. After negotiations with major publishers failed, he decided to self-publish *The Visual Display of Quantitative Information* (Graphics Press, 1982). The book, after he mortgaged a second home to pay for it, became a commercial success and he pivoted his career accordingly to focus on visual information design.

Even though I'm intrigued by his arguments around visual design and his corresponding arguments against PowerPoint, I am more interested in him as an entrepreneur. He reaches his audience, by and large, through his one-day seminars, which he has been delivering across the country for several years. I attended one of his seminars over a decade ago, paid for by my employer who sent several of us, and watched him present his arguments for the difference between strong visual design and ineffective, or worse yet, dangerous presentations of information.

I did a back-of-the-envelope calculation with a friend and colleague who was also there, which is almost hard not to as you sit in a day-long seminar watching this blended performance and educational seminar. We estimated that about 500 people were at this one-day seminar, which cost somewhere around $400 a person, and that he had hosted approximately 35 workshops across the country that year. Over a 15-year period, he probably hosted about 500 workshops. You don't need to have an MBA to understand this is a successful financial model for a lean business. Design-for-scale evangelists would call this a flawed business model in that the business is dependent on him to scale, which represents an upper bound on the growth. Instead, I consider Edward Tufte a brilliant entrepreneur and a highly successful one both in terms of his financial returns as well as in his thought leadership and impact on visual data design. Not everyone is built for that kind of schedule or that sort of repetition of the same iteration of a presentation, but if you are, then this model works just fine.

Edward Tufte is a Third Shift Entrepreneur through and through, having pursued his interest in visual design though ordained a political scientist. He has created experiments, proved there was a specific interest and market in the thought leadership he offered around information design, opened up the space with his customers through one-day events and created the repeatable model along the way based on the pull he observed. Undoubtedly, he experimented with, used, or at least considered other modalities including more traditional publishing, longer format events, online content, or having other people perhaps teach the content on his behalf. He arrived at a model that worked for him, one that gave him a lot of leverage and continued to be repeatable.

Nancy Duarte is another leader in visual information design who has built an extraordinary business, different from Tufte's, with a team of consultants, digital toolkits and a range of consulting services that allow her vision and services to scale beyond her personal involvement, similar to Dr. Brené Brown's approach to leading her business, The Daring Way. That works for her and serves her clients in distinctive ways.

Another technology entrepreneur, Craig Newmark, the founder of Craigslist, has stuck with a business model that worked well with a small number of employees, rejecting typical Silicon Valley refrains that success must be defined by scaling, going public, or facilitating toward an exit of some sort. Craigslist continues to serve customers, which is Craig Newmark's passion, along with generously donating to military veterans' causes, and the site continues to grow in popularity with sustained revenues and profitability.

Your end game as an entrepreneur can be freedom, impact, time with your family, growth, profitability, or a sale of your business and a liquidity event someday. These are different but valid aspirations.

For Kirby Atwell, he had to rediscover why he became an entrepreneur in the first place. "For me, the intent of starting a business and getting into real estate investing has always been freedom. When I was flipping houses, I lost sight of that and our decision making was based on growth. After five years, I realized that I was no closer to financial independence than when I started and vanity metrics had become the focus. When I started Green Vet Homes, I was really intentional about continuously growing the equity and cash flow from the investments, so ultimately the investments will eventually pay for my expenses, and I can work purely because I enjoy it."

Success, as such, is yours to define. You may choose to create leverage to grind harder on your passion projects, spend more time with your family, build a large business you run and take public someday, build a business that creates passive income, or build a business that is you without any employees. These decisions are yours to make, and you must have a vision. After all, this is the fun part. This ability to create leverage requires making turns so your business consistently creates magic for your customers and so you can do things more on your terms for what ignites you every day. It's an invitation to offer the world a little more of your best and most authentic self, to do the work you are built to do and to construct days that optimize your talent and passion. Ultimately, I believe it's about how you show up to be of service to the world. To be of service by virtue of doing the work we are each built to do is, in my view, the greatest gift to ourselves and for the people we will serve.

Observation: As the business grows, I am creating more capacity for myself.

Part III

The Entrepreneurs

Every success story starts small and improbable. Your story, today, is small and improbable. The start of Bunker Labs was small and improbable. The start of other things I have launched, including The Collective Academy and Emerson House, were small and improbable. Seeing successes in retrospect and hearing the stories of those founders can have us believing that the thing was pre-ordained from the start, but alas, we know the story has more to tell us. "An overnight success, 10 years in the making," is a common sentiment among founders.

Part I, the story of Matt and the *Third Shift Entrepreneurs*, shares a fictional story about how Matt pursued his entrepreneurial aspirations alongside others. Part II of this book explains the 12 Observations that provide the framework for self-inquiry and a business diagnosis to know, "Is it working?" This third and final part, which I call The Entrepreneurs, broadens the array for the kinds of businesses you might be thinking about starting. I use this to pressure test the 12 Observations as they might show up for different entrepreneurs starting different types of businesses. As a thought exercise, consider writing a character application about your own life, following the 12 Observations, and brainstorm and ideate toward a successful outcome. What are you seeing?

What would it take to tell yourself a different story about the possibilities for your life? What would it take to illuminate a new path, one full of small steps forward to demonstrate the validity of the idea you have, the network you have, the things you know and the resources you possess? How can you design a vision for what is possible even if you do not have role models whom you can point to specifically? Consider these characters and then create your own. The better we get at seeing the patterns or even brainstorming what the entrepreneurship patterns could be, the better we will become at making similar moves in our own lives. Anybody can take initiative and start something; therein lies your power.

Executive Coach

Nia is 38, has worked in various HR leadership roles for a mid-sized company, at various points overseeing hiring, diversity, equity and inclusion (DEI) and talent development. She is a strong performer, particularly gifted at coaching rising leaders and she would love to focus more exclusively on coaching women who have the potential for executive leadership.

1: Obsession — Nia has been passionate about people development, coaching and specifically helping to prepare women for leadership roles. In particular, she is interested in small peer-to-peer coaching formats as a way to create community and build leadership capacity.

2: Your Internship — Nia has worked in various elements of HR over the last 12 years and has informally coached a number of colleagues as well as friends. They have offered to be testimonials for her.

3: Personal Readiness — Nia is single and has a five-year-old daughter. She appreciates the stability that her career offers her and, generally speaking, she also enjoys her colleagues and the work she does. She does not want to quit her job until she has something that solidly generates revenue. She has time within her day and some flexibility on the weekends to invest in this effort.

4: The Space to Discover — Nia asks if she can launch an optional women's leadership development program for employees who have been with the company for more than three years and who are serving in middle management roles. She proposes the program be voluntary, that she will organize it free, and that the women will meet over lunch or after work to participate in developmental group experiences Nia designs and leads. The head of HR offers her support and some internal resources to move this opportunity forward for the company.

5: The Team — Nia has asked another one of her colleagues in HR at another company, also a certified coach, to consider supporting her in developing this women's program. She pulls in a friend who has built basic websites before and asks if he could help on the marketing front in exchange for bartered coaching services.

6: The Hypothesis — Nia believes that if she can get this offering right, companies would hire her as a consultant to implement this coaching program and others like it at their companies.

7: Running Experiments — Nia launches the optional peer mentoring network at her company and surveys 15 other HR leaders she knows through her networks to see if they would be interested in something similar.

8: Proof It Works — The women in the new peer mentoring program report having a great experience, forging new personal relationships and feeling a stronger engagement with the company. Nia also gets a strong response from her personalized outreach to other HR leaders and discovers a demand for coaching services specifically as part of an onboarding package. She creates a powerful video, with company resources, that demonstrates the impact of the experience with participants speaking in their own words.

9: **Observing the Pull** — Nia gets inquiries from other women at her company on how to participate in her beta coaching program. Though some women have fallen off or are no longer interested in participating, Nia has a better sense as to for whom the program is a right fit and how other companies could implement her approach. She has invited HR leaders at other companies to observe her peer coaching session to gauge their interest in launching something similar. A few women in the program have hired Nia privately to be their executive coach.

10: **Packaged and Productized** — Nia gives her group coaching program a name, "All Rise," and develops a one-page overview of the program, who it serves and what it costs, and she includes testimonials of women who have been through it. Nia shares this collateral with peers outside of her organization to start conversations about the possibility of her helping them launch similar programs.

11: **Repeatability** — The branded "All Rise" program becomes increasingly popular at Nia's company and has become an annual program with a competitive selection process. Nia has developed a journal, methodology and workbook to accompany the experience, and since sharing what she has done with other professional contacts of hers, two HR contacts have asked if Nia could implement a similar program at their company.

12: Create Leverage — Having secured one prospective first client, Nia then talks to her supervisor about the possibility of moving to part-time or becoming an outside consultant for her to focus on growing her business. Nia knows, from her work hiring other outside contractors, she could negotiate for approximately 60 percent of her current year salary as a retained consultant to facilitate a few leadership programs and, in the process, give herself significant time and freedom to grow her business.

Management Consulting Business

Micah is 36, has an MBA and has been working for a large management consulting firm. She likes the work she does, but she has grown weary of the travel schedule. She sees her path to partner, but she would rather own her own business, control more of her own schedule and get more engaged in her local community along with her school-aged kids. She has typically been a strong generalist with a few projects on her résumé that focused on consumer-packaged goods (CPG) companies, and she is thinking about how to specialize or package her skill set.

1: Obsession — Micah is an entrepreneur at heart. She has a natural sales instinct, work ethic and management consulting skillset she has cultivated over the last eight years. She has noticed she is regularly called upon by friends who work at small and mid-sized businesses, mostly family-owned, to address the challenges they face, which interests her.

2: Your Internship — Micah offers to a couple of friends who run small businesses that she would be willing to lead an offsite strategic planning retreat, on her own time and for free, to help them develop their strategic plan. One of her friends takes her up on the offer.

3: Personal Readiness — Micah is still working full-time, but she has committed to this personal pro bono assignment to help a family-owned small business develop a strategic plan. She fits this into her work schedule, and she commits to taking a day or two off each quarter as required for offsite strategic planning meetings.

4: The Space to Discover — To get closer to prospective customers, Micah finds out about a monthly gathering of family-owned business owners and offers to present topics of strategic interest each quarter, such as "preparing for sale" or "succession planning." She offers this same group pro bono visits to their businesses to talk to the business owners about their needs.

5: The Team — Micah finds two other management consultants who are looking to leave large firms and start their own business as well, and she invites them in to participate in the pro bono project she has initiated. She also seeks out a few mentors: people who have left large consulting firms and started their own boutique management consulting businesses.

6: The Hypothesis — Micah thinks that for the right company profile, which she hypothesizes is a family-owned business with fewer than 250 employees that is considering selling itself to a private equity firm, there is an opportunity to become a trusted and engaged boutique management consulting partner the CEO can use regularly for various projects. These companies, she theorizes, want smart, outside thought leaders to come in to drive efficiency, growth and market positioning.

7: Running Experiments — Micah successfully helps one family-owned business develop its strategic plan over the course of six months. She commits to asking 15 other contacts who work in private equity, or who run small but growing businesses, if developing a strategic plan is something in which they would be interested.

8: Proof It Works — The family-owned business is thrilled with its strategic plan. As an added bonus, Micah produces a document and a short video to talk about the path forward in implementing the plan. Micah shares the testimonials of that project and other projects she has completed through her firm into a portfolio that she can share with prospective clients.

9: Observing the Pull — Over the course of a series of conversations, Micah lands a new potential client that is a small private equity firm who wants to bring Micah in to help one of its portfolio companies develop a strategic plan. The firm specifically want to focus on positioning the company for sale.

10: Packaged and Productized — Micah develops a capability deck, or PowerPoint, that focuses on strategic consulting to maximize the value of small businesses preparing for sale. She creates a retainer pricing model less than what a large firm would charge, that offers more personalized support for the business, including ongoing report-outs with the private equity firm and other investors. She creates a visual process map that demonstrates how she works with clients, the key deliverables she will convey, the duration of the engagement and the pricing model.

11: Repeatability — Micah secures her first client, allowing her the financial runway to leave her day job at the management consulting firm, and focuses on creating a great client experience while creating templates for the key deliverables so she can use them in future engagements. She focuses on defining a standardized process for client intake and assessment, strategic planning, running offsite retreats and implementing a management oversight system.

12: Create Leverage — Other client opportunities come Micah's way as she becomes known for doing these types of projects. She hires a virtual assistant to help with some of the scheduling tasks and other processes, looks to bring in a junior associate to help with PowerPoint creation, and is talking to another former colleague about becoming a partner with her. She sets a goal for doing three projects, and only three, in the following year doing similar strategic planning work for similar clients.

Technology Services

David is 54 and has worked for the same public relations (PR) firm as an information technology (IT) manager for the last 15 years. He enjoys the work but does not feel challenged, wants to create more flexibility for himself and would rather focus on helping smaller businesses with limited technology sophistication implement cloud-based solutions.

1: Obsession — On his own time, David seeks additional certifications and loves to be an evangelist for different cloud-based solutions. He works well with people and, in particular, loves breaking down complicated technology applications to non-technologists in ways they can understand and use.

2: Your Internship — David is working in this field, which is a strong start. To get closer to the right opportunity, he joins an industry association of other PR professionals figuring he might be one of the few people with an IT background amid these PR professionals.

3: Personal Readiness — David does not plan to quit his job. His wife is a teacher. They have one daughter in college and one son who will be a junior in high school. He cannot afford to quit his job, but he has plenty of time to pursue this idea. His wife supports him using more of his nights and weekends to explore starting a business.

4: The Space to Discover — As a new member of the PR industry association, David approaches the committee that oversees programming and offers to start a virtual lunch-and-learn series to talk about technology trends specific to PR firms. As part of this series, he's decided to survey PR executives about their technology pain points, in turn building relationships and learning about their pressing needs.

5: The Team — David seeks out a mentor who launched her own boutique IT services firm to learn how she did it and to ask for introductions to other people who could help him with other aspects of setting up his business. In the event that David secures a larger client, he establishes an agreement with his new mentor that he will leverage her firm, for a fee, to help complete any contractual work.

6: The Hypothesis — David has a theory that for many PR firms, they are not big enough to hire their own IT professional, yet they have specific needs and want someone on - call for IT support who understands the nuances of their industry.

7: Running Experiments — David approaches three different CEOs and has conversations with them, based on the survey they completed for him previously about their needs going forward. He asks them whether what he assumed about their IT needs is correct. For the most part, they say it is. Two of the CEOs are interested in what David has to offer, and one expresses that it would not be a priority for her at this time.

8: **Proof It Works** — David offers to conduct a pro bono audit to one of the PR executives and to develop a road-map for cloud-based technology solutions that could have an outsized impact on the company. Following the audit, the CEO takes the recommendations and asks David to implement some of them that he thinks will have an out-sized impact. David in turn creates a case study with quotes from the CEO about this successful project.

9: **Observing the Pull** — David's beta client comes back and expresses interest in implementing the remaining recommendations. David leverages this experience and sets up a lunch-and-learn with other PR executives in which he and his client talk about the impact of imple-menting these cloud-based solutions. David shares this case study with individual executives in his network, and people are interested in similar free technology audits of their PR firms.

10: **Packaged and Productized** — David develops a Pow-erPoint to explain his approach, names his company Public Relationships Technology Strategies,' publishes a website and develops a pricing model that includes a free audit and assessment of technology opportunities. David also articulates his baseline fees for implementing cloud-based solutions.

11: **Repeatability** — David standardizes his approach to assessing baseline technology capabilities using a check-list of questions he has developed, and he creates stand-ard templates for how to provide data to clients. He offers clients a retainer model, and he finds subscription services to handle things like billing clients, managing workflows and his own email. He implements his own project management tool to monitor his client engagements and his cloud-based solutions.

12: Create Leverage — David's pricing for his second client is higher compared to his first beta client, and he is looking for a third client. He and his wife have decided that when he secures his third contract, he will leave his current job but offer to continue to work part-time on retainer to support his current employer's technology needs while creating more time for himself to pursue his full-time business.

Residential and Commercial Cleaning

Joe is 26 years old and has recently left active duty in the U.S. Marine Corps after eight years. He just moved back home to Detroit and knows he does not want to work in a job where he cannot grow his potential and his income. He's eager to prove himself as a business owner, and having worked during high school cleaning office buildings, he sees an opportunity to start a business in that field where hard work can differentiate you from the competition.

1: Obsession — Joe has been talking for years about how he wants to work for himself and about owning his own business where he can "see" the impact of his hard work. His passion is in wanting to build a business, create a culture, do a great job for his customers in whatever it is and in turn prove that hard work can create financial opportunities for himself.

2: Your Internship — Joe used to work in high school cleaning office buildings, and he decides to contact his old employer, who is something of a mentor to Joe. Joe tells him he wants to run a business, but he is unsure how to start. His old employer tells him that though he does not have the budget to hire Joe full time, he can give him part-time employment whenever possible, and beyond that, he can hang around as often as he wants to learn the business.

3: Personal Readiness — Joe decides to live with a room-mate to minimize rent, work as a bartender at nights and on weekends and elects to stay in the U.S. Marine Corps Reserves to create supplemental income. He also decides to pursue a job working in building manage-ment to understand how cleaning services are con-tracted and how to build a differentiated business in that sector.

4: The Space to Discover — Joe aggressively networks, some of which is made possible by his old boss and some of which he pursues on his own. He ultimately gets a job working for a landlord who owns six commercial buildings in the area, which gives him a front row seat how the industry and contracting process works.

5: The Team — Joe makes contacts from the place of his new employment including one cleaning crew in par-ticular that is dissatisfied with the management of their employer and is looking to switch companies. In addition to his old boss, Joe seeks out other mentors who run small businesses for their insights.

6: The Hypothesis — Joe develops three hypotheses that take hold. The first is that his mentor and former employer does not have a succession plan for his own business and retirement. The second hypothesis is that, rather than cleaning services, there seems to be more frustration and pain points for reliable security guard services. The third hypothesis is that, in the commercial cleaning space, a shortage of evening crews exists who can come in on a more flexible schedule and at a reasonable rate, which is a frustration he was hearing from building landlords.

7: Running Experiments — To test these hypotheses, Joe goes out to lunch with his mentor and tells him, with humility and after a conversation, he is interested in taking over his business and buying him out when he is ready to retire if the opportunity ever presents itself. His mentor tells him he is not ready to retire, but when Joe shares he saw a market in creating a security services offering, his mentor offers to help Joe build that line of business from within his company.

8: Proof It Works — Joe recruits a crew of military veterans and develops a security service that is less expensive and more professional than the current service provider. Joe personally works through exiting the current service provider and bringing onboard his newly recruited team. After a few months, Joe presents to management how it can improve results for a reduced price. The management team agrees to enter into a multi-year contract with Joe's new service offering.

9: Observing the Pull — Joe's mentor, happy with this new business line, approaches other existing clients of his to offer this Joe's security service. Though many are satisfied, some have stories of unprofessional security staff with whom they didn't have direct oversight. They share that if they had a better option at a reduced price, they would be interested.

10: Packaged and Productized — Joe assembles the service offering under the umbrella of his old employer but calls the security guard offering Patriot Security Solutions, appealing to the use of military veterans as the security personnel with a higher level of professionalism. He spells out the pricing model and how the security guards are managed. He includes the case study of his current employer and how happy the landlord has been with the results. Joe's mentor and old boss takes this two-page marketing piece and mails it to all his current clients with a personalized note inviting a follow-on conversation.

11: Repeatability — Joe develops a process to standardize recruitment, training and placement of military veterans who have returned home and are looking for temporary employment. Joe leans on the back-office support of his old employer for billing, legal and sales while he is focusing on streamlining the capability to serve multiple clients simultaneously.

12: Create Leverage — Joe and his mentor work out a deal that if he can get two clients for his new security program, Joe will have a business he is running as well as a full-time job. Joe has stopped bartending while this new effort is accelerating. Now running a security division for his old boss's company, Joe continues the conversations around the opportunity to take over the entire business someday.

Wellness Retreats

Esther is 33 and burnt out from her job working in medical device sales. Her passion is self-discovery, wellness and plant-based eating. Having actively participated in various yoga and spiritual retreats, she wants to make her living doing what she loves.

1: Obsession — Esther has been a dedicated practitioner of yoga as well as other spiritual and healing practices for the last six years. She regularly participates in group retreats and online wellness communities and has built a network of personal friends who are similarly interested.

2: Your Internship — Esther has participated in a few teacher-training workshops, has been active in the local community through the yoga studio where she is a member and has applied to teach yoga part-time. Desiring to understand the business model of wellness retreats better, she has reached out to people whom she knows lead wellness retreats to ask if she can support them for free by managing the logistics, registration and marketing aspects of future retreats.

3: Personal Readiness — Esther is not in a position to quit her job but has flexibility to use her nights, weekends and space throughout the weekdays to become closer to the community she hopes to serve through wellness retreats. By applying to work part-time at a yoga studio, she will be in a position to get paid while being close to those who might want to participate in retreats.

4: The Space to Discover — Esther is launching a free community series in which she brings people who have completed wellness retreats to share and offer a review of their experiences. She holds this monthly event and rotates the location of where she hosts it among yoga studios, a local natural food market and other venues that allow her to expand her network and relationships. She's hearing from people firsthand what they love about different wellness experiences while meeting those who are interested as well.

5: The Team — Between her part-time work at a yoga studio and the free community series, Esther is surrounding herself with like-minded people. She has also assembled a personal advisory board of informal advisors who can help her think through any business-related tasks with which she is less familiar. In some instances, she gives private yoga sessions in exchange for free services.

6: The Hypothesis — Esther has heard about some amazing retreats happening in other exotic, but faraway, locations in other countries, and she thinks people might be interested in something more local and only three days in length as a sort of easier-to-access retreat experience. She thinks that potentially hosting experiences from a Friday afternoon through a Sunday, which does not require taking off from work for most people, in an outdoor setting and at a lower price point, could be of interest.

7: Running Experiments — Esther identifies the perfect six-bedroom farmhouse approximately one hour away with a detached bunkhouse sleeping for another 10 people. She contacts the owner and asks if she can hold a weekend event, pending sign-ups. She markets a wellness retreat experience with fliers and social media posts and gets eight people to sign up. She only charges participants enough to cover the costs of the weekend.

8: Proof It Works — The participants have an amazing experience and share their thoughts in the monthly community series Esther holds. They share photos on social media with their networks, which Esther does as well. Esther puts forward another weekend she will be hosting at the same property.

9: Observing the Pull — Esther receives strong interest from people who saw the photos and heard about the last retreat. Some sign up immediately, others love the idea but had conflicts on the date and others wanted to talk in more detail before committing. Esther secures enough people to host the second retreat, cover her costs, and even make a little money for herself.

10: Packaged and Productized — After hosting her second retreat, Esther develops a brand for these retreats as a quarterly "Healing with Esther" series. She negotiates with the property owner for a reduced rate for recurring rentals, develops a website and publishes a digital brochure that articulates the retreats for the next calendar year, pricing, and discounts for people who commit to participate in all four quarterly experiences.

11: Repeatability — Meanwhile, Esther continues her monthly community series hosting guest speakers who talk about retreats they have been on as she sells her quarterly wellness retreats. She adds featured practitioners to her retreat schedule. She increases the price and explores a corporate offering for companies to provide this quarterly healing experience for their employees. She now has data she quantifies in terms of new people attending her free community events, how many convert to retreat registrations and how many people sign up for subsequent retreats after attending one retreat.

12: Create Leverage — Having pursued these retreats on a part-time basis, Esther looking at working full-time in the wellness space after her last retreat was sold out and had generated a nice dividend. She discovers other revenue opportunities, such as selling retreats to corporate groups, curating private wellness retreats for recovery groups and supporting the property owner with whom she has built a relationship for how to market the space for other wellness experiences.

Catering

Ana is 53, works as an administrator running a physician's office and has a passion for entertaining and for cooking.

Friends regularly approach her to cook prepared trays of food for Super Bowl parties, graduation parties and the like. Her daughter, in particular, has encouraged her to start a catering business, which she dreams of doing but feels unsure about her ability to turn this hobby into a business in spite of her strong business acumen.

1: Obsession — Ana is an extraordinary cook, and her Sunday night dinners, which she opens widely to extended friends and family, are a popular affair. She has a talent for cooking for large groups of up to 40 people and can do so even though her kitchen is small. She researches old family recipes and offers a consideration for the occasion that brings family stories into the meal being prepared.

2: Your Internship — At her office, she and her co-workers typically order lunch once a month from a local restaurant. Ana has asked if she could, for the same price as they would pay a restaurant, cater these monthly lunches. She proposes the same offer for another friend of hers who manages a different small office. Between these two standing engagements, she is getting regular exposure to developing menus, collecting payment and being a caterer.

3: Personal Readiness — Ana's children are grown, and she has some additional time and capacity to think about how to build this passion of hers into a business. She has been careful to spend no more money than she needs to while she is evolving this into a small business. On occasion, she needs additional kitchen capacity and has worked out an arrangement to use her next-door neighbors' oven.

4: The Space to Discover — Through the monthly prepared meals for the two offices, she is discovering more about her customers' needs, including dietary restrictions, which dishes are popular, which ones travel easily and what else she needs to make these luncheons successful. She has started attending the Chamber of Commerce monthly meetings and has begun to share that she runs a catering business specifically for office lunches.

5: The Team — Ana's tight-knit family has offered to help her in various ways, including marketing, creating a Facebook page, legally incorporating the business and securing an Employer Identification Number (EIN). She asks a few colleagues at the office where she works to give her feedback on the catering she offers and to post pictures on social media to generate more awareness.

6: The Hypothesis — Ana thinks she can find another 20 small offices that want similar lunch catering once a month. That would allow her to build a consistent monthly schedule using the same menu on a monthly basis, allow her to perfect her dishes, create economies of scale and create a predictable financial model.

7: Running Experiments — Ana has decided to post a formal announcement on Facebook and in the Chamber of Commerce newsletter that she is offering catering on a monthly basis to offices. She lists prices per person and invites people to try her catering once for free. She asks people to "like" her post or tag other people she thinks should see it and then follows up with 10 different people who have expressed interest.

8: Proof It Works — On social media, Ana shares pictures of her catered meals, complete with decorative touches, such as small desserts for employees celebrating birthdays or other milestones. She gets quotes from office managers who talk about how this small investment has strengthened employee morale and become a monthly highlight for the office.

9: Observing the Pull — Between posts on Facebook and other referrals shared verbally, Ana has more conversations with small businesses and office managers about catering lunches. She senses people hesitating to sign up for a 12-month commitment, which is what she wants, but she sees people are interested in weekly catering option as well.

10: Packaged and Productized — Ana leans on her niece, who is good at graphic design and Facebook advertising, to make a clean brand for "Lunches by Ana," which includes a picture of her wearing a chef's apron and photos of her spreads. The graphic includes pricing for trying her service once, pricing for a monthly catered lunch, a weekly catered lunch, and offers different ways to get in touch. The flier is simple and complete, with all the necessary information about options, pricing and how to sign up.

11: Repeatability — After securing four new offices, Ana began to build a system around designing the menu on a monthly basis, easing the schedule for her growing list of clients, and streamlining and simplifying the process by which new clients can sign up. Ana notes all the exceptions that seem to pop up or require her direct involvement and designs systems, such as a survey that goes out to office managers the week before, to ensure there is more predictability in how she runs her business.

12: Create Leverage — Ana does advanced menu planning for the month ahead, has a predictable revenue forecast, and leverages a friend to do more of the cooking so she can focus on securing new customers and getting them onboard. She is thinking about going full-time into her catering business. With these moves, Ana can focus more on building the business, rather than working in the business, without accruing personal debt.

Hazardous Waste Enterprise Technology

Scott is 40 years old and works in IT for an insurance company. He was at his kids' soccer game talking with a friend of his, Dwayne, the head of facilities for the local school district, about a challenge he has in managing hazardous materials generated by the chemistry lab, kitchen, and custodial services. On a whim, Scott offers an idea of how to build a hazardous waste management tracking tool that could manage the hazardous waste. He's always wanted to start his own business, is bored in his current job, and believes a simple technology tool could have an outsized impact for this hazardous waste challenge.

1: Obsession — Though Scott does not have any experience with managing hazardous waste or working with the local school district, he has become energized by this challenge shared by his friend Dwayne and is invigorated by the opportunity to build a technology solution that could solve this problem. Scott's wife has even observed him early in the morning and late at night researching OSHA standards, other technology applications that exist, and the various hazardous materials that might be present in a K-12 school district.

2: Your Internship — Scott agrees to help Dwayne figure this out and given that Dwayne starts work at 6:30 a.m. and works until 3:30 p.m., Scott commits to stopping by first thing one morning or so each week before he goes to work to familiarize himself with the IT platforms the school district uses for other maintenance projects. Dwayne introduces Scott to another contact of his who runs facilities for a neighboring school district to see if they have similar challenges.

3: Personal Readiness — Scott keeps his current job while spending the occasional morning visiting the school, and he spends nights and some weekends designing a technology solution to solve the challenge of managing hazardous waste for the local school districts. He believes he will incur some costs to build the tracking tool, but he decides he can revisit those things later as a business expense or a charitable in-kind donation to the school district.

4: The Space to Discover — Between the two contacts who are the heads of facilities, plus an association he joined and what he learns online, Scott is getting close to the customers and the information he needs to design the right solution. He has built a relationship at Dwayne's school district with the IT administrator who is in his 60s, looking to retire soon, and appreciates the opportunity to talk technology with someone else who understands his field of expertise.

5: The Team — Scott is building his network of school-based personnel who can provide input as potential users, and he is making more contacts through his new industry association membership. Where he lacks familiarity with existing school-based technologies, he asks for introductions to vendors who can articulate what the technology does and how it has been built. He befriends another technology entrepreneur who sells to school systems, and who has become a mentor to Scott on how to build a business in this sector.

6: The Hypothesis — Scott thinks that if he can solve this hazardous material tracking challenge with a technology solution for the local school district, he might be able to package this solution and sell it to other school districts.

7: Running Experiments — Scott creates a number of wireframe displays on PowerPoint to get feedback on whether or not the displayed level of information is helpful. He gets good feedback and then designs a process using shared spreadsheets to manage hazardous materials. Both schools agree it would be a good solution for them if it works.

8: Proof It Works — Scott builds the waste management tool per his wireframes, largely with shared spreadsheets, that Dwayne then begins to use. They find small challenges along the way, from a process and technology standpoint, which they learn from in order to tweak and improve their solution. Once the beta test feels stable at Dwayne's school district, they bring it over to his friend at the neighboring school district for implementation. Between the two schools, Scott is seeing great results, which they put into a one-page case study.

9: Observing the Pull — Scott decides to go public and shares information about the platform that he has built and the results he is seeing through an online forum hosted by the school facilities industry association, and he puts out a request to see if others would be interested in participating in another beta test or talking about what else they might be needing. He finds a couple interested new school districts where he initiates conversations.

10: Packaged and Productized — Scott formalizes his business that he calls HazMat Safety Tech and calls his platform SchoolSafe. He assembles marketing materials and creates a pricing strategy that includes a one-time implementation and consultation fee, followed by a monthly retainer model and two-year contract. He also develops a website and an intake process for interested physical plant and custodial managers.

11: Repeatability — Scott is improving how he interacts with school districts and has created checklists for consistency on how to do an initial consultation, conduct an onboarding and monitor the ongoing experience for clients. He's also looking for opportunities to automate things like monthly billing and client management. He is making product improvements to enhance his clients' experience.

12: Create Leverage — Scott estimates that if he can get four paying clients, he would be able to quit his job and focus on this business endeavor full-time. He aspires to grow a larger business, but his immediate task is to demonstrate the efficacy of SchoolSafe, get to four paying clients, and hire his first employee to manage the implementation process.

Videographer

Jay is 19 and fascinated by creative arts, filmmaking, and storytelling. He is particularly skilled at creating short creative films, which he has done for various student projects with some equipment he owns and other equipment he has borrowed. He is in school part-time studying filmmaking, but he wants to begin to build a portfolio and business for himself learning the art form that he loves, rather than getting a job in some unrelated field.

1: Obsession — Jay knows he has a natural passion and interest in filmmaking. His social media feeds are a source of comedic videos, clever montages, and other original video assets he has created. His friends regularly ask him to make videos for birthdays, event announcements, or as a form of social commentary.

2: Your Internship — Jay is formally enrolled in an associates program for filmmaking, but more importantly, he is building a brand for himself on social media and through the videos he has created for his friends. He seeks out a couple boutique brand production studios that focus on creating videos for corporate marketing departments, and he approaches them about interning one day a week in their offices to get exposure to their work. BridgeBeyond, one of the studios, accepts his offer.

3: Personal Readiness — Jay has a full plate between being a student, working a retail job, and spending one day a week in his self-appointed internship. In time, Bridge-Beyond recognizes his value and offers to pay him an hourly rate. His hours grow from 8 to 15 hours a week. Jay is not saving money and is accruing some student debt, but he is able to live simply and comfortably.

4: The Space to Discover — Through his internship, Jay is discovering the nature of how boutique film studios work for corporate clients, and he is meeting creative directors for a number of companies. He continues to do creative projects on the side and through his social media channels, which he also shares with his new colleagues. It turns out that a number of his new colleagues similarly do creative filmmaking on the side while supporting themselves financially by working with corporate clients.

5: The Team — Jay has access through his school to film students and professors of various creative and business disciplines, and through his internship to professionals working in film production and editing. One woman at BridgeBeyond has had success independently producing creative films, and she becomes Jay's mentor. Jay understands that his age and his status as a student affords him a unique opportunity to build mentor relationships.

6: The Hypothesis — Jay believes in the power of storytelling through film, and he believes if companies could tell more authentic stories about young adults between the ages of 18 and 25, they would attract better talent and build more relevant brands. He also believes that if he can demonstrate how companies could do this, they would be eager to invest more resources.

7: Running Experiments — Jay becomes familiar with one client who has retained BridgeBeyond to announce a significant merger. Jay asks if he could create some short films, eight minutes each, that follows a few of the new employees under the age of 30 to tell their authentic stories. The client seems intrigued and authorizes this idea, which is built into the existing contract.

8: Proof It Works — Jay creates these short films and sets them to music in a way that celebrates the employees and the company at which they work. After getting internal feedback and tweaking them, Jay and the BridgeBeyond team show these films to the client. The client loves the films.

9: Observing the Pull — The client shares that it wants to have a series to cover a broader set of diversity considerations for employees under the age of 30 to use for an upcoming CEO townhall. It requests the films be shorter, more optimistic, and branded differently based on the new merger.

10: Packaged and Productized — BridgeBeyond crafts a formal proposal and Statement of Work for the new film series, calling it "Beyond the Breakroom." This looks to be a lucrative contract opportunity, and Jay is assigned to the project and credited as being the creative director. Jay uses the video assets as part of his student work portfolio, showing a number of his professors what he has produced working from what was initially an unpaid internship.

11: Repeatability — BridgeBeyond considers Jay a differentiated asset, as someone on their team who can authentically represent the youth perspective. After securing the first contract, it productizes this video series as an offering to spotlight young employees and drive employee engagement for other potential clients. Jay is working with the sales team to present this video series and other youth-authentic content for other potential clients.

12: Create Leverage — Though Jay is enjoying creating valuable content for clients at BridgeBeyond, he still has a desire to focus more on creative short films. He is using the assets of BridgeBeyond, including the equipment, studio and the volunteer capacity of some of his colleagues to create more interesting and artistic films on the side. He has left his retail job and is exclusively focused on filmmaking and going to school.

High-End Athleisure Line

Valencia is 34 and has been a personal trainer for six years after quitting an office job working in graphic design. She loves fashion as well as being a personal trainer, and friends and clients regularly ask her where she buys her clothes that she wears to work and when socializing with friends. She knows she has a great style aesthetic, and she would love to build a new athleisure brand, but she does not know how to start.

1: Obsession — Valencia sees the intersection of athletic clothing that is highly functional yet also sophisticated fashion and can be worn out socially. She has an eye for thinking about how outfits can come together. She spends hours shopping online, noticing new brands and seeing what popularly followed Instagram models are wearing, and she is generally a style icon within her local fitness network.

2: Your Internship — Valencia works as a personal trainer, which gives her access to some clients and builds credibility for her personal fitness brand. She decides to pick up a part-time job at a local high-end boutique, The Goddess & The Garb, which is not fitness focused, so she can understand how brands get sourced, what draws customers in, and to learn the economics of running a small boutique.

3: Personal Readiness — Valencia has a good baseline income, between personal training and working at The Goddess & The Garb, working about 50 hours a week. She plans to do both while discovering how to launch this business.

4: The Space to Discover — Working part time at the boutique, Valencia now regularly interacts with people who could be her customers. Valencia asks Mara, the boutique owner, if she would be open to staging a few athleisure items at the shop that Valencia thinks her customers would love. She hosts a monthly evening open house to talk about new athleisure products she advertises on her social media channels.

5: The Team — Mara has become her mentor and teaches her retail and customer preferences. Valencia joins a local entrepreneurship network with monthly meetups, some online programming, and free mentor matchmaking. She specifically networks with people who know digital branding, e-commerce, HR, legal and finance as she fills in her knowledge gaps.

6: The Hypothesis — Valencia believes there is a retail market for high-end athleisure and an opportunity to build a recognized brand through an e-commerce platform. She thinks her target customers are women in their 30s and 40s with disposable income who regularly purchase other luxury accessories and wear other athleisure brands.

7: Running Experiments — Valencia uses the boutique where she works to discover the ideal products for her customers, in particular jackets and bags, which she thinks are distinctive. She sources about 15 different products in her store-within-a-store experiment, and she sees what products women purchase and what other products they would love to see made available.

8: Proof It Works — Valencia sells her product, captures the customers' names and emails, and stays in touch with them to determine if they are happy with what they purchased and what feedback their friends are giving them. Mara, the boutique owner, is happy with this additional growing line of business within her store because it diversifies her offering and makes her store more attractive to her existing customers.

9: Observing the Pull — Valencia accrues dedicated customers, asks them what products they like and sources those products accordingly. She stocks popular items in Mara's boutique for sale based on the customers' feedback.

10: Packaged and Productized — Mara and Valencia agree to a partnership in which Valencia gets more of the retail space within Mara's store, in turn establishing a revenue sharing agreement. Valencia launches her website, makes business cards offering personalized style consultations, and creates more of a branded space within Mara's boutique. She launches a digital catalog of items she thinks will be popular sellers, which she publishes four times a year.

11: Repeatability — Mara is happy with the growing traffic to her store and the additional revenue from Valencia's products. Valencia begins to track her newsletter growth, the number of personalized style consultations she's conducting and the average revenue that results from those style consultations. She establishes working relationships with key vendors and brands to create more proactively the digital catalog and sourcing calendar.

12: Create Leverage — Valencia turns her attention toward growing the newsletter, sourcing more exciting products and building out the brand of her business. Her income increases through sales within Mara's store and through personal training, but she is focusing on growing her business through online sales. Though her company is small, Valencia now has a retail presence, an online storefront and a growing customer base that is excited by what she continues to offer.

Banana-Based Ice Cream

Eddie is 52 years old and has been making his own banana-based ice cream for the last 15 years after he faced some health issues and committed to going gluten and dairy-free. His niece, who works in product development, has encouraged him to package his banana ice cream and launch a business. Though he currently works as an assistant principal at a high school, his passion is healthy eating and, in particular, his banana ice cream. He would love to turn this passion for cooking and healthy eating into a business.

1: Obsession — Eddie became an evangelist for healthy eating after he suffered a heart attack and had other health complications in his mid-40s. He has been passionate about helping other middle-aged men take control of their health and their diet. His ice cream, which started as a side hobby, is his annual Christmas present for friends and family.

2: Your Internship — Eddie has spent the better part of 15 years perfecting his one-ingredient banana ice cream. Considering growing this potential business, Eddie has experimented with additional flavors, created a dedicated weekly production schedule and has purchased a deep freezer to make and store larger batches of ice cream. In addition, he has applied to Future of Food, a virtual six-month business accelerator program.

3: Personal Readiness — Eddie is recently divorced, and he appreciates the distraction of making ice cream while continuing his day job working as an assistant principal, which he also enjoys, though some days can be exhausting. He has additional flexibility in the summers when school is out, and he can spend more time on the business. He does not plan on leaving his job at the high school anytime soon.

4: The Space to Discover — Eddie has applied to a local farmer's market to host a booth each Saturday throughout the upcoming summer, sell the product and get close to his potential customers to build relationships and gather their feedback. He has asked some people who have positively responded if they would be interested in signing up to get a few pints of banana ice cream at-cost each month as he works on introducing new flavors.

5: The Team — Eddie has been accepted into the Future of Food virtual business accelerator program and is meeting relevant and helpful people, including an entrepreneur who has developed a frozen food product in the healthy eating category that has national distribution. Eddie's niece has agreed to help him as a business partner, putting pieces of the business together, while Eddie is focusing on being a brand ambassador for healthy eating.

6: The Hypothesis — Eddie thinks he can create predictability and profitability in his business by getting people to sign up for a monthly subscription service. He also thinks he could partner with a local not-for-profit organization that focuses on diabetes or weight loss and could create a fundraiser that covers both the cost of his product and raises money for the designated charity.

7: Running Experiments — As part of his accelerator program, Eddie conducts 20 customer interviews and asks them whether they will buy his product, which flavors they prefer, and whether they would consider the monthly subscription service. On social media, his niece encourages people to buy gift subscriptions for the upcoming holidays for Eddie's banana ice cream, particularly for people who have committed to losing weight.

8: Proof It Works — Between these direct appeals and customer interviews, Eddie gets eight friends and family members to sign up, and his niece gets another seven new customers through her outreach on social media. These beta customers give strong reviews about the quality of the ice cream and the consistency of the delivery experience. Eddie captures these customer testimonials.

9: Observing the Pull — Eddie conducts a survey and finds out that certain flavors are less popular than others, the pint-sized packaging feels too small for many customers, and some customers want the option for more frequent deliveries, such as every other week. He also learns that about half of his customers are buying the annual subscription as a gift for others. The farmer's market grows in popularity, and Eddie has built a relationship with another vendor who sells frozen desserts at several farmer's markets. They have agreed to a profit-sharing agreement for any of Eddie's ice cream they add to their product set and sell.

10: Packaged and Productized — Now that Eddie has a few sources of income through direct sales, the monthly subscription, and the revenue sharing at the farmer's market, he decides to invest in a better brand for his newly named business, "I'm Telling You, It's Bananas!" He meets a boutique brand agency through the Future of Food accelerator that has marketed and branded other ice cream products. He develops a rate sheet to articulate retail and distributor pricing for his ice cream. His web-site has more information, and he's established a social media presence in which he shares where to find his ice cream and what new flavors are available. He also offers direct links for people to purchase the monthly subscrip-tion option.

11: Repeatability — Eddie invests in a sales management platform that tracks customers, renewal dates, flavor preferences, and other identifying information. With his niece, they build automated email campaigns to cre-ate a complete and consistent user experience. He has invested in more deep freezers and is borrowing kitchen capacity from a co-op community kitchen.

12: Create Leverage — Eddie hires a part-time contractor as his sales grow to focus on streamlining and automating aspects of the business that do not require personalized interventions. He is working on stepping beyond the daily operations to think about the overall brand and business growth. He re-invests any money he makes back into the business to grow the infrastructure required for him to make and distribute banana ice cream at scale. Within two years, he expects to begin paying himself.

Helping Military Families Relocate

Nicole is 47 and has been married for 19 years to her husband Jorge, who is in the U.S. Army. During that time, they have relocated five times, and in each case, they have struggled to build a new community of support. As her husband is nearing retirement at his last duty station of Fort Bragg, North Carolina, Nicole wants to ensure that future families transitioning between duty stations receive more support than her family has received.

1: Obsession — Nicole has informally served as a welcome party and guide for new military families moving to the communities in which she has been located throughout Jorge's 19 years of service in the Army. She earned a reputation for being a go-to source for questions about schools, housing, on-base resources and social networks to plug into. She's passionate about the mission of supporting military families.

2: Your Internship — Nicole has had several friends express to her how invaluable she has been for them and even a Base Commander comment, "Every duty station needs a Nicole." Recently, she has seen an opportunity to formalize her efforts into a more defined program. She decides to get involved with the base Welcome Center and organize a free, bi-weekly potluck dinner for newly arrived families. She also decides to get involved with another veteran not-for-profit as a volunteer and board member to understand how not-for-profits operate.

3: Personal Readiness — Jorge is ready to leave the Army, and though his military pension will not be enough to fully retire on, it will provide a baseline income for him and Nicole while he is seeking full-time employment. Nicole has not worked while supporting her husband's military career, but she does have a passion for serving the military community. Now that they will be separating from the military in North Carolina, they will be able to call Fayetteville home for the next several years, allowing her to plan her own career.

4: The Space to Discover — Through her now bi-weekly potluck dinners and through volunteering to lead seminars welcoming people to Fort Bragg, Nicole is more connected with families who are arriving on base. Her partnership with the base Welcome Center ensures she is meeting hundreds of newly arriving families each month. Through her volunteer work, she learns about how not-for-profits operate and meets some of the local funders who support the military community with grants to local not-for-profits.

5: The Team — Nicole quickly gets a number of other military spouses to join her in the effort to support arriving families on the base and leverages their skillsets for everything from marketing, creating a digital brand, event planning, and aggregating other resources. With the CEO of the organization for which she volunteers who has become a mentor, the other spouses who constitute her fellow volunteers, the relationships she is establishing on base and the arriving families who represent her clients, she is building a strong network and reputation to launch her organization.

6: The Hypothesis — Nicole believes she can create a highly effective transition organization to support military families with various volunteer-led programs. She believes military families can support other military families better than Department of Defense (DoD) run programs. She also thinks that if she can build a strong and scalable model, she could get funding and launch a not-for-profit of which she would become a paid employee.

7: Running Experiments — Through the potlucks, programs and matchmaking, Nicole gets feedback on what most impacts the ability for new arriving families to get "plugged in." She learns that matching families with school-aged kids the same age gives quicker, more powerful results, and the connection is greater if two "welcoming families" are assigned to each "arriving family." She learns that the more she outlines the expectations for the welcoming families, the more consistent the experience will be for the arriving families.

8: Proof It Works — After several months of implementing a program model, Nicole is able to ask the families who have arrived and participated in her program for testimonials on their experience. One of the other spouses who volunteers is particularly good with marketing and creating video assets and chooses to create a few different short videos that highlight five families' unique stories. Another volunteer creates a website to show the stories and starts a social media campaign to welcome families to Fort Bragg.

9: Observing the Pull — Nicole, who has informally been a go-to resource to help families get settled, is getting more attention with the base officials whose responsibility it is to support the families. They see her videos, notice her social media campaign, and ask for ways in which they can better partner and elevate her efforts. Other spouses who have since transitioned to other military installations ask if they can implement her program or something similar at their new bases. In addition, potential sponsors to whom she has been reaching out circle back to her with questions about her program and impact.

10: Packaged and Productized — Nicole names her new program and initiative 90 Days to Home, which promises all military families in her program will feel at home in their new community within three months. She develops a PowerPoint that explains her support model and her volunteer model and she shares the testimonials of all who have been through her program. For potential sponsors, she also develops a version of this PowerPoint that describes the results she has gotten and the cost to sponsor one arriving family or an entire welcoming operation for a military base.

11: Repeatability — After successfully implementing the program at Fort Bragg, Nicole asks a good friend and volunteer to implement the program at Fort Campbell, Kentucky, where she has recently transitioned with her family. Between the two sites, Nicole is learning what parts of the program model to tweak, how to close potential sponsorships and how to create a more consistent pot-luck dinner experience. In both locations, she is getting consistent results of families feeling at home in 90 days.

12: Create Leverage — Nicole has secured a few small grants, and she is able to pay herself and her colleague who is running the program at Fort Campbell a small, contracted salary. She has formalized and incorporated this not-for-profit and is getting more sophisticated about how to secure additional sponsors and how to recruit the right volunteers for the effort. With a DoD contract now pending, Nicole may soon be able to hire two more staff.

Encouraging More LGBTQ+ Candidates

Dustin is 27 and identifies as a gay man. He is passionate about advancing LGBTQ+ equality, particularly in his home state of Montana. While he is working as a research assistant at a university in Bozeman, his passion is discussing politics, working on political campaigns and getting younger people to get involved in the political process to advance LGBTQ+ equality.

1: Obsession — Dustin grew up in a rural community and felt ostracized, and he sees political activism as a core part of his identity and what his contribution to society needs to be. His friends are politically active, and

329

The Entrepreneurs

his social life is largely built around LGBTQ+ causes he organizes and fundraises for.

2: Your Internship — Dustin, a research assistant at the university, serves as a faculty advisor for various student organizations focusing on LGBTQ+ equality and does it during his working hours. Beyond that, he has chosen to become involved with the local Democratic party to meet candidates running for office, learn how campaigns are organized and funded, and to get closer to the policy-making process.

3: Personal Readiness — Dustin lives simply, has a room-mate and has a relatively stable job working at the university. His job allows flexibility for him to work nights and odd hours as long as he completes his work. He has some latitude for how he spends his days, and between his volunteer activity and his job as a research assistant, he typically puts in a 50-hour workweek, though he still feels he has the time and space to do more.

4: The Space to Discover — Dustin has started a monthly meet-up in the community to bring together different networks of people to discuss how to get more LGBTQ+ candidates to run for office. Sometimes, the meet-up is simply a networking event; in other instances, he brings in different experts or elected officials to talk about public policy issues.

5: The Team — Between working on political campaigns and being connected to the LGBTQ+ community on campus, Dustin sits at the intersection of seeing how those communities can come together. He has never run for office, but he has been pulling together a group of candidates who have run for office and are willing to help other LGBTQ+ candidates run for office. He has a few students who have offered to volunteer their time and others who have offered to serve as volunteer advisors.

6: The Hypothesis — Dustin knows of organizations in larger cities that help LGBTQ+ candidates run for office through training, organizing and PAC giving. He believes that Bozeman, Montana, while smaller than some other cities, nonetheless has enough local support to sustain a similar type of not-for-profit as seen in larger cities. If so, he sees himself as being the founding executive director of whatever gets created.

7: Running Experiments — Dustin has to experiment to ensure that the potential funders and those whom he would serve see the need for what he is proposing to build. He announces and promotes a candidate training workshop and gets 12 people to sign up. He solicits funding to receive in-kind or direct support, which he receives. Though he does not have enough financial support to hire staff, Dustin at least receives a signal from candidates and funders they are interested in what he is doing.

8: Proof It Works — Dustin holds the candidate training, and people talk about how impactful it was. He organizes volunteers to gather the necessary signatures to get these same candidates on the ballot. He shares his strategy and progress to date with prospective funders. Though the election is some time away, there is a noticeable effort under way as a result of Dustin's initiative.

9: Observing the Pull — Dustin begins to have more LGBTQ+ candidates express interest in running for office and asking for things, such as campaign training, technology support and introductions to potential donors. He has conversations with potential funders who see the work he is doing and are interested in funding him as a 501(c)(3), instead of a PAC or direct donor, to candidates which they see happening through other organizations.

10: Packaged and Productized — Dustin formally announces his initiative, "Out to WIN," which includes a picture of the state of Montana with a logo and a website. He announces himself as the executive director, though he is not yet paying himself, and includes 15 other people on the website with various titles and responsibilities even though they, too, are volunteers for the organization. He assembles a sponsorship package he can send to other potential funders with giving levels and the impact associated with sponsorship at each of those levels.

11: Repeatability — Dustin begins to map the new organizations' annual planning calendar, assigning specific tasks and milestones to ensure they are recruiting and training candidates. He organizes a conference that serves as a mechanism to raise sponsorship dollars. Though this is the first fundraiser he has done, this will serve as an annual fundraising event for which he can secure sponsorship. In the first cycle, two of his supported candidates win their elections and they give him significant credit for the support he and his organization provided.

In the following year, his applicant pool increases and his annual conference has twice as many attendees as the first year.

12: Create Leverage — Within a year, and after a few sponsorships are secured, Dustin begins to pay himself and one other full-time staff member. Dustin becomes tied more closely with other national efforts under way and with funders, activists and candidates who can help. Dustin leaves his job at the university and spends more time as a public speaker, advocate, political activist and founding executive director of his nascent not-for-profit organization.

About the Author

Todd Connor is a speaker, thought leader, and consultant who leads individuals and organizations to unlock their full entrepreneurial potential. Todd is the founder of Bunker Labs (www.BunkerLabs.org), a national entrepreneurship organization supporting the military-connected community with chapters across the United States. He is also the founder of The Collective Academy (www.TheCollective-Academy.com), Emerson House (www.ExperienceEmerson.com) and other small initiatives. For speaking requests and access to additional thought leadership, visit www.ThirdShiftEntrepreneur.com.